Exposure Anxiety – The Invisible Cage

also by Donna Williams

Autism: An Inside–Out Approach
An Innovative Look at the Mechanics of 'Autism'
and its Developmental 'Cousins'
ISBN 1 85302 387 6

Autism and Sensing
The Unlost Instinct
ISBN 1 85302 612 3

Nobody Nowhere
The Remarkable Autobiography of an Autistic Girl
ISBN 1 85302 718 9

Somebody Somewhere
Breaking Free from the World of Autism
ISBN 1 85302 719 7

Like Colour to the Blind
Soul Searching and Soul Finding
ISBN 1 85302 720 0

Exposure Anxiety
– The Invisible Cage

An Exploration of Self-Protection Responses in the Autism Spectrum and Beyond

Donna Williams

Jessica Kingsley Publishers
London and Philadelphia

First published in the United Kingdom in 2003
by Jessica Kingsley Publishers Ltd
116 Pentonville Road
London N1 9JB, England
and
325 Chestnut Street
Philadelphia, PA 19106, USA
www.jkp.com

Copyright © Donna Williams 2003

Library of Congress Cataloging in Publication Data
Williams, Donna, 1963-
    Exposure anxiety–the invisible cage : an exploration of self-protection responses in the autism spectrum / Donna Williams.
        p.cm.
    Includes bibliographical references and index.
    ISBN 1-84310-051-7 (alk. paper)
        1. Autism. 2. Anxiety--Treatment. 3. Selfinterest. I. Title.

RC553.A88 W5455 2002
616.89'82--dc21   2002072928

British Library Cataloguing in Publication Data
A CIP catalogue record for this book is available from the British Library

ISBN 1 84310 051 7

Printed and Bound in Great Britain by
Athenaeum Press, Gateshead, Tyne and Wear

*In memory of Sparkling Arkie
and in dedication to my husband
Chris the bear.*

For the colour and surrealism
For the map and the realism
For the mistakes and the survival
The the tough love and detachment
In spite of, and because of

Here stand I

Contents

The Invisible Cage

If I could draw you a picture of Exposure Anxiety,
I'd draw you a rainbow unseen within heavy stone walls.
Places in the stone where the cement had crumbled,
Chipped away and some of the colour had come streaming out
Like a ray of light into the world.

I'd draw you a picture from inside a prison,
An invisible prison with replica selves on the outside,
Each a contortion, a distortion,
Of the one you can't see
Who can't get out

I'd draw you a face with a plastic smile,
Perfect movements,
A learned handshake
And a gut full of despair and aloneness
In a world that applauds the 'appear'
At the expense of 'self';
Suicide without a corpse.

Exposure Anxiety: a definition

Exposure Anxiety is the internal parent watching its vulnerable and exposed baby being stolen by the world outside or given away by 'the self'; being robbed of control by what are felt as 'outside forces'.

Exposure Anxiety is a self-parenting survival mechanism, an intense often tic-like involuntary self-protection mechanism that jumps in to defend against sensed 'invasion'. When it becomes chronic, it is self-perpetuating – like a boulder hurtling down a hill, gaining momentum. Chronic, uncontrolled, acute Exposure Anxiety is about addiction to your own adrenaline.

We all experience stress and some of us are more driven, more passionate, more fixated and intense, more independent, more controlling, more dominant or passive, more jumpy or aloof, *naturally*. In most cases where Exposure Anxiety goes hand in hand with the metabolic, digestive and immune system disorders that co-occur in the largest percentage of people on the autistic spectrum. The chronic stress of Exposure Anxiety exacerbates physiological problems which then affect information processing as well as throw neurotransmitter balance into a state of chaos, forming a self-perpetuating loop. The person with Exposure Anxiety who lives and works with those who do not understand the condition are bound to find the self-in-relation-to-other, directly-confrontational approach of the environment seems to make Exposure Anxiety worse. This cycle can be broken.

Exposure Anxiety has two faces and is the heaven and the hell, the lure of sanctuary and the suffocation of the prison.

The 'buzz junkie' is one of these faces, addicted to the high of one's own excitement, attractions, fears, or tortured by the constant over-stimulation of sensory flooding and overload. Its other face reflects a hyper-aroused self-protection mechanism that is compelled to protect from invasion. That invasion can be social contact, conversation, the sense of others or their things in your own territory, physical contact not controlled by yourself…even love.

Exposure Anxiety is a mechanism that craves the extreme and retaliates against any sense of impending invasion. It is like taking a feeling of severe shyness and multiplying it by fifty, yet its presentation is extremely confusing to onlookers. People with severe Exposure Anxiety can be frozen, or they can be manic and high. They can be prone to despair and depression, driven and creative, or unable to connect. They can be obsessive or fiercely indifferent, compulsively helpful or aloof. They can be passive or controlling; bombastic or phobic; deeply empathic or compulsively violent; open and honest or secretive and intensely private. Exposure Anxiety is likely one of a range of conditions relating to what has been coined 'Reward Deficiency Syndrome', essentially relating to reward feedback and impulse control mechanisms in the brain. Exposure Anxiety has many faces. My own forms of it are only an example, a caricature that helps to paint a picture of how Exposure Anxiety works.

Exposure Anxiety makes it difficult to dare 'expressive volume' in a directly-confrontational (self-in-relation-to-other) world

Most of society is geared toward making you notice you have noticed: something people call communicating, sharing, and interacting.

In the face of sensed invasion, the self-protective response of acute Exposure Anxiety can reduce a scream to a mutter. It can turn a capable person into someone who needs prompting to do the simplest thing for him or herself. Someone creative can seem inactive and indifferent. It can turn an affectionate person into someone indifferent, even rejecting. It can turn a focused, interested person into a compulsive distracter and clown. It can turn a gentle person into someone compelled to provoke, antagonize and retaliate.

Acute Exposure Anxiety is like an invasion switch, triggered not just from the outside. In very severe cases it can even be triggered from the inside by too strong a sense of self-awareness, the invasive jolting of consciousness caused by thought, in self-protection against consciousness-jolting body messages or social-contact-driven emotions such as feelings of love and attachment.

Exposure Anxiety is about feeling your own existence *too close up,* too in your own face.

This triggers instinctual involuntary aversion to conscious awareness/responsibility for your own expression, both in acting on those feelings which would connect you with others (sensed as impending threat of invasion) and responding freely to the attempts of others to connect with you.

Like conditions such as agoraphobia, the more the Exposure Anxiety is challenged, the more the person sides with their anxiety against the environment and this compounds the condition. This progressive identification of selfhood with the condition means it becomes increasingly hard to stay self-motivated to initiate speaking, to look, to express a need or want, to share an interest or even dare to stay aware you have one.

> **Acute chronic Exposure Anxiety can create such an emotional obstacle to connection to mind and/or body that the person develops islands of expression in which they can't do for themselves, can't do as themselves, or can't do by themselves.**

Whilst they remain capable in those areas of life to which Exposure Anxiety has not become sensitized, it is often the case that the person's capabilities get eaten away piece by piece until their life choices are limited and Exposure Anxiety runs their life more than they do.

> **Pushing beyond the limits of will's tolerance, Exposure Anxiety heightens and can result in islands of ability that become 'off limits'.**

This often happens in those situations the person most craves to be part of. Many people with Exposure Anxiety are extremely lonely, even when surrounded by others. On their own, the person may crave contact but life teaches them that involvement comes at a price. In company, Exposure Anxiety responses may be all others see and the person is associated with those responses they cannot control. There is no greater sense of isolation. Acute Exposure Anxiety teaches the self that, in spite of the craving to be social, to seek social contact is futile.

Exposure Anxiety in the general population

Exposure Anxiety affects all of us because we all experience fluctuations in our hormonal and biochemical states in response to times of high stress. Puberty is a good example here but not the only one. We all have known the excruciating self-consciousness that compels us to pull away, divert attention, retaliate as though we would otherwise suffocate. Everything that occurs in 'autism' occurs in those who are not autistic. The difference is degree and frequency.

Degree and frequency of attacks of Exposure Anxiety affect everything.

Where Exposure Anxiety is severe and chronic it affects how we appear, how we experience the world, how we experience ourselves and it affects how our personality, language, behaviour and social–emotional skills develop through adaptations within our prison and between the spaces made by the bars.

There are people who don't have autism who experience extreme Exposure Anxiety. Their self-protection mechanisms are, for a whole range of reasons, too sensitive, too easily triggered. Some adapt by becoming reliant on alcohol or drugs, relying too heavily on props, even living through somebody else. Some are persistent clowns, others workaholics or clinically detached intellectuals who can't 'let people in', or can only do so within controlled, prescribed boundaries.

※

If I could draw you a picture of acute chronic Exposure Anxiety, I'd draw you a rainbow unseen within heavy stone walls. There'd be places in the stone where the cement had crumbled, been chipped away and some of the colour had come streaming out like a ray of light into the world.

I'd draw you a picture of someone inside a prison, an invisible prison with replica selves on the outside, each a contortion, a distortion of the one you can't see who can't get out. I'd draw you a picture of someone avoidant with a social person waiting inside for the keys and a way out. I'd show you the compulsive, with a face manic in the midst of a diversion to distract you, to control you, from getting in. I'd draw you a face with a plastic smile, perfect movements, a learned handshake and a gut full of despair and lone-liness in a world that applauds the 'appear' at the expense of 'self'; suicide without a corpse.

I might show you the workaholic, the alcoholic, the compulsive DIYer, the agoraphobic who takes her children out of school to go shopping, the compulsive reader who just doesn't want to be interrupted, or the compulsive helper, diverting successfully from any attention to self. I might show you the flag waver who draws attention to everything they are not or the raging materialist who runs away when you try to get close. I might bring you the train-spotter who has all his lines down pat or the compulsive comedian who can't be caught being 'real'. I might show you the 'autistic', the self-abuser, the anorexic. I might show you the activist who can't 'just chat', the lawyer who never knocks off, the teacher who's always being useful, the mother who advertises how much she loves her kids and the father who can't stand to pick them up. We can all experience Exposure Anxiety but, for some of us, it controls us more than we control it. Exposure Anxiety is on a sliding scale from self-preserving to inhibiting, from annoying to dangerous and tragic.

Exposure Anxiety and 'autism-spectrum' conditions

People with Asperger Syndrome (who live in the literal and struggle for the significant) provide a clearer picture of the links between the autistic and non-autistic world regarding the effects of Exposure Anxiety. The detached 'fact-tition', the involuntary impressionist, the hyper-lexic who lives in books, the obsessive who tightly controls where all interaction or conversation is *allowed* to go, according to the silent inner laws laid down by Exposure Anxiety.

So-called apparently 'low-functioning' people with autism are more primitive in their display of Exposure Anxiety, its appearances in them less diverse. In people with autism (who live in the sensory and struggle for the literal), the avoidance of eye contact or of verbal initiation for their own need or benefit are expressions of managing information overload and often also of the social–emotional response of Exposure Anxiety. The inability to make the transition from 'in front of' or 'at' to 'with', is part of being mono, having information processing problems, but is also a social state that gets co-opted by Exposure Anxiety. The self-payback for breaking those inner laws and daring beyond the limits of what Exposure Anxiety will tolerate is the self, which interacts with Exposure Anxiety in an inner non-verbal dialogue, arguing over the emotion-politics of striving for, inviting or allowing contact with the world.

> **The only difference between the apparently 'high-functioning able' and the apparently 'lower-functioning less able' person with autism is not always that one has less Exposure Anxiety than the other, but that one has been pushed into diversifying the Exposure Anxiety responses.**

Through this, one becomes 'incidentally' more functionally able, while the other, however equally capable inside, does not.

> **There is no one type of 'autism' or Asperger Syndrome. Exposure Anxiety is one face of these conditions and yet it is shaped by the way the environment compounds, works with, challenges or expands the condition, on a physical, environmental and interpersonal level. It is one face with many expressions.**

Exposure Anxiety is shaped by personality differences that affect how we identify with or rebel against the condition. The condition may be the same, but adaptations to it vary enormously. So answers need to be tailored to the individual. Work with what he or she presents and listen to the language of their behaviour, yet look beyond it to what appears within the cracks speaking of the self beyond the confines of the condition. Be imaginative, eccentric, and surreal. Don't be held to emotional blackmail and dominated. Be challenging yet be respectful. Be bold in the face of your limitations in understanding, yet be humble enough to say, teach me.

My first experiences with Exposure Anxiety

My first experiences with Exposure Anxiety were so subtle, I didn't even notice them. I didn't yet know who I was as opposed to who I was not. Even as I bit myself, pulled my hair and tensed my stomach muscles, coughing against the pressure compulsively till I brought up blood, I still took this as being 'me'. I buzzed, my emotions without boundary as I became obliviously entertained over a play of light or a sound pattern, compulsively indulged in a niggle which flooded straight into a blind rage, or laughing over an unusual shape form till I could hardly breath. I didn't distinguish this from 'self'. I knew there were moments in between such states but these were few. This other stuff must, therefore, be 'me'. Up to six times a day, the hysterical screaming waking emotional fits blew my fuses and disintegrated all sense of environment or sensory cohesion and all remnants of meaning, including the memory of it. I was left over and over and over again with the impression that the external world could neither help nor save me. I hadn't yet linked the sensory flooding with the Exposure Anxiety.

I was a social kid: social with the dirt, the trees, the grass, the birds in the aviary, the rolls of carpet at the hardware store, the tinkling of pins, the books of wallpaper samples and the smell and lickable surface of patent leather. I felt the world deeply and passionately. I was cheerful in my own world and I had a fascination with anything that was not directly-confrontational and which would allow me to 'simply be'. People too often failed the criteria. They were looking for concepts such as 'to-gether', 'with' and 'us'. They were not worlds unto themselves within the world, as I was. They needed to be taken account of, to interact in a directly-confrontational way that they called 'normality'.

When the world asked for more than to be allowed to exist, when it expected me to respond, I gave it the message that it had invaded; I went into aversion, diversion and retaliation responses; 'I' stopped existing. I found strategies to tune out awareness; awareness of the environment and of myself. This freed things up again. Still, when things did free up, they did so without much ability to direct this wild horse within me.

The world didn't take a hint. When it watched too closely everything seized up. It was hard to breathe. I couldn't connect to take myself to the toilet. I couldn't think. Eating before others was like doing a solo perfor-mance in the Albert Hall. Showing the need for the toilet was like baring a huge vulnerability before those so eager, so waiting, hungry for purpose, they were like bears waiting outside the cave I was in.

I was fine chattering away to myself, singing or making sound patterns, in order to close out the impact of the invasiveness of others, and being told to shut up only heightened the desire to surround myself with the sound of my own voice. If I was expected to reply, however, this was the complete antithesis. Hearing myself speak in my own voice in acknowledged connection to the world was excruciatingly personal and felt like fingernails down a blackboard.

It wasn't that the volume was too loud so much as that in the grip of an adrenaline rush everything was sensorily too much. The intense 'pain' was that the personal, individual, me-ness in it was unbearable. I was allergic to the experience of my own existence and the experience of hearing my own voice speaking from connected expression as me could, at times, be far worse than the terrible feeling you get hearing your own voice on an audio tape or answerphone.

When I wasn't using my voice to close others out, I felt repelled by it as if it was a sell out, a disgusting statement of the desire to exist and claim life. Exposure Anxiety made me determinedly indecisive or indifferent about commitment to life. I felt a disownership so compulsive and so strong that it hurt every muscle in my throat to persist in trying to speak in my own voice with my own feelings.

It was so much easier to use someone else's voice, to speak in TV commercials, stored lines, to wait to be told to go to the toilet, to starve and grab food I wasn't being expected or seen to take. Although Exposure Anxiety was defensively, divertingly, retaliatively verbal, I hardly ever heard me as myself. My strongest voice and a voice always free, was the one I discovered through typing.

It was always easier to go without than ask or answer. If I rejected whatever was causing the Exposure, however much I liked or wanted it, then I felt relieved as it let me go. The panic subsided. This reward of refusing to care became something welded so strongly together, so inter-twined, it became almost impossible to conceive of any other social reality. I had been intensely conditioned by my Exposure Anxiety responses and a cognitive take on the social–emotional self-in-relation-to-other world would remain alien, difficult to imagine or comprehend, even once the information-processing problems were addressed.

The sanctuary of 'my own world' was becoming the prison as well, the battle swinging between the desire to join the world and the desire to keep it out. Worse, it was being controlled by something beyond me: the reactive mechanism of will and overactive sense of survival, and the constantly triggered reaction to a directly-confrontational world. I was being brought up by the brutal mechanisms of Exposure Anxiety as my parent. Socially I may as well have been taken away and put in prison. This is what progressively happened to my expression before others and, at one time, even to myself. Nobody else could see the mechanisms. They weren't subject to them. Their 'normality' was not based on them. Their theories and textbooks were not informed by the experience of them. So nobody could help.

Though I was held to ransom by it, I didn't actively or consciously feel imprisoned by my Exposure Anxiety until I tried desperately, too consciously, to fight it. Then not only was the environment the enemy of its 'self-protection' responses, but I was as well. It was as though I was a foreign body fighting against what was 'for my own good'. Never was this so bad as when I began to comprehend interpretive meaning at around the age of nine. I was driven to seize a world I had never conceived of beyond sensory pattern and Exposure Anxiety and I entered into an internal war. Ironically, it was at nine that, in addition to the immune and digestive system problems I had had for years, the years of severe chronic stress led to the development of juvenile arthritis, an autoimmune inflammatory response in which the body attacks its own tissue. There are those who believe the physical is a manifestation of the emotional dynamic, but it is equally true that severe chronic stress will exacerbate pre-existing healthy issues of all kinds. I can only say, the two states did reflect each other, and rather than cause and effect, I think it more likely to be a causal loop; the stress causing ill health, causing poor processing and overload, triggering Exposure Anxiety and exacerbating ill health.

At its worst during this struggle between freedom and 'protection', I stopped being aware I had any thoughts at all and the more I fought to be part of the world, the harder it became. In late childhood I sat eight hours lost in a spot on the wall until told to move. Exposure Anxiety was partly responsible for me being unable to process information so I was virtually meaning deaf and meaning blind to conversations and other people's actions – hearing and seeing without being able to interpret. I had an instinctual aversion to any connections which would trigger awareness and, thereby, a sense of Exposure. I felt like an island. I starved myself for days on end, abused the body that had imprisoned me and punished me for every attempt to break out, peed all over my room in an attempt to move out beyond the confines of my body.

At worst I have felt murderous against the world that taught me to perfect a smiling façade and create the impressive glass coffin of a compulsive comedian, intellectual and 'helper'. I have despaired at living with those I despised under the word of 'love' and despaired as I watched myself compelled to reject/be indifferent to those I loved truly.

I have known what it is to be buried alive, to give up completely and to find it painful to keep believing. Happiness was only connected or consistent when neither I, nor anyone else, was noticing too much. Then I was free. In a waking dream, but free.

I learned to trust that mine would have to be unknown knowing, that I could be intelligent, even if it would always constantly surprise me. I learned I could work with the progressively reinforced addiction to tune people out and my own consciousness which had always been the key to freeing up and being. I could learn to use tuning out when I needed it, not all the time, and give myself a chance to know the world as others do. I learned to laugh when I could at my aversion, diversion, retaliation responses, got playful, negotiated, learned self-calming strategies and mastered the tricks of mind which would shift perception, alter identification with Exposure Anxiety. I have learned to celebrate the buzz junkie but not let it run my life. We shared fifty-fifty, each tolerating the disruption of the other.

I have survived its other half, the self-murderer within, to ask for help and to help the world to help me when it didn't know how. I have made the most of my 'day release' in between getting caught and imprisoned again and again and have found strategies to ensure that what I need and want won't be allowed compulsively to be thrown away without strategic opposition. I learned to expose the Exposure Anxiety itself and trigger the compulsion to disown it, setting me free. Mine is a story of extreme Exposure Anxiety, a tic-like response so pervasive and so extreme it has been called 'autistic'. But it is just an extreme example of the mechanisms that at one time or other affect us all. If I can manoeuvre this untamed 'Id state' that is Exposure Anxiety, then there is hope within the invisible cage for others who live with it too.

CHAPTER 1

The Mechanics

Faces of Exposure Anxiety

People with chronic Exposure Anxiety are sometimes expressive if left to their own devices, albeit in a self-directed way. You might catch them chatting to themselves, looking into the eyes of their reflection with affection, curiosity, questioning, despair or entertainment. You might catch them wandering about in the dawn before everyone else is awake or making all kind of experiments and creations as soon as you are out of the house. Those who appear unable to talk may be heard stifling, mouth shut, the tones and patterns of sentence structures you can barely hear or humming to themselves. Others have come to use assisted typing as a way in which to 'speak', and have expressed that they spent years talking inside, disconnected from body.

Why can someone with Exposure Anxiety be expressively and naturally laughing out loud out in the back garden but somehow 'stuck', compliant, or performing when in front of others? Why they can't get it together to make breakfast once you are up, or run the bath, or get dressed, but can seem to do a whole range of things which might prove they were capable of these? Why might someone with Exposure Anxiety be able to initiate communication with their own reflection and yet unable to respond as themselves when shown affection? Or be able to initiate an activity, but when you try to initiate exactly the same activity with them, appear uninterested, distracted or disowning? Why, although they have an ability, do they appear to freeze and become incapable in front of others or when asked to perform a task on command?

People with Exposure Anxiety are confusing. They can appear to hold you to ransom, to be control freaks, to be playing hard to get. They can appear unforgiving, stubborn, rejecting and selfish. They can appear obnoxious, out of control, passive as well as aggressive. They can be seen as backward, naïve, formal, fiercely intellectual or compulsively other-oriented. They can be seen as funny but sad, as performing but lonely, incapable or fiercely independent. They are enigmas.

As someone with Exposure Anxiety, I have found my own functioning everywhere from hilariously amusing to infuriating. I find it both an extremely complex system to understand in a world which is not domi-nated by it on a day-to-day level and which has no words for it, no way of understanding or explaining it and no hints for working with it. But it is also an extremely simple system, a system which has its origins before the development of mind.

The trademarks of Exposure Anxiety are, 'can't do it as myself', 'can't do it by myself' or 'can't do it for myself'. Exposure Anxiety makes it extremely hard to ask for personal help verbally and face to face, as oneself, for one's own benefit. The child who takes your hand to open the door when she seems easily physically capable of doing so for herself, and may even do so when you are not present, is one face of acute chronic Exposure Anxiety. The child who sits and rocks or makes a tune over and over to close out the fact he can't get into action because he is blocked by Exposure Anxiety is another. The child who seems to be giving in to her want or your request but then tears off across the room suddenly, inexpli-cably focused with great conviction on something obscure and far removed from what she was about to do is yet another face. The child who gives away or offers to you everything he wants for himself is another.

The performer with a hundred stored lines, put-on voices and stances, who never gets off the stage is another face. The person who attributes all responsibility to the objects around her or carried with them, the person who slaps, bites and tries to escape his body in response to being approached or even in response to feeling his own want, the perfect but wooden puppet-person compulsive in her self-control are others.

Parents, partners, friends and professionals despair in trying to understand or work with people with Exposure Anxiety, disarming one strategy only to find it replaced by another. The person herself is often given the feeling that she not only has a problem but is a problem and this negative self view only compounds the trap she is in and her isolation.

Can't do it for myself

Many high-functioning people are desperately eager to please, to follow the rules, to get things 'right'. They are often far more able to do something because another person needs it than to do something because it occurs to them that they need it themselves. In fact, for some, Exposure Anxiety can mean that even recognizing the need causes an expressive dilemma and the unseen, unexpressed need either stays unmet, causing frustration and despair, or it becomes subject to 'aversion', 'diversion' or 'retaliation' responses. So if the need apparently 'disappears', the person suddenly becomes very interested in…something else, or she actively defies the need, simply because it demands her attention; holding on instead of using the toilet, starving or going without drink, intentionally going without a coat or unable to initiate taking it off. Doing something 'for oneself' can be a non-concept, a constant distraction or an imprisoning, bullying, self-hate relationship with an invisible prison warder/saboteur. Why doesn't he just do it for himself? Those who don't have to tackle severe Exposure Anxiety can't imagine the obstacle because it's not visible.

When I was younger, I found it very hard to hold onto the concept that body was part of me. It didn't obey me, and I failed to identify with it properly as 'self'. I mostly didn't care what it felt, its needs weren't relevant. It was impinging on me, the person, demanding my attention, but I simply retaliated against the demand, insisting on tuning it back out and letting it know it could not penetrate through to the me. It was 'other', I was 'self' and I saw its messages not as feelings but as invasions. This was once my daily reality. Gradually, I developed a relationship to body. I had intensive highly-structured, ritualistic classical ballet training of several hours a day from the age of five to seven or eight. Being able to fall into the pattern and lend will to the ritual itself probably helped me accept I had volition over my body rather than it purely having volition over me, and I think it helped me to externalize my war, focusing instead on the demands of the environment to use body or mind or react to it. If I hadn't been helped in this way to make the transition, I think I'd have been far more disturbed in my relationship to body. I could at least treat it as functional. If someone is attacking body as 'other', I think they should have serious structured intervention in the form of occupational therapy of some kind. We generally don't think of working with people with autism from a physical training perspective. But when it comes to Exposure Anxiety, the first war between internal self and external other is primarily with the body, then later with the world in causing reactions via the body.

Being detached from body meant I was tortured by its most extreme sensations, blocked by an Exposure Anxiety response from acknowledging and then responding through action or expression to its needs. The earliest way I can remember dealing with these 'invasions' was avoidance responses – 'nothing was happening'. I let body do whatever it would, as though it were a Siamese twin I was forced to share space with. Later, I learned to use diversion responses to allow some other, purely logical part of me to take care of practical needs such as using the toilet or eating mechanically. The emotional part of me, however, took much longer to connect to these pragmatic skills. This part was somewhere else in a state of self-hypnosis or involved in something quite incidental to the action. So whilst the logic mind would be using the toilet (which I experienced as a separated mind-self, 'I'd' be busy with movement rhythms, singing tunes or exploring the structure of the toilet cubicle. These ways of tuning out made actions more possible; for to not employ them lead to far greater struggle with avoidance.

Around the age of five or six echopraxia came to the rescue. I would merge with the movements of my older brother. If he spoke, the sound came out from me too, if he moved, my body went with him, if he lifted a hand, my hand went up too. I don't know if this was a Tourette trait (because I also had spitting, coughing and movement 'tics') but it meant I was able to use his use of blinking, is body as a map for my own. If he got food, my hand took it too.

Later, if someone left the room for the toilet, I followed. If someone grabbed a piece of fruit before leaving the house, pulled back the curtains, grabbed a coat, then whether I wanted to or not, I found my body following. In separation from self, survival had necessitated its linking with someone else's selfhood. For me as a detached self inside, it was remarkable, sometimes amusing, sometimes scary, and always curious to watch my body doing this. Later, as this became not only progressively embarrassing and annoying but also a source of sadness rather than freedom, I moved into another strategy. Envious of the freedom of others to act voluntarily for self, I could not get there, but I could do the next best thing. I projected my own volition onto them. If I was hungry, I asked if they wanted to eat, then I'd do as they did. If I wanted the toilet, I'd ask if they needed it. The problem was always that if they said 'no', I was stuck. I couldn't physically connect. Exposure Anxiety would jump in, sensing a heightened sense of exposure and 'protect me', freezing me. These days, things are easier, but, until recently, Exposure Anxiety was still a big issue (even in writing this book, I was still plagued by Exposure Anxiety and had to constantly remind myself why it was important to other people or I found I couldn't get near it).

Being unable to do for myself meant I may still have been able to 'fix the crease in the curtain' (the curtain needed it), 'feed the cat' (even if it couldn't feed itself), ask 'do you need the toilet?' (often meaning, I wish you'd go to the toilet so I could go 'as you'). The more anyone watched, the more Exposure Anxiety compelled me to pull back from 'feeling' compliance in doing 'for someone else'. So, small doses, play hard to get, be pragmatic and casual; these were ground rules. 'Oh, could you pick that up for me', 'Ta'. No fuss, no surprise if I do so. Next, if I could do for someone else, to get me to do for self. 'Oh, those feet need to go outside, off they go' (casual, get on with your own thing, don't watch or the person with Exposure Anxiety will often freeze). 'Oh, oh, there's a pee needs to go into the toilet, it doesn't have anyone to help it, you'd better take it.' 'The body wants a coat, a caring person would give it one.' Eventually, 'There's a person in distress, they need to give themselves a rhythm, the hand wants to help, OK hand, give the person a rhythm, great' (again, be busy, don't watch, get on with your own thing). And, 'Poor hand. Gentle biting. It needs gentler biting.' Remember that to command 'no biting' to someone with Exposure Anxiety often triggers retaliation responses then or later in which they will be compelled to defy the 'no biting' command. To permit, even force repetition on the person, on the other hand, is to trigger their rejection of the unwanted action as much as externally initiated praise often inhibits a repetition of a wanted act.

The role of getting someone to do for self is not that of a teacher, but of a facilitator. The transition from doing for someone else to doing for self involves helping people to experience 'self' as a 'thing', 'something external'. This reduces the sense of claustrophobia which drives someone to avoid, divert or retaliate against even 'self'. Eventually 'the arm' becomes 'the person's arm', becomes 'the boy's arm', 'becomes the arm of Michael Jones', becomes 'Michael's arm', becomes 'Michael', 'you'. Similarly, terms like 'Mummy', 'Daddy', even using first names, can trigger Exposure Anxiety by forcing the person to feel a self–other relationship too sharply.

Many children with Exposure Anxiety refer to their parents by their formal names, first names, a made up name or nothing. In my case, my mother got nothing unless I screamed to get my brother out of my room, in which case I mimicked him screaming 'Mum' at the top of my lungs. Later she got her first name, formal, in its full form, later shortened, still now never Mum. My father got a made up name, Jackie Paper (from Puff the Magic Dragon song), later his first name, full form, formal, later the relaxed familiar version of his first name and two weeks before he died (I was thirty), I called him Dad. My brothers had names – I referred to them in the third person – but I still found it hard to get their attention using a name. It was easier to just walk in front of them. Teachers rarely were given any name. To try to name them caused such a rising self-directed rage, I gave up trying. It was easier just to walk in front of them.

Facilitated Expression is another helpful technique. It is about hand over hand, shadowing their opening of the cupboard, their holding of the pen, their pulling up of the socks. It is not about doing the activity for them but about allowing them, if necessary to attribute the responsibility for the action to your control. It is an interactive dance of responsibility. First shadowing the person's actions as though they were your own, then beginning to hold back, even pull away from the target if necessary, to provoke a retaliation response in the direction of the activity itself. The person who needs to use your hand to open the cupboard will allow themselves now to open the cupboard with their own hand because they tell themselves you are in control of the action, not them; it's not their responsibility, their expression any more. Progressively, having won this 'trust', you begin to hold back a little here and there, play hard to get and let them privately experience their own frustration and prompt of your involvement. They begin to lose the sense of which side they'd been fighting on. Eventually, the facilitator's support becomes lighter, more intermittent, less controlling, playing harder to get. Progressively, the hand over the hand becomes the hand supporting the hand. This progressively becomes the finger touching the hand, becomes the hand supporting the arm, becomes the finger 'supporting' the arm. Progressively, this becomes the finger just touching the arm, then becomes the hand on the shoulder, becomes the intermittent tap, becomes the vocal reassurance of presence from nearby, becomes the reassurance of presence from the next room. There are some people with severe Exposure Anxiety for whom this technique has led to a gradual broadening of ability in doing things for themselves in ways compliance models can only achieve in getting someone to do things as someone else.

When I was three I was in a hospital crèche and I was fine with the approach to the building, I was fine with the glass door, I was fine with the entrance. I was fine until I felt the slightest external attempt to control or directly include me. Then I made straight for the cupboards.

There were long cupboards that ran the length of the room. They were like a long corridor. The nursery nurse kept trying to get me out and I just scrambled further along the inside of the stretch of cupboards like a cat escaping attention. Eventually, Exposure Anxiety would subside and I'd make my way out of the cupboard into the room. As soon as I was approached I made a line straight for the cupboards again. As my mother has said, 'Control Donna? Have you ever tried to control her?'

Children sat on the mat at the front of a kind of classroom. I couldn't sit with them nor could I be made to. Even to try felt like being stuck with pins and anxiety had me restless and aloof. I would stand off to the side and look at anything else but I could not control the feeling of agitation inside me that warned that if I sat among those children chaos was going to be the result. No amount of efforts from the nursery nurse was able to counter this conviction. Something in me could sense her expectations were recklessly uninformed of the chaos that would result from my compliance with her expectations. Some kids can control themselves without 'the payback'. I knew I couldn't. I felt I was saving both of us. She left me standing. It was probably the best way to keep me from being straight back in the cupboard.

The nursery nurse brought over a crate full of tiny milk bottles and, ignoring me, placed them in front of the children sitting on the floor. I didn't go for one. She began to give out the bottles, one by one. She took my hand with hers over mine as though she was using it as hers and used my hand to take out one of the bottles that she then walked over to one of the children, who took it from me. I didn't experience this action as being me or mine and she didn't address me directly over it nor praise me for it. It felt like a pragmatic event. I was simply given a job, a role, nobody had made me be a person in relation to them. She gave out the whole crate of milk using my hand, going from child to child. I'll never forget that. Eventually, I just had to hear the bottles in the crate and I made my way to the area up the front and handed out the milk.

The other place I used to go in this crèche was to the prams. They had curvy metal handles, all the same, all in a row. I was drawn to the order, to the curving form of the shiny metal and the feel of it and the sound of it chinking against my teeth. Sometimes the babies in the prams would start crying and it probably set me off a bit because I still find the sound really agitating.

This same nursery nurse took my hand and put it, puppet-like, on the handle of the pram and tugged gently and rhythmically to a count of about twenty, then moved me along to the next one, then the next. As she did this she didn't speak to me. She spoke out loud to herself as though for her own sake, not mine, and said 'Rock the babies, rock the babies, rock the babies', focused not on me but on the babies. Over the four months I was in this crèche, my two jobs were giving out the milk and rocking the babies. I never said anything about the milk, but I did use the phrase, 'Rock the babies' (said out loud but mostly inside myself) for many things, including calming myself down or expressing in my mid- twenties as an adult that I needed to be 'tamed'. Now, in my thirties, I say 'tame me' or 'give me taming'.

In *Somebody Somewhere* I wrote about a boy I called Jack. Jack had extreme Exposure Anxiety and was said to be 'non-verbal' and had the label 'autistic' and was not considered high functioning. Jack needed the toilet and had taken my hand to delegate the responsibility of his need to me, using my hand as though it was his, like the nursery nurse had. I began to shake. I felt Exposure Anxiety in being given, by him, the responsibility for his expression of his need for the toilet. He stopped still, looked straight up at me and said very clearly and audibly, 'Don't worry, I will come with you'. I managed to take him but he had obviously sensed my Exposure Anxiety was higher than his and this brought his own down enough to tackle the situation as though I was the one needed help more than him. He had begun to go to the toilet as though it was my responsibility but had shifted to being my assistant.

As carers, most people either expect a person capable of an action simply to use their abilities for themselves or they expect to be asked for help rather than be handed the entire responsibility for the expression.

When my younger brother was about three, I was about ten years old. I'd begun to make meaning out of spoken sentences with some consistency at about the age of nine and could now understand three sentences in a row but that was pretty much the limit. Before, everything would tumble about and sound meaningless again.

Much of the entertaining of my brother was made my job and this gave me a focus of being responsible for someone else rather than dealing with dodging focus on myself.

When my mother wanted something she generally didn't come up to me as if to ask me and she didn't insist on eye contact. She didn't ask in fluffy sentences of 'Would you like' or 'what about…'. She made statements, strong definitive, assuming statements like 'Make your brother a sandwich', 'Play soldiers with your brother'. Though relatively directly-confrontational in nature, her statements didn't feel self-in-relation-to-other. I didn't feel 'asked' or 'watched'. She didn't make me feel 'personal' about these requests and she didn't offer me a way out.

She had absolute expectation but somehow the 'me-ness' in the expectation seemed absent. I felt like a tool in the request and this worked a hundred times better than being addressed more personally (which triggered a strong response to 'disconnect'). She also gave these commands with a kind of assumption directed to herself. She didn't wait or watch to see and often I remember her taking the statement as though it would do the work on her behalf and instruct my brother 'Right, Donna's making it for you', 'Right, Donna's going to play with you now'.

I had been railroaded into 'a job'. She had walked off leaving the responsibility on me. From there, she left my little brother to see to it I followed through. If I didn't, he screamed because I wouldn't 'obey' what he'd been promised and I'd then be used, not to please her, but to shut him up. It was a very successful triangle. Once he knew you were there for his needs, that was it; there was no escape, he took charge but in a way so focused on himself that little Exposure Anxiety ensued. The point was that this was like a 'job' and the activity of making a sandwich or playing was not taken to be 'for me' in front of others (where it would have triggered much more aversion, diversion or retaliation) but for someone else for *their* own sake.

I remember recently a young boy who had improved quite dramatically since being on an amino acid treatment. He had extreme Exposure Anxiety that we were still tackling now we had the sensory chaos reasonably managed. He was beginning to dare an interest in the people around him now but it seemed that he had never been expected to clean up after himself.

I was sitting at the table with him, not focusing on him directly and focused instead on the plate and the food on it in front of him. It was very clear that when I looked at the plate he could look at me; when I looked at him, it triggered an aversion which quickly escalated into diversions of attention onto anything else but me. As he grabbed for food on another boy's plate I continued to be indirectly-confrontational in how I managed this and addressed his hand, not him, in having the food put back.

At the end of his meal, he sat there and tuned out, probably aware this was where the direct attention usually comes in as the staff come around and check who's eaten, and take away the plates. I took his plate, looked only at his hand, took his hand and put the plate in it, closing the fingers back around it to hold it. I then gave him a physical prompt out of the chair and said 'Plate wants to go in the sink'. The boy seemed quite surprised but took the plate as though it was the plate's need, not a request of him. He stopped a few times as he crossed the big hall full of children. I walked behind but off to the side of the boy, like a shepherd herding. But I did this as though I didn't notice my effect on him, as though this was for myself. This made it easier for him to continue ahead of me, doing the plate's volition. He made it all the way to the washing up bowl and stopped.

Without looking at him at all, I tapped the plate and said out loud to myself as though I was the plate, 'Help, I need to go in the water'. I gave the boy's hand a slight physical prompt, again not addressing him directly and giving him no personal reassurance (which would be counter-productive in working with someone with such high Exposure Anxiety and would probably trigger it). He dropped it gently into the wash bowl and then put his hands in there with it. He seemed so happy being with the plate that I left him there. I could have taken the plate out and made it say, 'Go away, leave me alone now, bye', but I didn't.

Had I asked the boy to do this for himself it would have become at best a matter of compliance. By doing it for the plate, he seemed to be able to be a real part of his own actions. It was his uncertainty as he hesitated, it was his choice and enjoyment when he used the situation to keep his hands in the warm water.

In middle childhood I had lots of activities in the house. I loved tying myself up in the beaded curtain on the pantry, making it tinkle for maybe an hour at a time. I could throw myself backward into the armchair in the lounge room, over and over again, feeling my body fall through space and the involuntary pull of my head back against the cushion as I fell. I traced the pattern of the flocked raised wallpaper up the stairwell and down the stairwell, up the stairwell and down the stairwell. I walked around and around and around the boundary of the pool in the yard or along the side fence and back again. I jumped down patterns of stairs to various felt mathematical patterns and went up and back down and back up. I dropped things from heights for an hour or more at a time, rang the doorbell and got so high on the repetition I was blissfully oblivious. I spent hours indulged in the reflection of my own face or the turning movement of my own hands. In between I did my TV commercials, my endless monologues, my jingles and the occasional 'interesting' word-association sentence.

My mother had no hesitation in directing me into systematic activities that at least gave me skills. I spent ages with the vibration of the washing machine and related to it personally, seeing it as expressing 'agitation' and assuming it 'enjoyed' its movements (or it wouldn't have been so set on doing them). I spent hours putting everything in order on the shelves. I was handed washing and heard 'this goes to the washing machine', handed shopping and told 'this goes in the pantry', handed dishes and told 'these go in the sink', handed clothes and told 'these go upstairs'. I wasn't addressed personally. I was addressed simply as though these were facts about these things that I was being handed. I didn't feel it was about me. Later, the skills provided carried over and this was such a dilemma for me. Why did skills carry over when it was the object which was addressed, but when it was me who was addressed, the lesson remained context bound and didn't transfer into new situations? I figure it was precisely *because* they were addressed to the objects, not to me. Directed at me, these skills become bound to the particular times and places in which these were requested. In a defensive, self-protective state, the lesson is blocked from being open information, free to *affect* other days, other places.

Directed at the object or the issue and not at the person, lessons didn't become context bound. Not being about me, the lesson becomes object or issue bound – washing always goes to the machine, clothes always go upstairs, shopping always goes on the shelf. It may have meant the rule got applied very rigidly but it was always more functional than when nothing got carried over and I was still frozen out of 'thinking for myself' in deciding what to do in a new situation.

It's important to acknowledge that whilst severe information-processing problems may co-occur, not all of the cognitive issues affecting people with severe Exposure Anxiety come down to the information-processing problems alone. In the acknowledgement of sensory and information-processing issues, we have to consider whether we may, in some cases, be letting Exposure Anxiety hold us to ransom. Are we condoning it for using its own blocking capacity and adrenaline rushes as we say, 'Oh but the person can't help their information-processing and sensory issues'? Identifying Exposure Anxiety, teaching self-calming and self-hypnosis techniques to stay involved, an indirectly-confrontational approach and addressing self-indulgence in learned dependency and adrenaline addiction can reduce the way Exposure Anxiety compounds information-processing and sensory issues.

Can't do it as myself

I have a photo – taken when I was less than three months old, one eye turned inwards, my feet turning in awkwardly, my fists clenched and arms pulled in protectively against sensed invasion of being the focus of attention. The photos of me taken before the age of three often stare through the person taking the picture as though I can't see them. Those from the age of four show a social child with a short fuse for tolerating self-in-relation-to-other social contact and a very tentative and fragile ability to comply and stay present.

Those taken around the age of five show a tight pinched-up mouth, the use of peripheral vision to tune in without inviting invasion. This was the face of what I thought of as my defender, my protector. Looking back it was almost a face of Exposure Anxiety as self, except that that aspect of self was not me. I had dissociated from this protector and by this age interacted with it from inside. I had a name for this compartmentalized aspect of self. I called him Willie. He had dominance over my presence in my body. I would have feelings: my like, my want, my happy, my sad. What would show would be another self, a reactive one living by the rules dictated by a hypersensitive self-protection mechanism. I wasn't attached to having a body and it hadn't yet occurred to me that letting this self-protection mechanism operate the body in my place would progressively sever the links between self and body, taking almost a decade of work to try to recover.

By the age of six something else had distinctly changed. Although I was almost completely meaning deaf until the age of nine and still almost completely meaning blind, I saw something quite different emerge by the age of six. It was a contrast to the wilful, steely, protector. It was a per-formed, almost painted-on smile – a plastic smile, learned comical phrases, postures taken from sixties American sitcoms of the time, including Gilligan's Island and The Brady Bunch and an ability to perform to push button order without the slightest self-consciousness. It was like watching my body from the inside, being run by a conservative, driven purist now competed with by a cheesy, American, talent-show construct. My fight and flight response had formed into two compulsive, ticcy personae. And I knew exactly whose this plastic smile was. It was Carol's.

Like my parents, I seemed charged with adrenaline all the time. The self-protection instinct of Exposure Anxiety was already so highly tuned I was bound to be expressively challenged in connecting with my body, whatever my circumstances. My home environment, living with two parents probably similarly challenged, kept this volume turned up so high, so consistently, that I became unable, in the end, to connect with my body. Simultaneously, however, the environment meant my fight and flight responses were so ever-present I went where many never go. I learned that even if I couldn't live connected with body and expression as self, there was still a semblance of life and ability that was possible. Both Willie and Carol were remarkably autistic: Willie the traditional stereotype impression of someone with Asperger's Syndrome; logical, purist, literal, pedantic, rigid. Carol was so like the high-functioning 'autistic', stored, reactive, a compulsive detachment and performance of a disconnected self to divert from the inner emotional and personal reality. In both modes, there was the awareness that I existed, in neither mode did I feel there was any reason to give up control of the body and expression because both were, after all, there to protect as a matter of survival in the world.

What I knew as 'me', 'Donna', was someone whose movements were natural though not conventional. This was someone whose sounds were expressive, though not usually through words, who had experiential concepts for which conventional language did not exist and who had a capacity for deep attachment and empathy that these reactive, protective façades could perform but never connect with internally.

Like those with Tourette Syndrome, many people with severe Exposure Anxiety also switch to stored voices, learned lines, pieces of advertisements, gestures picked up from characters on TV, showing intermittent 'ability' as though they suddenly 'come to life' by being someone other than themselves. My father used several techniques that tapped into this mechanism of being able to act as someone other than self. He would make all manner of objects suddenly interact. He would suddenly address an issue by having the fork start an argument with a matchbox, using put-on voices. It worked in promoting a sense of play-hard-to-get exclusion that compelled me to gain control and get closer, listening in, ready to grab the objects and stop the dialogue, later trying to make it continue. Using these things as 'puppets', talking via objects, addressing the object/issue but not me as the person, using put-on voices so there was no longer any sense of 'other' in relation to me as self, was able to get me to my social self where nobody else could.

My father was the only person able to trigger non-defensive, non-hiding, non-diverting communication as self. Where my mother was able to force compliance and get me to do 'as her', he was able to get me to do as self by turning down any sense of self-consciousness by himself, acting as someone other than self.

My father's own Tourette-like modelling of communicating via objects allowed me to attribute responsibility for my communication to all kinds of things that were not self. Experiencing my communication as self would have instantly triggered my over-sensitive self-protection mechanism, trapping me inside. But thanks to a combination of what he had modelled and my mother's technique of leaving things in my room to be discovered I was able to begin to type. I was about ten years old and had only discovered the year before that words had meaning. I'd been reading fluently but delayed information-processing meant I didn't connect that written words, let alone heard spoken words were linked to real things and experiences. But I began to explore this thing left in my room, tapping its keys and watching it move. I wasn't typing letters, my fingers were doing it. When the letters began to appear on the page, it wasn't me who was typing them – my fingers were moving independently of me, showing me through my eyes what the patterns were. Soon, paper magically appeared in my room for my 'discovery' and I did what the typewriter needed and fed it some paper. The letter patterns became word-line-patterns. These became sensory-experience words like crunch and crack, brittle and glass, words with strong feelings about them, good sounds, good textures when said. In the next two years they became word-list-poems, then (described dismissively by my mother as 'psychotic') prose (written in the detached and compulsively hiding language of Exposure Anxiety).

When I couldn't move, colour to take me somewhere. When I couldn't scream, I told voice to let noise out. When I couldn't show I needed food, I allowed hand to feed me. The ability to do as other saved my life. Whatever else they were responsible for, my parents, knowingly or otherwise, also provided keys with which to navigate the condition. In their indirectly-confrontational way I believe they got more variation out of me than anyone using a directly-confrontational, self-in-relation-to-other approach would have got. I'm certain they'd have said the same of themselves. Neither could cope with being 'shown' or 'helped' and were insistent on being in complete control of their own lives. Both were from very large, overburdened families. Both saw themselves as having 'brought themselves up' and I cannot recall any memory of any tone of self-pity about this – they just took this as 'how life is'.

When I was about three, I would escape to my grandparents in the shed outside, where they lived. I was capable of climbing out of my window and going to the park. I was capable of taking myself into the lounge room and getting into a blanket in the chair. When it came to escape and going wherever my feet took me, I was quite capable.

In company I could be physically prompted into compliance and could snatch things that were not meant for me. The thing I couldn't easily do was to take an action for myself when I experienced a sense of focus on me. I simply cut off, lost connection to self. The only answer was either to tune out awareness of 'other' and find I came back on line, or merge with 'other' and let my body do as 'them'.

If noticing I needed the toilet (or being made to notice) caused a shutdown in the connection to body and its sensations, then it was always possible to 'shadow' someone else. It wasn't conscious nor even voluntary. It was simply a crack in the wall through which light streamed through, a gap in the bars.

What was needed simply followed. My brother would leave the room and my body, no longer subject to the laws of Exposure Anxiety, would fulfil what was my otherwise blocked desire, and leave with him. Where I couldn't ask or initiate the desire for food or where there was any sense of audience to such acknowledgement or action, I could still eat 'as my brother'.

I was reminded of this experience in watching the film, *Awakenings* where the patient was in a kind of waking coma state. The patient, was able to cross the floor by following subconsciously the dictate (the 'will') of the pattern of the floor tiles, but where these ran out, simply ran out of the con- nection between volition and action.

The first person whose 'will' I came to borrow was that of my older brother and I merged into his actions not as conscious copy but as involun- tary but welcome echopraxia. His days were filled with 'Mum, stop her, she won't stop copying me'. It must have been infuriating for him, especially as although I seemed unable to simply 'interact' with him as the playmate he needed I was clearly able to be capable 'as him'.

As I got older, the television adverts and sit-com characters provided the vehicles. I learned to brush my teeth *as* the *Colgate* commercial (thank you *Colgate*). I learned to wash myself as the *Lux* commercial (thank you *Lux*). I learned to do dishes as Madge from the *Palmolive* commercial ('It's Palmolive. Mild on your hands as you do dishes'), to iron as the *Fabulon* commercial ('*Fabulon* makes ironing easier') and to dust and clean windows as the *Mr Sheen* Commercial ('clean wax and polish as you dust with *Mr Sheen*'). I learned to complain as the Skipper from *Gilligan's Island*, to initiate as Gilligan, to be girlie as Marianne, to be intellectual as the Professor. I learned to throw a teenage strop as Jan from *The Brady Bunch*, to act cute as Cindy, and to be the cleaner as Alice. I learned to eat lettuce and celery as our rabbit, ate dog biscuits both as and with the dog and ate honey by the jar as Fred Bear in *The Magic Circle Club*. I projected onto my reflection all I wished to be and then moved forward to 'do life as her'. I was not thinking, this will be fun, I think I'll copy this, I will play at this idea etc. I learned to close out awareness of others and of self in focusing on objects and speaking through them. I just found the mergence with these things so natural and a road to freedom. In front of others, there was progressively so little self-initiated self-expression left that there was nothing to close this stuff out, compete with it or make it 'a choice'.

These things remind me so much of so many echolalic, echopraxic people; ingenious and brave people tackling an invisible opponent. I have experienced those able to speak as puppets or object, to speak as the dog, or as Postman Pat or Thomas the Tank, the weather girl, the recorded phone message. The freeing art of self-delusion it may be, for the reflection in the mirror is our own, the voice, whoever it may mimic comes from us, the body, however much it feels freed of the imprisoning impact of felt volition, it still actually, physically ours.

I've seen many patchwork people with fragments of self that slip through the cracks where they can. What I see is survival and it impresses me. I don't see 'semantic-pragmatic disorder', I see people using whatever mechanisms they have to get free in whatever limited way that may be. To work on the behaviour, we must get away from the blinding nature of the labels and work on the underlying cause. For with Exposure Anxiety, more than any other condition I can imagine, compliance is not a long-term sustainable answer if our goal is independence in capable people who cannot handle the awareness of self.

Can't do it by myself

I was one of those characters who would wait for people to mind read or wait till I sensed nobody around and found myself coordinating whatever it took to climb to that shelf, to scale that fence, to lift that piece of unsymmetrical furniture. I remember getting my head stuck between the railings of the staircase. I stayed there, waiting to be discovered for ages before starting to make a noise in the hope it would be explored. I was discovered, much to my mother's restrained self-amusement. I was helped to get my head out and, of course, having got the sense this behaviour was stupid and unwanted, after she'd gone, I was driven to do it all over again. Whilst I could do 'my world' things by myself. It wasn't so easy when it came to demonstrating before others that I could do 'their world' things for myself, as myself or by myself.

Being out in public, however, gripped my gut with dread and there was nobody I could turn to for help. Where many children with severe Exposure Anxiety will make a connection with a 'special person', my special people, my grandparents, had died or been sent away before I was five. This was one event I know strongly compounded the justification to identify with and side with my aversion to getting close to others again. Until recently I still struggled with the phobia that getting close to someone meant they would die, with the vulnerability of being left with that suddenly severed attachment.

The only person I felt could get me through the terror of being out in the open in front of people was my own reflection, and my sense of company with my characters, Carol and Willie. At times, I was near the surface, terrified someone might say hello or initiate the kind of robbery of control that would trigger dissociation, shutdown and chaos. At other time, I felt like an invisible dog being walked by those who possessed my body at the time. Yet these invisible 'others' gave me a sense of being in company without which it would have been impossible to initiate so many things. Many children do this by referring to themselves in the third person or by their own name as though they are watching the behaviour of a stranger with their name. Others have been known to make up names for different aspects of themselves.

Being with my reflection allowed me the strength to stand being in company. I used to tap glass windows wherever I went, feel reassured by the presence of my shadow as a familiar, completely predictable, non-invasive other. I'd had a mirror for as long as I could remember. I'd spent hours looking into the eyes of that girl in the mirror, connecting with her, seeing each other beyond our bodies and our trappedness, seeing the sad in spite of the smile, seeing the laughter which was suppressed for fear of other-heard noise. Her every move was familiar to me and clearly mine to her. I felt family with her, best friends, deep understanding, empathy and love. I didn't know her as me, I knew her as other – my special person. When I couldn't sleep, I'd check she was there, having the same problem.

When I was seven my family moved to a large house where my attic bedroom became the showpiece for visitors and a way to demonstrate how cared for, and lucky I was. My parents had the entire wall of my bedroom tiled with mirrors. Then the bathroom followed with three of four walls all mirrored. The lounge room followed, from floor to ceiling, wall to wall on one wall – mirrors. Now I would use the bathroom, sit in the lounge room and eat my dinner with my best friend – my reflection.

When I couldn't do alone, Willie would take over. Even if I didn't get what I wanted, I got something. Later, in my twenties, I had to get these reactive states to stop assuming my incapability and justify themselves taking over at the first sign of imperfection or nervousness. Eventually, I was capable enough as myself to stop depending on them and (especially through addressing information overload and anxiety through diet) I'd changed my chemistry enough to claim my body and my life as mine. I felt a great sadness and loss in letting them go. They were my bridges to where I am now. I remember them as ghosts of an internal family that both imprisoned me and held my hand through a life I was unable and unready to claim.

Nature as company and objects as company were both extremely important to me. I felt in company with trees. I couldn't distinguish between the sense of company in being friends with a tree versus a person except the company with the tree was easier. I didn't just climb a tree, I was in company with it like two friends sharing beingness together. I felt protected by them like one might a silent person with very fixed boundaries with whom you always knew where you stood. In my first book, *Nobody Nowhere*, I wrote, 'my favourite tree lived in the park' and this was pointed out as quirky but delightful and became part of a conversation in which I learned other people usually didn't think of trees in such a way. To me, this was the residential address of my friend the tree, my favourite of tree friends at that time. My experience with trees is social. My social relationships are about sensing the feel of something and its edges, so in that sense of knowing social experiences through my body rather than my mind, they are what some would call 'spiritual' (a topic I wrote a lot about in *Autism and Sensing: The Unlost Instinct*). I used to cry and stroke our old palm tree in my front yard, telling it in silence all my feelings of despair and rage, but also sitting at its elephant-like trunk-feet and jointly appreciating the day and good feelings too. The tree, unlike people, lived a self-in-relation-to-self world. Unlike the self-in-relation-to-other world of people, the tree was by nature indirectly confrontational and good 'simply being'.

Relying on sensing in the absence of the ability to rely on interpretation my relationship with objects was intensely social. I spent hours standing stock still staring at a colour, resonating with it until I could feel nothing but the experience of it, devoid of any experience of me – a pure communication, a communion of extreme empathic experience others couldn't fathom the purpose of. I was the same with wallpaper patterns, patterns in carpet, the beaded curtain in the kitchen, most coloured glass, tinkling sounds, symmetry, shiny surfaces, marble, pink street lights… These experiences made me feel intensely 'in company' and sometimes carrying objects with me which were part of or represented the feel of these 'friends' gave me a kind of strength, just like having a close friend nearby might. An interactive human friend as support would have frozen me unless they were utterly self-owning but these object friends were self-owning entities and gave me company without ever triggering Exposure Anxiety. Others may have seen my merging behaviour in relation to them as an obstacle to interaction, but they may never know that many times I could not have moved except that I felt in company with the button or sleeve I was holding. They made me more myself.

Exposure Anxiety creates a vicious circle in social–emotional development. Severe information-processing problems meant I couldn't actually process a sense of self-in-relation-to-other. I couldn't communicate and understand myself at the same time, so building confidence in my communication in my teens and adulthood whilst being meaning deaf to my own communication was hard. Then, having stopped speaking, I'd start to catch up on processing an idea of what I'd just said, at which point the other person would be speaking and I couldn't understand a word. Then they'd stop and as I was trying to make some sense of the tumble that was their meaningless blah blah, I was expected to reply. Often, instead, I'd be covering my ears, grimacing in pressured polite tolerance, causing a diversion of attention onto something or anything else, or walking off to save myself from the ensuing behavioural problems. The only things that could actually lend support rather than add to incapacity were things like objects, nature, reflection or the sense of myself in the third person as a form of company. Essentially these 'autistic' self-reassurances made it more possible to dare communication, expression or involvement of a true self-expressive kind (as opposed to avoidant, diversion, and retaliation responses). It's important to realize here that what I was probably trying to get around was not an emotional development issue, but the interference of my own chemistry mechanisms which were triggered too easily. Many people think that getting through to the person is the answer. When you are looking at underlying physiological problems and their impact, there may be very little the outside world can do to reassure. It maybe more a matter of doing what one can to help people chemically and understanding how the behavioural approach may interact with that chemistry to the benefit or detriment of the person's cognitive, communication and social–emotional development.

'Want to go to the toilet?' 'Want a biscuit?' 'Want to get dressed now?' 'Want the curtains closed?' As an adult this was my way of expressing the need to do things when in front of others. I tried to simply 'do' but the doing would freeze.

When the other person answered 'no' to my unintentionally other-directed question–statements, I would be stuck. Often I'd wait a moment, get flustered and say–ask again. The response of the other person would become progressively more annoyed, and he might answer, 'Why, do you want the toilet?' This didn't work either most of the time, because being asked directly and personally only compelled me involuntarily to reject the offer of a way out. The response of 'No, you have a biscuit if you want' was not a command but an invitation to demonstrate publicly I had a want. It generally got rejected too. The only response that consistently worked would be 'No, you go to the toilet'. Having been commanded I was relieved of the sense that the action was my own expression. Exposure Anxiety would go and I would comply, thereby achieving what I wanted in the first place. Getting to this point was very hit and miss and most often I simply had to wait till the other person went to the toilet, took a biscuit, got dressed etc to move 'as them' and share the joint responsibility for my actions. This meant there were a lot of responses like 'What are you following me to the toilet for. Get out' and 'Do you have to do *everything* I do?' The rejection worked because the more the other person pushed me away, the greater the decrease in obstruction to my actions. It often freed me up to drive forward of my own volition like nothing else could and as an adult living with others I did push my way past people to beat them to the toilet.

The same was so of wanting to make a statement of feelings. 'Do you love me?' was my statement of reassurance to the other person, often if I feared they were going to hurt or abandon me. 'Do you like that?' meant 'I like that'. The response of the other person was often appropriate to the question they heard but inappropriate to the statement I felt I made. My response was to ignore their response and make my statement again, of course, heard again as another directed question the person felt they'd already answered.

Aversion responses

At six months old, I was able to bounce in my cot to the rhythmic, jolly tones of my father singing in my room. At three I was able to smile when things amused me without becoming overwhelmed by the exposure of my own emotional expression. At four I was able to sing to myself whether others could overhear me or not. I was able to dance with the air currents I could see all around me without a sense exposure closing me off.

At this earlier age, Exposure Anxiety was not so obvious or intense. The space between the bars was still enough to slip out through the gaps before climbing back in where it felt 'safe' in my own world. The walls were not steel, they were warm, not cold, I sided with them more than they imprisoned me. The response of closing down connection with the world outside of me felt natural and I was not fighting it nor did I experience it yet as severely fighting me.

I was two and a half when I was taken for testing at the hospital. I had physical symptoms, bruising very easily, coughing up blood and I appeared deaf. I was kept for three days before being released. I had been found to be obsessively tensing up my stomach muscles to cough against the pressure, persistently enough to bring up blood. I was found not to be deaf and the bruising was found not to be the result of leukemia as thought.

It was less than a year later that I first remember 'the big black nothing-ness' coming to eat me. I know this now as sensory flooding triggering such a degree of information overload as to cause an epilepsy-like total shut down on the processing of incoming information. These 'emotional fits' were probably raging hormonal rushes and would happen about six times a day and were terrifying. Exposure Anxiety begun its conquest over my soul. The only comfort was to give up all attachment to meaning and let the world go. When I stopped fighting the shutdown it didn't disorient me. I didn't feel the world being 'ripped away'. I sided with my withdrawal as my saviour from overload. The walls of Exposure Anxiety were getting harder and colder. My excursions outside of the bars, shorter, the terms of my momentarily releases subject to stricter and stricter rule. The punish-ments were my own involuntary paybacks for pushing the boundaries beyond the internal sense of safety – I found myself at the hands of a terrible abuser: myself.

Aversion responses saved me. They saved me from retaliating against myself. They also imprisoned me but they changed my life. I developed an exceptionally highly developed skill of being 'the fly on the wall'. I could use peripheral vision, peripheral listening, like a videotape recorder. I became progressively less and less consciously present in this state. The lull and peace of this was hypnotic. It became, by contrast, progressively more painful and infuriating to be expected to respond with a consciously accessed response when required by someone else. The basis for a war with the world for the next two and a half decades was sealed.

Today I work on undermining children's identification with their own Exposure Anxiety. I work on reducing the sensory flooding experience that justifies the over-development of the hormonal-driven survival response. I work with the families on turning around the sense of with-drawal as peaceful and rescuing, to building the sense of it as a redundant prison, not justified by the response of the world outside. This approach is multifaceted and sometimes feels like an act of secret service intelligence in undermining the other side. But it seems to work.

Aversion responses can make you appear deaf. They can make you appear unintelligent, uninterested, unempathic, helpless in the face of an accident or emergency. They can make it not only hard for the world to know who you are but for you, yourself, to know who you are. The very fact a response is frozen out of connection with the body builds an almost hyper-awareness of one's desires and externally-unheard internal commu-nication the screaming inside of what one wants. At other times, Exposure Anxiety can freeze not only the expression and action, but any conscious awareness of the desire to express or act. I was certain others *must* know what I was feeling so strongly inside. How could something be so almost overwhelmingly forceful and loud internally and not be experienced by others outside of me? One of the results of years of imprisonment at the hands of Exposure Anxiety was that I developed intense despair and retaliative apathy at the same time as passion. I became as capable of the height of self-calming detachment as I did the emotional depths of the manic-depressive. What was on the outside said it all. I was 'Dolly'. I looked like a doll.

Diversion responses

By the time I was five, my Exposure Anxiety had become both more entrenched in its links with identity and more diverse. Like a new enemy to the battlefield, new experiences didn't decrease its power, they simply challenged its power and forced it to forge new adaptations. The prison remained small but the labyrinth within its bars and walls became increas-ingly complex, more confusing to me, the person trying to navigate it, and more confusing in its presentation to the outside world. My Exposure Anxiety, in its ever-growing complexity, had me on the run. I became so much more involved in interacting with it than with the world itself that it was often hard to grasp the slightest glimpse of what was going on in the external world, let alone the relevance of wanting it.

I spent three years in my first junior school class. The photo for this class is on my website. I'm the one in the front row with the pinched up mouth looking rather promisingly retaliative toward the invasion of being photographed. At first I was able to jump as others jumped, run as they ran. In between, I bit myself so hard I left bruises and teeth marks. Then, relieved after my payback for daring, I'd continue my involvement.

My class reports referred to me as disturbed and I was described as constantly disturbing the other students, constantly out of my seat and chattering constantly to myself. I remember these years quite differently. I remember swinging sharply between enjoying myself for moments in the external world and then enjoying myself for much longer moments in my own world where the external world was very external. This swinging, though, interrupted everything. Nothing was perceived with flow or cohesion unless I sang or provided a rhythm. I had such a short attention span I could not stay involved long enough to grasp the point of most activities nor expand them beyond the point I'd experienced them the day before. Each re-visit to letters or blocks or numbers was back to the same place I'd been before the diversion which took me out of the activity. I developed no sense of continuity and the big buzz for me was the daring return to the familiarity and attachment of what I'd known.

In this class, far from being compelled into avoidance responses, I did not seem uninterested and aloof. I was giggly, outgoing, constantly active, very distracting, very hard to keep on task. It was only when cornered that I attacked myself. My Exposure Anxiety had moved from predominant aversion strategies to diversion strategies and I was like a monkey. The fact I was dairy intolerant and now being given milk every day which got me high as a kite probably helped me. Had I not been so 'drugged' by the milk (which mimicked LSD-like effects) my sense of exposure would probably have been much higher. Instead of giggly and distracted, I'd have been frozen and shutdown. Of course, these days, there are better alternatives.

In this diversion state, the ingrained rules of Exposure Anxiety still governed. If they said yes, it jumped no. If they said no, it jumped yes. If they were indifferent, some working together was possible. If they got enthusiastic, there wasn't a chance. If they were firm but detached, like an army officer, I could comply like a good soldier. If they demonstrated any personal desire for my response, there wasn't a chance. I appeared, by my disruptive, distracting actions, to be attention seeking. But if you tried to use attention to get me to do something, you were sure to have war declared upon you.

The greatest success I had in this class was when the teacher left the room, leaving us to respond to the dry formal tones of instruction coming through an overhead speaker. The class was called The Country Infant Room and was designed to teach city teachers how to teach as though they were in the country. Like following instruction given by a TV, I followed brilliantly. For this reason, I am a strong supporter of video and computer instruction for children challenged by severe Exposure Anxiety.

This was the stage of Exposure Anxiety where I felt like someone daring to pass notes out of the prison. It built a sense of the rebel and this contrasted sharply with the sense of myself as being protected by my own Exposure Anxiety. I was dipping my toe in the water and running away, reassuring my captor I was only playing with that outside world. I wasn't selling out. This was the time of learning the skills of devil's advocate.

Retaliation responses

Through progressive trapped intermittent involvement with others and the way this triggered diversion responses, I had developed a wide repertoire of behaviour, albeit almost all of it involuntary. This allowed me to form fragments of relationships with others and a sense of social desire. I was always of a happy nature and almost a blind optimist in my take on life but I had now, unwittingly, mostly through diversion behaviours, got used to some level of social connection. I began to feel the desire not to close other children out but to join them. But I had no skills to socially initiate, just to react.

By the time I was eight or nine, all the children had already grouped socially. They had their ideas of what's 'normal', what games they liked to play, what things they liked to talk about and a sense of who their best friends were. A weirdo with surreal behaviour whose form of enjoyment amounted to wild sensory extremes didn't hit it off with most children at a mainstream school. Where at five or six the games seemed simpler – run, hide, squeal, dance about like a wild thing, they had become progressively about replaying 'situational contexts' and conversing so being 'different' was not the trend. Children looked to each other to be 'the same'.

This became a very quiet and introspective period, full of uncertainty. At the other end of it, at about the age of ten or so, I began to become aggressive, pushy, and by the age of eleven I was violent.

The biggest problem was that my social desire had so overtaken the level of social–emotional development that I couldn't easily combine feelings with being social. I was being driven as strongly outward as I was inward, attacking myself and attacking others, diverting attention onto everything and being as confusing as I was confused. One moment Exposure Anxiety and I were one, next it was my captor. One moment the world was the enemy, next it was only the world that could help me. One moment it could go to hell, the next I mourned for it. One moment I embraced the world of meaning, the next I denied to myself that I'd ever shown an interest.

Those who most got a retaliation response were not those who hurt me. I really liked my class teacher, a woman who had a warm and under-standing feel to her. But it was the very fact I had warmed to her that meant I would throw my chair, spit, stamp, swear. Her attempts to get me to talk to her only made things worse. The only time it ever worked was when she tore up pieces of paper with names on them to help me to decide what to do about a dilemma regarding some of the children. I took them out of a jar but then was able to express myself with regard not to her but to the papers. This and other incidents which facilitated communication make me a strong supporter of the use of indirectly-confrontational media through which people with Exposure Anxiety can express themselves.

At home, the more I liked something, the more I would actively and publicly reject it and the same went for people. It was a source of extreme frustration but this frustration pushed a deep desire to understand in order to conquer these invisible saboteurs. My father would talk through objects as though for his own benefit, playing hard to get, speaking in a whisper and compelling me to fight his mock-rejection of my interest and involve-ment. My aunt was invited to sew in my room (on the newly appeared sewing machine) and I began, through *lack* of direct encouragement, to watch and eventually butt in. None of these activities drew retaliation. Yet a simple compliment, or statement about what I wanted or liked, drew both self-directed, and later other-directed violence, with me punching myself, slapping myself in the face, pulling my hair, tearing things or throwing the chair. Again, though my actions appeared attention seeking, I was far from being someone who enjoyed attention.

Why me?

I am often asked why I developed such skills of analysis and insight into my own mechanics. Everybody faced with such a challenge makes their own adaptations, finds their own way. Savant memory skills meant I had a resource for tracing something back, mapping its progress. I have very little short-term memory. Everything becomes part of serial memory as though all I have is mostly long-term memory covering in the absence of short-term.

A very cheerful nature meant I optimistically believed in a way out even when things were very dark. In many ways, it helped me broaden my adaptations to Exposure Anxiety and autism-related issues. Certainly having high adrenaline levels has two sides. One is that of being highly anxious and easily triggered into self-protection. The other is excitability. In spite of extreme lows as well as highs, I seem to have always maintained a sense of great optimism. Some of this surely comes down to feeling tremendously self-owning. I had a strong sense of the world being completely open for exploration.

Being extremely eccentric meant I tended towards quite surreal and unexpected solutions and avenues of dealing with challenges. Being a natural rebel with a sense of claustrophobia and love of freedom meant that whatever I sided with, I would eventually need distance from it to know I had 'chosen' it rather than been 'taken' by it. I also had the advantage of an eccentric environment that lacked any conventionality in its responses and approaches, teaching me by accident what worked and didn't work, beyond the scope many families would encounter. I also found myself in social circumstances which constantly challenged me (beyond any control of my own) to deal with a great deal of predictable unpredictability and social change. The pattern of advantages and disadvantages, motivations and anti-motivations will be different for every individual. My experiences are a guideline but for a program to work with Exposure Anxiety it has to tackle sensory flooding and overload and be tailored to the individual.

From my teens onwards, Exposure Anxiety has meant being unable to express or respond verbally as myself, leaving involuntary characterizations to passively comply and mirror the sexual desires and antics of others, eventually leaving me one very angry and suicidal teenager and, later, adult.

At seventeen, the social–emotional inability to simply open the door and greet whoever was there resulted instead in an elaborate social contortion. I met anyone who knocked on the door with 'Hiya, woman, how's your hormones', then slammed in their face before, having now diffused the Exposure Anxiety, reopening it. At eighteen, after complete failure at secondary school, the inability to express myself as myself in any way eventually led to a love affair with intellect. The lesser prison and expressive hiding place of text books and academia became my salvation and expression for the next six years before churning out of university as someone who could argue intellectually but still not ask you for a drink of water or say 'hands off'.

At twenty-four when asked once to kiss someone on the cheek, I diverted into kissing their hand, grabbed his arm which I then did not kiss but bit before throwing it back at him. (When I say now, 'I don't shake hands' or 'no thankyou' to the suggestion of a congratulatory kiss, it is not an insult but a favour). In the absence of any ability to discuss and resolve a problem with the person concerned, I was by now an habitual 'runner'.

At twenty-five I was launched into the public eye by my own hand when I wrote my first book. I discovered that journalists could help me, not to explain myself to the outside world, but to build up the ability to work with and eventually win against the mechanics of Exposure Anxiety through talking about myself 'as a topic'. I dropped characterizations and via typed communication was eventually able to disarm Exposure Anxiety, gradually then taking away the safety net and speaking out of my notes, to the point I can now just speak about myself with the feeling of an observer. I still find it hard to ask for a glass of water or a jumper if I'm cold or stop people in their tracks to say I need the toilet or answer someone in my private life about what I like or want without going into 'professional' mode.

At thirty-seven I proposed marriage via a letter to the man I knew I wanted to marry. He answered out loud to himself 'the answer is yes'. It's still hard to finish a breakfast without more diversions than I can count. I still find myself waiting up to two hours to get it together to initiate going to the toilet (unless someone else tries to go). I still go out without my coat because I can't stop anyone so I can grab one. I still find it hard to stop working because it is easier to do for others than take personal time for myself let alone show or ask for what I want or like.

An Italian journalist wrote, on seeing me speak, one of the most insightful and moving observances I'd ever experienced from someone who isn't challenged by the contortions of severe Exposure Anxiety. He wrote that he had observed how someone severely challenged was able to parody who they would be had they not been so challenged, giving the appearance of being extremely able. I have never heard anyone get so close to the point. It still amazes me that the people with autism who attended my lectures sometimes wrote to me of the terror they saw in me. Yet the parents saw me as capable. I know I was both but, yes, sometimes it was not me up there but the parody and I slipped in when I could, sometimes more, sometimes less, with the parody holding my space.

In the last few years I have spoken around the world in front of hundreds, even once in front of thousands of people. I put myself through it persistently. I hated it, my body hated it, but it gave me a great sense of achievement. I am glad others got something from it but for me that was just the medium through which I did what I did for the most basic of personal reasons: it helped keep Exposure Anxiety desensitized and the result was that through exposure by choice, I had a fuller, freer life, at least professionally (in my personal life I was more challenged than I appeared professionally). I have invited other people with Exposure Anxiety (diagnosed as 'autistic') to speak at my conferences, either directly or via typed communication. They tell me they are terrified and ask why they'd want to and how I could want to. 'Because it will get you free', is what I'd like to have said. But put on the spot, I often didn't say something so personal.

Exposure Anxiety and consciousness

When a baby is unable to keep up with the rate of incoming information, its threshold for involvement or attention is not great before aversion, diversion or retaliation responses step in, or plain and simple systems shutdowns: nobody's home.

There are a number of strategies someone can develop to tolerate involvement. One of these is the splitting off or compartmentalizing of incoming information. I call this 'being mono' and contrast it with those who are able to keep up with the rate of incoming information, even left wanting more – people I call 'multi-track'.

The adaptation of mono

Being mono can mean using sensory channels in a non-integrated way. You might take in what you are seeing, but have no conscious awareness of what you are hearing, be aware of a tactile sensation but have no idea of what you are seeing, be aware of the sounds or actions coming from self but keep no simultaneous track of the responses coming from someone outside of yourself or vice versa.

Another form of being mono is about taking in pieces of information but each piece remains separate, instead of linking with other related pieces of information. When you hop to the next 'island' of information, awareness of the last one disappears. Many islands may exist but only one or two exist at a time, making generalizations very hard but reducing information overload and its impact. Exposure Anxiety makes information-processing problems much worse. It is very hard to connect and let information affect you, even to process or synthesize it when you are compulsively, phobically geared to protect yourself from such 'impact'.

The person subject to mono-ism as an adaptation to overload may not show severe Exposure Anxiety until they begin to attempt to combine sensory modalities or components of related information, or fight to retain awareness and struggle to stay on line in spite of physical responses warning of shutdown.

Certainly some severely overloaded, mono people, reject their own involuntary adaptation, pushing fiercely beyond their will's own tolerance in pursuing a multi-track reality they can't integrate. The result for such tenacious people can be self-injurious or abusive behaviour as the system involuntarily retaliates against the individual, not responding to the warnings of impending shutdown.

The adaptation of using preconsciousness and peripheral
use of senses

Another type of adaptation to information overload, other than being 'mono', is that of using sensory channels peripherally.

In my late childhood, there were long phases when I would come into the lounge room and throw myself repetitively back into the chair, often whilst watching something in the big mirror tiled wall beside me. My older brother was majorly distressed by my 'annoying behaviour' as though I didn't care about him and his needs and had no interest in what he wanted to do. As a sister he saw me as pretty bad value. But I remember very clearly and accurately his behaviour and responses in the room. I remember what was on the TV, where he was sitting or lying, things he did and said whilst I appeared to be entertaining myself. Part of the appeal of entertaining myself so repetitively and so constantly in this way was it made the whole world move to the rhythm. It made it cohesive to my perception and it stopped the external information fragmenting. I couldn't break out and actually join it without causing myself fragmentation, sensory flooding, overload and shutdown, but the point was that I *was* involved.

At primary school my teachers found me unable to stay in my seat, constantly chatting to myself, singing or fiddling with something. I had severe muscle twitching (magnesium deficiency due to leaky gut) but my only coherent memories of the happenings in the class were *whilst* I was busy doing these things. When being directly involved I became overwhelmed and unable to fathom what was expected of me or any of the links between things going on – the information came through a blender. With other children, I could focus best when walking and not looking at them, tuning in to the sound of my own feet, especially in gravel, made it easier to 'hear' them and retain in sequence (no blender) what was said.

In my teens, on arrival at home I'd hear 'What happened at school?' and would launch into a self-directed litany, spewing forth every single event and utterance. Had I been watching attentively, listening and responding? No, I'd spent my day compulsively shaking my hands from my wrists, shaking my head to hear the insides move, making myself faint, doing adverts, buzzing on the sound of my many voices, spinning coins, buzzing on light effects with eye behaviour and being everywhere except in my seat.

I stand out as exceptional among people with autism because I found a means of letting out the information I'd stored in my first book, *Nobody Nowhere*. I typed it in four weeks and it felt not like my action but like an exorcism, a verbal typewritten vomit. I did not type it, I allowed it out through typing. The insight came not before I typed it but as I did. Much of my life was like this. I was constantly amused and shocked by what I heard or experienced as coming out of me

The question is, though, if this were so for me, does it remain something untapped in others? Have we imprisoned not just those who appear very disabled but perhaps also those who have built marvellous and complex façades to distract others from sabotaging their strategies?

Using your senses peripherally means that instead of focusing directly on what you are looking at, you focus on something unrelated and *see* what you are looking at elsewhere. So to look at someone's face you may focus up at the light fitting above them. To take in where they are sitting in relation to others you may focus on the opposite corner of the room. Similarly, to take in what someone is saying, you may sing a tune to yourself or repeat a pattern you are used to. To tune in to someone's touch you may pick something up and toy with that. By using your sense indirectly rather than directly you can actually take in a deeper sense of the information you are tuning in to peripherally. I have demonstrated this at many conferences and meetings, shocking and surprising people by the extent to which I can watch what I appear unable to see or repeat back with meaning what I appeared not to be listening to. This action is, for me, about an altered state, not of awareness so much as of consciousness. To take in happenings in this way is so lulling, so relaxing. But it is also not so conscious. For me, it feels like a half-sleep state, and it looks so as well. To others it looks like daydreaming, but for me it has a wholeness direct attention doesn't give. When I look directly, my brain processes what I've seen as though it came in via a blender. When I try to keep up directly with what is being said I struggle much more to hold the meaning than when I'm drawing or humming. And tuning in directly makes me so tired. I feel as if I'm running marathons. The opposite makes it appear that I'm taking in nothing but I process far more and retain it with far more sequence and sense of self and other than in direct use of my senses.

I call this a state of preconsciousness. The way it is accessed, too, is completely different. Where information taken in directly can be accessed in response to demand, information taken in indirectly (peripherally) is extremely difficult to access on demand. Instead, requests to access that information seem to cause a blank response, a freezing up as if someone is pressing the wrong keys or going to the wrong file. But if someone makes a statement rather than asks a question, gives multi-choice response possibilities or says what is opposite to what was experienced, the information is much more easily *triggered*. Yet all of the educational programs I've seen used with individuals who work in this way are programs designed to access rather than trigger information. Furthermore, children who use their senses in this indirect peripheral way are considered not to have taken in information unless they demonstrate they have done so directly. Yet psychologists are aware that we don't use ninety per cent of our brain. It is this part that takes in everything we are not looking at directly! Yet educational programs don't tap into the abilities of some people to collect this information. Techniques such as facilitated communication (FC) that focus on triggering information through an indirectly-confrontational technique of communication rather than expecting people to access and express it directly, are considered invalid. As the users of FC tune out direct awareness of their own typing, even speaking over their own typed communications, they are, ironically, seen to have been incapable of being the authors of their assisted (can't do it for myself, by myself, or as myself) typing.

Many people with Dyslexia don't read but can 'scan'. We acknowledge this ability but when a related tactic is used by a person with 'autism' to take in information about the environment, we fail to see the relationship.

Information overload and Exposure Anxiety

So what does all this processing stuff have to do with Exposure Anxiety? …Everything.

Exposure Anxiety as a tic response manifests as it does as a matter of sensitisation. So it is important to explore they key issues which can underpin this sensitivity.

Someone who relies on being mono to keep up with information often becomes subject to the involuntary self-protection mechanisms of Exposure Anxiety as they begin to put it all together. The loss of a simultaneous sense of self and other in their previously mono state leaves the person unaccustomed to the social–emotional impact of any sense of self-in-relation-to-other and other in relation to self. They remain too emotionally hypersensitive to handle ongoing contact in large doses. What's more, on top of the persistent internal bullying caused by Exposure Anxiety's avoidance, diversion and retaliation responses, there is little processing resource or tolerance left to cope easily with complex or dynamic other-initiated, social involvements. Without a program through which to desensitize to the sharpness of this experience of 'involvement' they remain unable to stand too much direct contact, especially when contact is not initiated and navigated by them. Without a program which demonstrates that they will always be left wanting, the more the likelihood that phobia of social involvement will become progressively more entrenched and acute.

Someone who has relied on peripheral and indirect use of their senses has rarely experienced direct acknowledgement of their social–emotional involvement (as they've often been wrongly perceived to have none). The result of this acknowledgement is that it is felt as so crushingly invasive it sends the person into the kind of aversion, diversion and retaliation responses that present as Exposure Anxiety.

The more you encourage the person into awareness and acknowledgement, the more the Exposure Anxiety responses heighten. Yet this is exactly what many behaviour modification techniques do in their directly-confrontational 'rewards' and 'attention' for the outward demonstration of a skill. Once that outward demonstration is linked with being forced to acknowledge awareness of it, the likelihood of the person repeating the action becomes less and less with each 'reward' of attention.

Those who have spent years building strategies to avoid attention in order to keep up better and experience the world around them more fully (without being seen to do so) don't respond well to this idea of 'reinforcement'. A program of intentionally 'overlooking' the display of wanted behaviour, 'under-reacting' to its significance and maintaining, regardless of one's own excitement, an outward display of distraction and a sense of one's own world, are essential, in my view, to building here a progressive eventual desire for recognition, and the expansion of social involvement from one's own 'want'.

I went through phases where I used to respond to compliments with violence, and when attention was drawn to my achievements I destroyed or disowned them. I responded best to an underplaying of interest with people giving a clear sense of their own world being important. I then became far more daring in combating Exposure Anxiety instead of siding with it. What I needed was not a building of self-confidence but a building of the desire to seek the attention of others. It still meant I had to do so on my terms and not when asked by others. This is why it is so important to realize that motivation and identity are key in building action from the inside, not outward compliance. One leads to independence, the other to performance that is not felt as one's own, to be too easily then disowned.

I believe strongly in the value of real change and that this comes from the inside. The desires and motivations that come from the inside are not unreachable or unworkable from the outside. They just require facilitating strategies. In working with people with Exposure Anxiety, remember that doing as you, for you or only whilst with you, doesn't mean being free as oneself. Weigh this up in the context of the techniques you consider using with people with Exposure Anxiety.

Exposure Anxiety and the system of sensing

The system of sensing is that place where we take in information without interpreting it. Imagine you are on the motorway and a vehicle comes past you at such a speed that it is out of sight before you can even recognize whether the driver was male or female, if it was a car or a van, or whether it had or hadn't signaled. This gives you some idea of what it is like to be subject to information-processing problems. People with such problems perceive the world as if it is a very fast motorway and everything is zipping past so fast that all you can do is get a sense of what passed you – the pattern, the feel of things.

The system of sensing is about impression but it is not just limited to what we see. It is about the impression of pattern and 'feel' of what we experience with our sense of space and movement, and the mapping in ourselves of physical shifts in response to the pitch, pace, tone and varia-tion patterns in what we hear. The question of 'why' is not part of the system and the question of 'what' hardly figures either. Things are simply what they are – their mapped patterns.

When someone lives by the system of sensing, it can be like a waking sleep state. It is a place of preconscious awareness. It is a place in which oneself and everything else is assumed to be self-in-relation- to-self. It is pattern driven – it's about 'the buzz'. When the directly- confrontational reality of interpretation-driven self-in-relation-to- other, generally ego-complicated people, impinges directly on the person who lives by the system of sensing, it can provoke a sense of awareness that is sharp and impinging…far from the gentle well intentioned visitation imagined by the 'invader'.

People with the involuntary responses of Exposure Anxiety, who live by the system of sensing, are sometimes seen as 'emotionally immature' or 'emotionally hypersensitive' in their emotional responses, even their extreme shutdowns. The impact of that Exposure Anxiety on the public outside impression of intelligence, in a world that relies on interpretation and conscious accessing, can be major. The way that assumptions of intelligence shape both the imprisonment and the hiding-place of people with Exposure Anxiety is something most people have little awareness of.

The problem of 'knowing'

An ability to 'map' patterns isn't usually seen as 'knowing'. I have said that if a dog had hands you might be able to teach it to drive, even to read a book, but you couldn't teach it to understand a story at the moment in which you tell it.

People who live by the system of sensing can read words, patterns of visual letters represented by sound patterns, but may have great difficulty putting mental pictures to those words or significance. They may enjoy reading, enjoying the forms and the flow as the patterns unfold across a page. Everyone has experienced reading fatigue when they can't remember what they have read. It's as though the meaning fell out. Yet you continued to be able to read. Later, if you put that book down, you might find that you came up with a mood, impulse or idea that seemed your own with no idea where it came from. Picking up the book again you may feel, 'Wow, that's just like what I was thinking about'. The lesson is, just because we don't keep up with what we are doing doesn't mean we don't 'map' that information. When we 'map' information, we don't have any sense of its relative or personal significance so our mind plays on it, in case it's important. It may not finish being worked with for five seconds, five minutes, five days, but eventually it is worked through, often beyond our moment-by-moment awareness. Then, something happens which triggers that information out of us and we are surprised.

That works fine for those who can turn interpretation back on at will. It is a mere visit to the world of sensing. But for those with information-processing problems this may be their ongoing reality and they are assumed 'stupid' because of it. The definition of 'knowing' is 'to have knowledge'. But in our proof-driven society that definition has become 'to have consciously accessible awareness of knowledge'.

Proof and Exposure Anxiety

If someone doesn't show an interest, they couldn't be capable of having one. If someone doesn't show they have learned how to read from the shop signs or product labels, then they couldn't have learned to read. If someone has never shown an interest in handwriting, then they certainly couldn't be able to type. If a person has been unable to speak as themselves in their own voice, they certainly could not be capable of speaking through song or the use of a puppet or character. If someone has never been able to openly initiate loving behaviour then surely they must be incapable of such feelings. All people hold back sometimes, too inhibited to show what they are capable of. Yet still, society in general cannot imagine someone so gripped by emotionally overwhelmingly involutary self-protection responses that they are often unable to connect and show what is in there.

In primary school I sang to myself throughout most of my first year. I was seen as being a constant disruption. In fact this was a way of being able to tune out awareness that reduced anxiety enough to reasonably manage my behaviour. By secondary school, I no longer sang all day in class. Now I sat in my seat more but indulged in more 'underground' diversions, tensing my stomach muscles with my breath held to make myself faint, compulsively playing rhythms using the muscles of my inner ears. I was still seen as disturbed. Yet I can recall the names of every teacher I ever had, name every pupil in my primary school class photo and describe the room in detail in pattern, texture, smell and acoustics and the number of steps it took to cross the schoolyard or the neighbours' front porch. Who was paying attention?

One of the most exceptional people I have met was the man I wrote about as Alex in *Like Colour to the Blind*. At about the age of fourteen, he was assisted in pointing to words on a word grid, later assisted in typing responses on a letter board. At school he used the technique to tell his teachers that he was sick of being taught ABC, he wanted to learn physics and art history. Yet all they could see was a boy whose verbal articulation was chattering in Exposure Anxiety – driven diversion communications about electric sockets and washing machines. They couldn't reconcile this self-abusive young man with someone capable of having taught himself to read from Sesame Street, a man driven almost to despair by his treatment as though he were retarded. He had to go to great lengths to prove his typing was valid, even speaking it onto a tape for his teachers so they could hear it spoken by him. Still, without his writing there to read, his mouth couldn't get to the words before Exposure Anxiety did so for him. This man later managed to do his secondary level GCSEs in Literature and Art History at an adult education college with the use of a hand-held voice communicator which spoke whatever he managed, with varied assistance (depending on the level of Exposure Anxiety in a given situation) to type.

Others have learned to speak as 'Postman Pat', as the family dog, or like me as a series of TV characters, through jingles, using advertisements or by going into character as someone else. Some of their communication diverts in the hands of Exposure Anxiety, some of it is theirs. This is intensely frustrating for the person with Exposure Anxiety and often will be misinterpreted as anything from signs of retardation to emotional disturbance or mental illness. In my case, my reliance on characters to handle both isolation and communication meant I was seen as emotionally disturbed throughout childhood, a view very common in the sixties and seventies when people encountered able people with 'autism'. In my late teens and early twenties, my ability to scan huge volumes of information (in spite of been very challenged by dyslexia) meant my once-crude characterizations diversified into 'intellectual personae'. I became able to talk 'shop' but still found it intensely hard to ask for the toilet or say directly whether I liked my breakfast or was enjoying life. This is so to some degree for many people with Asperger's Syndrome who have severe Exposure Anxiety.

Why some indirectly-confrontational approaches have worked

An indirectly-confrontational approach is one in which those working with someone with Exposure Anxiety respect that state and, whilst not pandering to it, seek to retain a level of interaction whilst appearing to be socially non-invasive. To do this successfully, the parent, teacher or carer has to acknowledge and respect the social–emotional and sensory–perceptual reality of the person with Exposure Anxiety as one in which the person often has no consistent sense of self and other and is essentially self-in-relation-to-self. Although interaction may be projected *at* or *in front of*, the person with extreme Exposure Anxiety generally can't sustain *with*. Furthermore, the person with severe Exposure Anxiety assumes this self-in-relation-to-self state to be 'normal'. When others attempt even tentative social contact that has a clearly self-in-relation-to-other feel to it, it inevitably triggers Exposure Anxiety.

A successful indirectly-confrontational approach involves mimicking the social–emotional developmental reality of the person involved, but not being in the person's face about it. The parent, teacher, carer needs to be 'self-owning' in their actions, self-in-relation-to-self and not self-in-relation-to-other, and this is where the approach differs so dramatically from that of Option and the Son Rise program, which are distinctly self-in-relation-to-other. The carer should model rather than teach, and should act as though it is for the carer's own benefit. This is part of playing hard to get. Address the object/issue and *not the person*. Address the shoes, the feet, the hand, the artwork, but not the person unless you want to inhibit motivation to participate fully next time. Speaking through objects, using characterizations, putting on voices, keeping things external, visual and concrete helps to take the pressure off crippling self-consciousness.

Leave the person wanting. This is essential. The biggest key to learning is to trigger motivation to return and take things further. If you wait until overload and Exposure Anxiety cripple the enjoyment and involvement in the activity you reinforce the self-protection response of Exposure Anxiety. If you notice the person is really into the activity without any signs of overload or Exposure Anxiety, it's time to go make yourself a cup of tea.

Be warm, be funny, but be aloof. Being indirectly-confrontational doesn't mean being cold or uninterested, but you may need to deal with feeling you are being 'rude' or 'selfish'– both of which are incorrect assumptions about the social–emotional reality of Exposure Anxiety responses. But if you get a great response, keep your excitement to yourself. It is yours. Don't put it onto them. When you do eventually get to praise, be warm but casual, however excited you are. Remember many people with Exposure Anxiety will fail or do things half-heartedly just to disown the activity or avoid praise (unless they actively came after it). When you do come to praise, don't pounce and, remember, small doses, praise the object/issue, not the person. Drop the enthusiam if it is responded to as an invasive infliction. Find a warm but blasé attitude. 'That typing was very impressive.' 'It's good when a person can use the toilet for themselves.' Don't wait for the smile. It's theirs, not yours. Have your own, for your own sake, but don't let it be taken as being 'for them' or 'in their face'.

Exposure Anxiety responses may fluctuate and this can be confusing. The person may show problems at home, but not at school; in sports but not in the library; in relation to using spoken language, but not typing; in relation to playing with dolls, but not when playing with gadgets. This often reflects how directly-confrontational the atmosphere was surrounding the things being avoided and the level of expectation. To remove Exposure Anxiety in a given situation, bring in an indirectly-confrontational approach in those situations until the person is able to desensitize to the level of involvement and attention. Exposure Anxiety can also fluctuate depending on external or internal information overload levels. Check for the complications of whether food intolerance, food allergies, metabolic problems such as Phenylketopuria or Salicylate Intolerance, sugar or caffeine are raising anxiety levels and messing with information-processing and further exacerbating neurotransmitter imbalance underlying Exposure Anxiety.

The other confusing aspect of Exposure Anxiety is where the person is able to initiate but doesn't cope when you do. This is probably because they have a 'map', a sense of boundary how far an activity can go when they have initiated. This means it doesn't trigger the sensed loss of control that can trigger Exposure Anxiety. When you initiate, it's another story, so play by the rules.

Exposure Anxiety and intelligence

Non-autistic people are generally able to keep up with the rate of incoming information consistently. They generally have the processing time to make coherent meaning out of incoming information, going beyond the sensory mapping of that information to the categorization and literal interpretation of it and then beyond that to processing the information for significance.

Before I was nine I lived quite squarely in the sensory, struggling for the literal. This wasn't just to do with how I understood verbal language, but also how I understood both visual language and the visual impression of objects and people. When I heard people speaking, I assumed they were mostly just making noise patterns. I assumed it was for their own self-entertainment, an entertainment I found annoying when it was directed at me but one which I sometimes found fascinating when it was something 'outside of me' with no sensed danger of it being directed at me. The speech of others was like a mosaic of tumbled sound, some patterned, some not, some with rhythm, some not, some with strange and interesting sound combinations, others without interest and purely annoying. Nevertheless, I felt confident in my ability to escape or exit any situation and this allowed me to feel more comfortable around this unintelligible noise than had I been expected to be an active part of it. In my first week of school, my mother was called in and told I wouldn't sit, sang to myself all the time and was a disruption to the other students. My mother's response was simply that if she was ever called in again for something so stupid, she'd punch the teacher in the face next time. She was not called in again and I was pretty much left almost entirely to my own devices, blending in progressively in a school with a high population of students for whom English was second language. Later, having achieved a label of 'emotionally disturbed' meant people didn't push responses too much. They were far more concerned with whether I seemed reasonably content and non-violent. Being left alone so much meant I didn't feel as trapped and retaliative as I might have, especially about language. I was generally not asked questions and all the questions I might have asked, I was generally unaware of. This was probably because I knew that even if I made myself comprehensible (generally via TV jingles, advertisements and stored lines) there was little point as I wouldn't understand nor emotionally tolerate the social connection in receiving the answer.

I never expected anything in particular from people but learned that if their actions were projected in my direction, the unexpected would probably come my way, causing overload. I learned to avoid encouraging the environment in its social approaches to me, but remained quite good at my own 'hit and run' form of tentative initiation. I also had a fascination for people's movement patterns, like watching dance – mostly ugly, sometimes wonderful. Sometimes I used these patterns back at them, to show them the feel of themselves they were showing me (as though this might inhibit them and they, like me, might have gone away). Sometimes I did some of these at the mirror as though they were posture-clothing I was trying on before the girl in the mirror. This humour and apparent cheekiness made me seem quite a character and either likeable or infuriating around others. I remember one of the Marx brothers with blond hair who behaved in a similar way (the one who didn't speak) and I remember feeling he behaved a bit like me.

People's facial expressions seemed idiosyncratic contortions. As faces, they were so very hard to recognize because they never remained constant. Instead I recognized people by bits of them rather than the whole. Having no visual cohesion meant I learned to rely on touch, acoustics and how something moved to make meaning rather than visual recognition. I generally didn't try to touch or feel people till I was an adult (except sometimes with hair). I got by instead by mapping the pattern of their movements, the way their foot struck the floor, the way their hand gripped a glass, their particular voice pattern as smooth, staccato, burbling, rigid. I mapped how they sat in their body, whether they frothed up like bubbles trying to get out, whether they were stuck in their body like steel walls, whether they let their expression out like sudden spikes, whether they felt like glass ready to break. I also went through phases where I didn't feel part of their world and had no drive to map them. Here, I got by generally by treating people with equal relative indifference (indiscriminately cold or cheerful depending on mood and chemistry).

Objects were known mostly by their placement, movement, acoustics or texture. Visually, it depended on which angle you came at them. They seemed ever changing and visual recognition was always so delayed that other means of ascertaining the use or familiarity of something was much more immediate. Watching me with objects, it was hard to see me as meaning blind because I was clearly not blind. Instead, I was seen as mad, often disrespectful. I don't remember being told not to touch things. It's possible I just didn't register being told not to touch things. Certainly, as a child with severe Exposure Anxiety responses, had I registered I was being controlled through being told 'not to', this would almost certainly have produced the opposite effect.

The number of times I was described as deaf, told to simply watch or listen, I cannot count but can still feel. Rather than seen as having severe processing delay, I was seen as not caring and being 'disturbed'. It is always possible that the eccentric and socially extreme nature of my parents influenced the way I was understood at school. Certainly, had I had very co-operative parents with strong moral values, middle-class manners and an expression of concern about my development, the school might have had a very different view. It was perhaps easier to see me as a disturbed product of a disturbed environment, as was the fashion in the sixties and seventies when I grew up.

At around the age of nine, I began to recognize pictures far more, although not line drawings because that's all they looked like – lines. I didn't interpret them and when I finally did it usually wasn't what they were trying to represent. The PECS symbol for play that involves two figures with hands throwing a ball between them was, to me, a spider. Because a spider was something round with long straight bits out at the sides, joined or not, the picture was of a spider. The picture for dinner looks like a face with a black eye. I did love pictures. I loved form and pattern immensely. But it took me years to realize a tall thing with lit up spheres on a long walkway was a picture of lamplights on a bridge. I drew, mostly patterns, but also exact replications of the structure of houses. I also drew cows. For quite a number of years, cows were a very important concept. I had seen them in the royal show, each pen with one cow and one name of breed. I then saw in an atlas the symbols of cows together with the same words for breeds I'd seen the form of at the show. The world made sense…at least cows did. It was this kind of cohesion I couldn't gather from blah blah or stories or pictures alone. Life has been a series of gathered networks of information. The networking rarely just happened of its own accord.

At nine, I began to ask one important highly-repetitive question – 'What's happening?', 'What's happening now?' Although my ability to process the blah blah response was only about twenty-five per cent interpretation, leaving the sentence tumbled and fragmented, I was asking for visual interpretation of actions on the television. Not understanding meaning blindness, I was told to 'Shut up and watch and I'll find out'. It didn't stop me. I continued to ask about every fifteen seconds as I watched figures go blah blah and move across the screen. I think I was about equivalent to a talking cat watching the football on TV. I could explain nothing and ask no deeper question.

At nine, I read the street directory and understood all streets had names. I read the telephone book. I read a pictorial dictionary and found that all things had names. I later got a sentence dictionary and I was on the road to being less meaning deaf. I still couldn't process incoming information at the rate it came in (my mind did play on it, processing it out of context hours, days or weeks later) but I now had a body of links through which to piece information together if I so chose. I shifted from someone compelled by pattern and repetition to someone compelled by category and collection.

Visually, the links between words and pictures began to help link the pieces of visual image into a cohesive whole as well. I could read in any language; I had no comprehension and no enjoyment but the sound of hearing myself articulate word patterns I could not process. I would highly recommend labelling every concrete tangible, visual object to link words with objects and model the naming of them as though for one's own benefit. I did this later in teaching myself German and then teaching a Chinese student English. It was then I realized how important this technique would have been.

I began to keep up with three sentences in a row. I could 'hear'. To hold meaning, I learned to act out the words as they were said. I couldn't hold them in my head. I didn't think in pictures. I thought in movement and use. I learned to mime sign covertly, and as an adult overtly to myself, to link incoming words to meaning and also to keep track of the meaning of my own words and retain the confidence that I was making sense even when my ability to process my own speech had fallen away. I had literal meaning. I made the transition from the autistic end to the Asperger end of the spectrum, from the sensory to the literal. I didn't just know the table as clonk, clonk solid thing with legs. It was 'table', a thing for putting objects on. An eye wasn't just jelly with colour, circles and a dot. It was that person's eye for looking. Still, the proof of this transition was largely kept to myself. I didn't share the excitement with the world. Exposure Anxiety kept it strictly to myself. I had broken out of one prison, but was still within the walls of the other. My ability to process information fluctuated constantly. At the same time, acute chronic Exposure Anxiety generally interfered either in that processing or in any direct demonstration of the knowing based on what I did process for meaning or significance. This meant I was seen intermittently in both categories, often depending on the familiarity of the challenge and how free I felt to leave at any time.

It would be years and years before I'd realize there was another level, the significant. That the table wasn't just a thing for putting things on but someone's table put there or kept clear for a specific purpose at a particular time. The eye wasn't just someone's eye for looking, it could give certain messages to people and be taken as part of attractiveness.

I was often called stupid, even more often seen as devoid of common sense, even incapable of it. Nevertheless, I was also seen as very intelligent. A friend of my father's had summed this up in describing me as a funny kind of backward genius. That people were able to see my intelligence, I put down to my environment. Before the age of four, a tightrope had been put up between two trees and I used to walk it. I could climb almost anything and often got up on top of my door to swing it and hide from anyone entering. I could find the tiniest thing, yet not recognize so many simple objects. I could repeat a very complex tune but not understand a sentence. I could sense and map a person's patterns to an incredible degree but virtually never asked a question. I would try to look and cross the road but walk straight out in front of the oncoming car. I could not process but I could feel the music of the traffic and walk in rhythm with it, avoiding anyone hitting me. I couldn't ask for food but I could rifle through the pantry and leave everything ordered by size, shape and colour. My repetitive games showed an entertainment with physics and an ability to be so unconstrained by the nature of an object that I could adapt most things into uses others might never consider. To watch me I was a mystery but I had the freedom in which to see a complex and intelligent individual.

The non-autistic person is able to keep up with that rate of incoming information not because they are cleverer than people with autism or Asperger Syndrome, but because in filtering incoming information they take in less information, so they have more time to process it. Because the non-autistic person can keep up with the rate of incoming information, it doesn't feel like an invasion and adrenaline levels stay low, leaving dopamine and serotonin levels relatively stable so that new information generally doesn't trigger survival responses such as Exposure Anxiety. The result is that non-autistic people learn to want more information and more of the involvement that brings this information. They appear to have 'learned' more, even though the 'autistic' person has taken in more information.

Exposure Anxiety and sensory flooding

As infants, we all experience sensory flooding. The world is in bits, for which we have not yet formed concepts. The concepts bring the bits together. The concepts form our perception. Perception then becomes the key to closing out all kinds of 'irrelevant' information – the stuff that doesn't fit the concepts. So-called 'normality' is about becoming 'closed-minded'.

As babies, non-autistic people keep up with the rate of incoming information (people's words and actions) and this makes them form concepts. The concepts close off their minds to all the stuff that isn't about the concepts. They stop experiencing sensory flooding and as a result get more and more comfortable with being given attention and shown new things. As babies or later as infants, people with autism have problems with the adequate supply of nutrients to the brain, generally meaning that they can't keep up with the rate of incoming information (people's words and actions) and this means they can't integrate information cohesively. If you can't integrate information cohesively, it is hard to form concepts. If you can't form the concepts, you don't learn to filter out all the stuff coming in. Adrenaline highs heighten the senses and promote sensory flooding.

I saw the swirl of energy particles in the air, heard the hum of the fridge in the other room, saw the fracturing rainbows of light like stars from a light bulb. I heard the sound of shoes scuffing the floor, the sound of my blood rushing with adrenaline, the reflection of shadow and shine carving up the visual impression of everything. I had constant noise flooding into people's words and the words tumbling in my head as if they came in through a blender, every pattern of movement mapped like an artist using my brain like a brush. That was my world, the world of sensory flooding, making a child meaning deaf meaning blind, unable to have the processing time and space to simultaneously perceive one thing in relation to another, even self-in-relation-to-the-world or it in relation to me. Whether the sensory flooding itself was the product of very high noradrenaline, putting me into a shock state in which I could not filter information, I can't be sure. What I do know is that from the earliest, these two states occurred together. This level of sensory flooding triggered an intense degree of invasion and an intense survival response to that invasion and overload. The Exposure Anxiety loop would escalate to a crescendo and the involutary responses ate me like a lion its prey.

Exposure Anxiety and emotional flooding

Exposure Anxiety suffocatingly over-protects the self not only from sensory flooding, but also from emotional flooding in a self-justifying, behaviour-reinforcing loop. From the earliest I can remember, I was flooded with sensory information in such fine detail I felt as if I was either lost in the bombardment or I existed but would explode if I took in anything more. I did often explode or implode, which took the form of severe total processing shutdowns, some publicly obvious, some not. When these happened, I lost connection to the meaning and connectedness of absolutely everything – a state I called 'the big black nothingness'. This was like having a fit but with conscious experience of your own disintegration. I would lose any idea of what my body was, now a thing stuck on me, suffocating me. I would lose any idea whose scream it was coming from my body and deafening me, raising my emotions to an adrenaline-rush pitch that felt like being stuck with pins.

As a toddler, these states happened up to six times a day, generally ending in self-injurious behaviours and despair. As I got older, I learned to stifle them, have them in silence, use self-calming and self-reassurance strategies, tapping, humming, rhythm, keeping something sensorily familiar with me at all times. It wasn't until I had dietary intervention and treatment for severe reactive hypoglycemia that I realized the problem was not merely that of sensory flooding causing cognitive shutdown. The heightened LSD-like states induced by dairy intolerance, combined with heightened cocaine-like effects of severe salicylate intolerance meant my own chemistry was inviting such intense sensory flooding and with it, extreme emotional states. Exacerbated by severe reactive hypoglycemia, causing constant adrenaline rushes, my emotional experience of these attacks was heightened. I experienced them each time at the kind of pitch you'd only normally experience in a threat of death. I used to describe this emotional extreme as comparable to walking into a room expecting a sense of home and predictability, but finding that everything you were attached to was smashed, every person you found comfort in, murdered. The state of dread, horror, terror and despair was extreme. I felt I was being murdered from inside and there was not a thing anyone could do to help.

This persistent emotional assault meant that the Exposure Anxiety became a chemical addiction on the lookout to justify its expression and the next 'fix'. Living in the grip of its intense persistent drives, I developed such a heightened self-protection response regarding emotion that I was buried alive even when I wasn't in this state. The response became so finely tuned that, although I was able at first to indulge in my own self-initiated emotional highs (especially with lights, textures, sounds, patterns), it was progressively in opposition to a rigid internal law not to allow others to provoke emotion in me. When they succeeded, I experienced the payback for allowing them to affect me. This feedback response has been coined 'Reward Deficiency Syndrome' and is thought to underly conditions affecting involuntary behaviours as diverse as alcoholism, compulsive gambling, drug dependency, schizophrenia, Tourette and OCD.

I don't know what my life would have been like had I been able to ask for love, to be unafraid of emotion, not to run in terror from the threat someone would make me feel. I do know I can ask for love now. Until recently I was still rigid, self-protective and unable to ask for that from almost everyone. But occasionally, although I couldn't take a hug, I had asked for caring and reassurance from a best friend. I was free with my husband Chris much of the time. It was harder however, when he initiated things, but he left me to initiate when I needed closeness and he offered it without making it his when he saw I needed it, careful not to trigger Exposure Anxiety.

Exposure Anxiety and one's own world

The more the person themselves wants a sense of social, the more Exposure Anxiety may seek to justify the pursuit of an adrenalin high by internally experiencing this as a threat from the self itself. The person then becomes able to initiate social involvement only under narrowed conditions, freed up in her expression, but generally only when it is within her own total control or when so obscure or obsessive the environment cannot truly 'join' her. She may be able to initiate connection but normally only when the initiation is aloof, indirect, peripheral and half-hearted in a fly-on-the-wall manner.

In infancy, among many other nicknames, my father told me I had been called 'Spook' because of the way I hovered about and then disappeared when approached – like a ghost. Most people find these approaches so aloof they perceive them as the child's 'involvement' and so come to doubt these are even initiations – taking them instead as 'hanging about', 'wandering in' etc. When approached directly in a self-in-relation-to-other way, the person with severe Exposure Anxiety gives a clear shrug-off message as if to say, 'What do you mean, I didn't give you any sign I was asking for your involvement'. To the parent who has experienced this response in the company of friends or visitors not used to such a child, this is embarrassing and makes them look like a fool. The answer is to initiate back not directly, triggering a sense of invasion into that person's world but, instead, as though for your own benefit, not theirs. In this way Exposure Anxiety is no longer able to justify any sense of invasion, no threat to enter the person's own world. Turning down the invasion-volume of your own self-in-relation-to-other approaches can cause someone with Exposure Anxiety to turn up their own sense of self-in-relation-to-other. In the case of people with severe Exposure Anxiety, this is a social dance that has many steps to get through before you can dance in front of each other, let alone dance later *with* each other.

Unless there is an emphasis on modelling rather than teaching, on accepting ability before having it proven and on being self-owning as a key to building people's desire to reach out, the world may challenge issues of information overload but it will have a long way to go before it can successfully turn around the restrictions of severe, chronic Exposure Anxiety.

Controlling Exposure Anxiety by addressing overload

One of the ways of controlling Exposure Anxiety self-protection responses is to reduce the sense that there is an overload to protect yourself from. Part of this is reducing the sense of self-in-relation -to-other as part of an indirectly-confrontational approach. Part is doing things in such digestible small doses that not only do you leave the person wanting more, but you also stop them consistently experiencing the stress of accumulative processing delay and sensory systems shutdowns. When people have shutdowns, the ability to make sense of incoming information, even the meaning of your own words, starts to fall away. You progressively can't make sense of what you are watching, what someone is saying, what you have just said, even your sense of where you are in space or the relationship between body and self. For those who can normally consistently process incoming information it can be bewildering, even terrifying, depending on the suddenness and extremity of the shutdown. If it is partial, it is just annoying, a little alienating, an inconvenience that creates a need to use adaptations to hold onto meaning and reassure oneself one is still intact in spite of feeling everything has 'altered'. If it's a total systems shutdown, it can be like dying with your eyes open. It is being awake and conscious as all connection with mind's ability to interpret strips away and you become reduced to an animal state until processing is back on line again. Many just go silent and still. Some go onto autopilot, continuing with stored communication or behaviour but with no idea what they have said or done. Others have panic attacks, screaming fits, episodes of absolute terror and despair in which involuntarily throwing or tearing things or attacking themselves is not uncommon. Still others simply cry in the desolation. I called this The Big Black Nothingness and in that state no words or actions mean anything. They cannot help. Only objects of sensory familiarity and rhythm are of consolation. Those able autistic people who experience these states fear the kind of social vulnerability this can mean. I have been slapped in this state, put under water, shouted at and shaken. Sometimes the greatest fear, in a state of impending total shutdown, is the fear of what others can do to you. As an adult, I began to carry a card explaining that if found in such a panic state, I was not to be handled nor excessively spoken to, and that providing a rhythm and objects of familiarity such as twigs, leaves or grass to snap or shred would usually help me get myself out of such a state.

Total shutdowns last anywhere from minutes to an hour at a time. As a young child I had about six a day. They became fewer as I got older. They ceased with dietary intervention and nutritional supplements to improve information-processing. Those who challenge themselves too far beyond their processing capacity, push themselves unwittingly into shutdowns, being 'punished' by their own desire to 'join the world'.

Environmentally reducing overload

When total shutdowns happen, Exposure Anxiety justifies itself to increase afterwards and long term. To avoid and progressively turn around this cycle, keep contact and learning in small doses, leaving the recipient wanting more. Provide 'time out' activities that involve the person having complete control of their self-learning. TEACCH is an example of a potentially self-regulated program which could be used to give regular timed breaks to open interaction, creating a mix of overload and control over information, overload, and control. Many people need processing breaks every ten to twenty minutes. Some very able people can cope for an hour without being on auto-pilot or relying heavily on 'strategies'.

The other way of reducing environmental overload, as a key to reducing Exposure Anxiety is reducing overhead lighting, which makes possible a huge amount of incoming information. Some children love the buzz of flooding their senses but only when they are in control. Some will even use it as a diversion response, taking the attention off an attempt to interact or communicate with them. Reducing overhead lighting cuts down on visual processing and lends processing time to other sensory systems such as interpreting what one hears or the sense of body connectedness. Coloured light bulbs can change light frequencies with a similar effect and lamps are better for reducing overload than overhead lights.

Keeping speech to a minimum, in slow digestible chunks, keeping it pragmatic, visual and concrete cuts down processing time in linking sounds with concepts. This is one reason why talking through objects is not just good with Exposure Anxiety in taking the focus off the person and onto the issue, but is also good in reducing overload by creating 're-playable mental movies' associated with the blah blah. Gestural signing can also help some children put meaning to blah blah. Temple Grandin talks of thinking in pictures. Those with severe visual perceptual processing problems may, like me, not think in pictures at all, but in movement and use. For others it may be their 'acoustics', smell or texture. For me, 'cup' is not an image, it is a movement and use. 'Toilet', is not a picture, it is an action. 'Love' has no picture or symbol, it has a flow of pattern.

Speaking through objects is also most important for cutting down the greatest source of overload which is jumping from all self–no other to all other–no self, as happens in verbal discussion or explanation when one hasn't got the processing capacity to keep up with both together.

Having a processing delay is nothing to do with being stupid. If you have to artificially filter incoming information for people who can't filter it, that doesn't mean treating people as mentally retarded. Even if they are severely retarded in their social–emotional development and the responses that spring from it, this has no necessary relationship with their intellectual capacity. Someone with severe information overload and severe Exposure Anxiety can sometimes be as intelligent, even occasionally more intelligent than you.

Exposure Anxiety and diet, digestion and immunity

Anything that raises stress levels raises anxiety. Caffeine, for example, which is not just in coffee but in cola and chocolate, not only causes the wild irritability and restlessness of restless legs syndrome (RLS) but raises anxiety-driven reactiveness and that's bad news for adrenaline-driven Exposure Anxiety levels. It also has excitatory effects on neurons in the brain, triggering chemical changes which can lead to neurotoxicity. Chronic stress reduces secretory IgA in the gut, leaving the person with an alkaline gut in which harmful bugs thrive and the gut's natural, good bacteria are diminished.

Sugar not only makes people more hyper than anxiety alone would do, but also feeds Candida, the fungal infection that sets up camp in the digestive tracts of people with immune system and digestive system problems particularly in those under states of chronic stress. What it does there, with the help of sugar, is to live off the vitamin B content of the diet, starving the brain of this essential nutrient it would otherwise utilize for detoxing the body and processing incoming information. So there's a very good reason why sugar increases, and in some cases, even triggers the chain reaction underlying the adrenaline addiction in Exposure Anxiety. If that isn't enough, a diet high in sugar also robs the body of magnesium – the mineral most crucial to managing our own stress levels and without which we cannot properly absorb the B group vitamins from our diet. The fact that children with severe Exposure Anxiety are 'rewarded' with sweets, biscuits and sugary drinks leaves me in despair. The child is soon off the wall or out of it and the carer feels it's such a shame as the child had just been doing so well.

I was severely addicted to sugar. I craved it like an addict. When I got it, I got high and hyper, oblivious to my obnoxious behaviour toward others. When I began to come down, I came down with a crash, into panic attacks and disorientation. When the severe plummet triggered an adrenaline rush I was irritable and impossible, and often self-abusive. And the whole time I already found keeping up with information a tremendous struggle. The roller-coaster sugar had me on contributed greatly to my experience of emotional states as extremely uncomfortable and uncontrollable.

When I came off sugar I was twenty-four. I ripped my clothes, tore the fence posts away and ended up in a face-slapping heap of tears as I went through severe withdrawal. I then became able not merely to suppress my wildness, oblivion and panic, but to live with Exposure Anxiety and more calmly manage it in its progressively more subtle form. I became safer and more able to let the 'me' out from inside instead of the compulsion-driven rote-learned façade I had left running on auto-pilot.

I was also severely intolerant to dairy products and a group of foods called salicylates. The severe drug-like perceptual fluctuations and sensory extremes I'd had all my life came almost to a halt when I came off milk products and reduced the high levels of salicylate-rich foods. Vision became less fragmented. I could begin to recognize objects more easily. It became easier to be in unfamiliar places without having to hide behind stored lines and characterizations. I could keep up better with what people were saying instead of pretending to keep up. I lost all sense of my body and its connectedness less often, and self-abusive behaviour became less instant and more controllable. I stopped having the major directional and background–foreground fluctuations that had always made places seem unfamiliar and made me either buzz or have sudden terror at the simplest things. If you've never seen the floor seem to bow or the sky jump through the trees you might not realize what I mean. The fracturing and shimmering of light decreased as did the drug-like highs. I began to lose 'my world' but I found 'the world' more consistent, more cohesive, more able to be held without struggle. I still had major work to do on the long-term impact of processing problems and Exposure Anxiety on identity, personality and survival strategies as well as personal non-stored communication, but dealing with food allergies and food intolerance certainly had me on my way.

According to research by Paul Shattock of Sunderland University, eighty per cent of people with autism spectrum conditions have undigested dairy and/or gluten proteins in their urine samples. Seventy-three per cent of those tested in studies by Rosemary Waring at Birmingham University were found to have low levels of sulphur transferase causing salicylate and phenol intolerance and twenty per cent of this group have identifiable immune deficiencies. Other metabolic conditions such as untreated subclinical Phenylketonuria are also commonly associated with autism and may cause kind of dopamine excess associated with chronic anxiety amd impulse control problems. Research into Leaky Gut Syndrome and Candida and an amino acid called Glutamine have shown promise in improving the lives of people with ME and AIDS and such treatments are beginning to show promise as well in the field of autism. There are a handful of medically qualified doctors able to treat Leaky Gut through natural or complementary medicine. However, in spite of extensive studies and research, these areas of treatment are not widely accepted and often not acknowledged by some mainstream, conventional doctors, who generally have no additional qualifications or knowledge in the fields of natural or complementary medicine. Whilst there are behaviour-suppressant drugs, there are, as far as I'm aware, currently no readily available treatments in the field of conventional western medicine known to improve information-processing. There are, however, a handful of qualified western doctors using holistic eastern medicine approaches such as naturopathy, homeopathy and herbalism, working with the links between digestion, toxicity, immune and auto-immune systems and neurobiology to help people back to equilibrium. By restoring the healthy supply of nutrients to the brain, underlying information processing problems are improved and this should reduce levels of Exposure Anxiety as well. Further, recent studies into an atypical neuroleptic drug called Risperidone, were found useful in treating involuntary behaviours in Tourette and OCD at doses as small as 0.5mgs. This drug, which regulates levels of the neurotransmitters dopamine and serotonin in the brain, have been recently used with people on autistic spectrum to control involuntary behaviours and may hold some promise, particularly in a combined approach which includes supplementation and addressing dietary issues (I have personally combined these two treatments and found that the involuntary responses of Exposure Anxiety have decreased, and some have disappeared). The chronic stress caused by the persistent freeze/flight/ fright involuntary responses of Exposure Anxiety could quite feasibly exacerbate predispositions toward gut, immune system or metabolic dysfunction with its obvious effect on sensory flooding and information-processing problems. Similarly, the drug-like highs caused by opiate excess in dairy/gluten intolerance or the cocaine-like highs of salicylafe intolerance seem bound to interact with a predisposition toward the hormone imbalances underlying Exposure Anxiety. This makes the two like a pair of cogs which come together to start the process of what now is known as 'autism-spectrum' conditions.

    After treatment, what is needed is a sensitive re-education program which addresses issues such as identity with the earlier developmental state should be able to begin the process of picking up the pieces.

Developing mind as a technique for managing overload

It had never occurred to me that the underlying cause of sensory flooding was the inability to form concepts quickly enough to cohesively bring fragments of information together as a whole. Then, one day when I was in Toronto, I was to speak in front of three thousand people at the Geneva centre. I went out on the stage without the slightest fear. I simply walked out with no one around me, enjoying the darkness of the stage and the sound of the wood and the structure above me. When I looked out at the ocean of people in front of me, I was amused at first. Every finger, every fold of clothing, every rustle of notes, every scuffing of a shoe, every movement and eye blink began to come at me like a frame by frame movie travelling at lightening speed. Suddenly, the amusement reached a fever pitch and I felt like I was going to scream, be sick or faint. It was as though each tiny piece of information was an entity in its own right. I hadn't thought, 'bodies', 'faces', 'hands', 'clothing', 'people' or 'audience'. I'd walked out there completely on my own track, not a concept in my head about what was coming in. When it came in, it had no structures to slot into. I felt like I was going to explode.

I put my head down, stifling a rising scream and calmed myself frantically, 'Don't worry, it's a people tree, just a people tree, look up, it's OK, they are just leaves, lots of leaves on a people tree'. Then I dared to look up. The three thousand people were no longer flooding me. I didn't see an eye and a finger, hear a scrape and a cough, see a fold, and a shimmer. I saw one cohesive people tree and all the sound and movement seemed suddenly 'related'. It stopped flooding me. It didn't occur to me what had happened. I was simply glad it had. But what had happened was that I'd used my mind, created a concept to control perception and manage overload by converting fragments of unrelated information into a singular context, just like combining files on a computer into an umbrella called a folder. I knew the word 'audience' but it didn't actually mean anything. 'People tree' meant the same thing, but I could relate to the concept as one singular thing made up of rustling noises and movement, form and colour.

It wasn't until I was in Orlando another year that I found the same thing happening but this time at the hands of someone else. A journalist friend and I were in an art gallery and I was buzzing on an array of free-floating coloured forms against a big white background. The forms had different edges and curves, seeming almost to swim among the white. Then Mary Kay remarked, 'Oh, you like the painting of the lion', and something freaky happened. The shapes stopped being just shapes. The whiteness stopped being a big square whiteness. I saw a lion, a lion on a white canvas. I was absolutely shocked, as though she had done magic. It was then that I had my first conversation about the power of labels to trigger the concepts that would cause visual cohesion to happen. It taught me many things. It taught me I could control overload in a new way, by looking away, tuning out, and struggling for an umbrella term, a folder, for a fragmented experience.

I used this last year in Australia in a shopping centre. I'm fine in places I know, like the blind person who has mapped their own room. As someone largely meaning blind, I have mapped what everything is by its place or use, sound or movement, or by feeling its texture or form. I do now have the capacity to see whole objects, thanks to specially tinted lenses which help with visual processing, but my brain, after twenty-five years of not seeing cohesively, doesn't automatically seek the concepts through the visual. I have to do so deliberately because what should happen automatically often doesn't. I'm still learning to navigate this connection between my eyes and my brain.

This new shopping centre didn't have a structure similar to any I'd known. I couldn't predict the use or nature of its stores, departments, sounds. My head was swimming and I felt eaten up and overwhelmed, trying to make cohesive sense out of the clashing forms of display and sounds around me. I put my head down. My husband Chris asked if I was all right. 'It's a circus', I said to myself, 'Look up, it's OK, it's just a circus'. The word 'circus' meant an experience in which there are many things going on at once, all competing for attention. Just like in Toronto, suddenly I had a framework. One shop and its displays, music, products, was like one kind of circus act, another shop, a different circus act. And all of a sudden, each piece of the chaos was suddenly a coherent part of the whole. I was in the midst of a 'circus'.

Why talking through objects can help

Talking through objects moves the focus off the person and onto the object/issue, reducing the involuntary self-justification of Exposure Anxiety and making it easier for someone to tune in. Talking through objects is good for two other things too: holding a simultaneous sense of self and other without triggering overload or Exposure Anxiety, and cutting down on translation time in putting mental images/experiences to spoken words. My father played so hard to get I stopped doing what I was doing in order to tune in, first peripherally, progressively more directly and he got quieter and more to himself about it. Like someone driven by Tourette he compulsively brought objects to life with voices, personality and characterizations. It didn't matter what they were. Sometimes he'd grab the cat suddenly and make it 'talk' to him. Sometimes it would be the cutlery having a discussion. Sometimes he'd talk to something he had hidden from view. The point was, he could get around Exposure Anxiety, raise issues, tell stories and get my attention, however much it was one foot in the door and one foot out. Whether I was able to process these interactions with meaning or not was not important. I could feel the theme and the content and the rest was processed outside of the context in which it occurred, mostly beyond conscious awareness and only realised to be there once such content was triggered back out of me. As a consultant, I don't see this approach being modelled around children with autism often enough. Most commonly I see many children with 'autism' who are not assumed to be 'equal' and 'normal'. I watch many parents, teachers and carers give off a feeling of waiting, needing, mourning, a fuelling which can sensitise Exposure Anxiety to the alert of 'impending invasion' and sometimes stifle even self-directed initiations in the presence of others. I can't help but feel this sense of being waited for, having others emotionally needing responses from me in order to be happy in themselves, to be watching me with a sense of loss or mourning, could easily promote, instead, a feeling of alienation and brokenness. It also promotes for me a mistrust of the verbal expression or display of love if I a sense that 'love' is about neediness, pity, ownership or control over others.

Typed communication and overload

Typed communication can reduce overload because making the connection between feelings and expression harder through spoken language than typed language. This has astounded many people, including myself. I wrote my first book in four weeks. I had just learned to type. The book was two hundred and fifty pages and became an international bestseller. I had no awareness of the words as I wrote them. I merely felt feelings. I just let the feelings come out of my fingers as my fingers, not me, spoke to the page. As the words came up on the paper, that was the first I knew of them. I shook and cried and felt ill to watch my words come tumbling out like someone possessed. This was not the personal expressiveness I'd known as myself. I had been able to speak within the learned persona of 'the intellectual' or let wild statements fly out unchecked as a diverting clown, but this type of stuff, never. I could give in the pragmatic role of carer, but was someone terrified of feeling emotionally connected or moved to love. I mirrored everyone and could not dare show a personal non-mirrored want without feeling I had to 'pay myself back' for such defiance of the laws of Exposure Anxiety. But my book felt purely from me to me. There was no idea nor intention to publish *Nobody Nowhere*. On my own, with little sense of exposure, it simply poured out beyond even my own capacity to keep up with what hit the page. It was like a fit, a literary vomiting episode onto paper. I felt terrified of what was in me showing itself. I later asked an Educational Psychologist and friend how that could have been when even to let someone know I needed the toilet was at that point near impossible. He replied that the part of the brain responsible for language and writing is not the same as the part of the brain that controls the connection between language and speech. Although I relied very heavily on 'stored' speech and speaking in characters, personas or roles, I could speak absolutely freely and personally from myself to myself through typing.

With typing one doesn't have to take in a simultaneous sense of self and other, so the three channels of self, other, and topic become two channels: self and topic. Furthermore, the visual overload of keeping visual contact with a moving face and body in front of you is gone, leaving you far more processing time for retrieval. It also takes far less energy to waggle your fingers out in front of you than to connect to ever changing patterns in your mouth with the feedback bombarding back at you in your ears with a distastefully heightened sense of excruciating individuality of self.

The importance of rhythm, time out, and self-calming strategies

Rhythm is one way of shifting perception. If things seem too in your face, a rhythm can make them more external, more outside of you, allowing you better to tune back in peripherally – noticing better because you are no longer compelled to reject your own noticing. Rhythm competes for consciousness, pushing the ever-ready, eager beast of Exposure Anxiety into a back seat. Rhythm also provides a framework to make segments of and sequence an incoming flood of otherwise tumbled information.

Time out provides space breaks to allow people with information-processing delay to catch up with the backlog without blowing fuses and experiencing partial or total sensory-systems information-processing shutdowns. It also removes someone from an activity whilst they are still wanting more and before overload reinforces the self protective social–emotional defence response of Exposure Anxiety. This action of small doses and leaving the activity whilst still wanting is an invaluable part of building want, countering the compulsive and addictive antimotivations of Exposure Anxiety and leading to independence rather than short-term compliance.

Self-calming strategies involve things like jumping, tapping, rocking, giving oneself a rhythm and then slowing the pace down before gradually getting back into the activity, but where it leads into a manic, oblivious high it has been co-opted and guided by the Exposure Anxiety response and can lead from calm into pleasure, into mania, into panic and finally the retaliative self-injurious responses of Exposure Anxiety in which the person gets an adrenaline 'fix'. Self-calming may be all you have when robbed of control and overloaded by the self-in-relation-to-other, in your face directly-confrontational interaction that so many traditional non-autistic behaviour modification programs naively recommend in cases where Exposure Anxiety is poorly understood.

CHAPTER 2

Relationship to Self

Exposure Anxiety is an invisible cage and to those who live with it, that invisible cage is either their prison warder–monster–saboteur or their saviour, helping them to cut off, shutdown and keep the world of overload at bay. To work respectfully and with grace in the realms where Exposure Anxiety is the ruler, you should know how delicately interconnected Exposure Anxiety is with the person's sense of self. It's like trying to remove a parasite which has become finely intertwined with the person's own functioning; they may respond to this 'help' as though it were an assault on selfhood.

Exposure Anxiety and will

Even those with severe Exposure Anxiety who have treated underlying digestive system problems driving overload may still rely rigidly on old Exposure Anxiety responses. So why can't they just 'get over it'? Is an addict, removed from one of the major sources of drugs, simply 'over their addiction?

There is the self of mind which may be free, and the self of will which opposes the desires and needs of mind. So someone can actually trigger their own Exposure Anxiety simply because they become such an intense audience to themselves. It seems to me no surprise that some of the most intensely driven people with 'autism' are the ones with the most severe Exposure Anxiety. It is sometimes the very fact that mind is so awake, so wanting, so frustrated and annoyed at being blocked in expression that it turns up this sense of audience to oneself. I have written a lot about having to trick mind out of awareness so I was able to counter Exposure Anxiety from defying my own mind. It took intense self-calming and highly refined abilities to shift perception enough to use this facility but I've seen it too in some so-called 'low-functioning' people and I am in the deepest awe and respect for their adaptations and endurance. Yet, unfortunately, in this world of praise-driven behaviour-modification programs, the environment actively sabotages such individuals by forcing their awareness of everything they manage to achieve. 'Good for you Peter. Look, you managed to pour yourself a drink.' Next time Peter has to try twice as hard to tune out awareness of his want to get his body to follow mind's desire and not will's Exposure Anxiety-driven counter action.

Being sabotaged and contorted by an invisible enemy which seems to know you and head you off at every turn shapes the whole idea of self, the whole relationship to the body, to the social world and to the idea of what 'enjoying oneself' is meant to be about. I hate writing about this particular face of 'autism', for Exposure Anxiety is a dark space in which the only humour is in laughing with oneself as one tries to outrun a cage one can neither name, describe or escape.

In the world of Exposure Anxiety the world outside of oneself is limited in its capacity to help except stop contributing to the triggers and build sensitive and respectful sensitization programs and model self-calming, self-hypnosis skills that help people escape their Exposure Anxiety. One of the things, though, that I have found does help on this level are the Bach Flower Remedies.

Where someone's very strong desire and drive triggers Exposure Anxiety regardless of the environment, Vervain is suggested. By lowering dramatic drives, it lowers, too, the countering of those drives in the form of freezing 'aversions', compulsive 'diversions' and self-sabotaging retaliations against what the person themselves wants.

Sweet Chestnut is suggested as good for despair in the face losing motivation to try, together with Gorse for discouragement, doubt and despondency. Similarly, Wild Rose, for lack of interest, resignation, no love or point in life, could help renew involvement – provided these were used in light of an approach which did not simultaneously trigger Exposure Anxiety. Willow is thought good for feelings of self-pity that the trappedness causes which lead to spiteful feelings against oneself or the environment, and Holly for anger. Rockwater is thought to be helpful in addressing feelings of self-denial, stricture, rigidity and being a purist. Vine is thought useful in changing the emotional state that makes someone dominating, a tyrant or bully who demands obedience. Whether this is self-directed in the hands of Exposure Anxiety or projected externally in being driven to control others, it might be worth a try. Impatiens seems almost made for the will-related problems of Exposure Anxiety: for being irritated by constraints, quick, tense, impatient. Mimulus, Rock Rose, and Cherry Plum are all meant to address fear. Cherry Plum might calm the responses of Exposure Anxiety to overload because it addresses fear of losing control and doing dreaded things. Mimulus might be better with phobic states and Rock Rose might assist with intense emotional over-reactions.

Cerato is thought to be for distrust of self and intuition when one gives up control to Exposure Anxiety. Centaury may be useful for problems associated with wanting to disappear by giving all power up to others; being anxious to serve, weak, dominated. Water Violet is thought to address the withdrawal of despair but also that of aversion responses in being withdrawn, proud, aloof, self-reliant; quiet grief.

Chicory might be helpful with people who give up on being able to rely on themselves and, instead, cling fiercely, possessively in a demanding state of self-pity and tearfulness. Pine is thought helpful for the person who blames themselves for being so 'out of control' in the hands of Exposure Anxiety, for being self-critical, full of self-reproach, assuming blame and apologetic. Crab Apple is thought helpful for self-disgust and the feeling of small things being out of proportion. Oak is thought useful for the person who fights relentlessly with the condition, never admitting to limitation but suffering for that intense endurance. Scleranthus is suggested for the person swinging between the battle to join the world and the battle to keep it out. It is for indecision and alternation to give balance and determination.

Exposure Anxiety and body

As a child I could see but processed everything bit by bit so only very small things were perceptually whole and most of the world was 'in bits'. My brain could only have my good functioning eyes see in bits. I was not only, therefore, meaning blind, but also context blind. I thought the point of the visual was to excitedly buzz on its form, climb into the experience of it and merge with it or mimic it in an attempt to know the experience of it from the inside without processing.

I also couldn't understand what people were saying. I was as meaning deaf as I was meaning blind. I thought the point of the auditory was pattern making. People drove me nuts with their chaotic blah blah sound and invasive self-in-relation-to-other expectation to respond and led me to mimic it, in the hope I could drag meaning out of it if it came from inside of me not from outside of me. My sense of self-in-relation-to-others was deeply disturbed. I felt constantly unable to hold sense of external other in the same context as sense of self. I knew social relationships existed in the world, even learnt to perform as others but was unable to perceive them directly in relation to myself. This was the equivalent of the blind person who looks at you whilst you are speaking, the deaf person who lip-reads and speaks. I couldn't cohesively perceive a sense of my own external body or internal body messages or emotions. I thought the point of externally provoked unexpected emotions was to torture me and rob me of the tiny bit of control over myself I had left.

I thought body messages were frightening impositions knocking from inside for attention when I didn't know what they were saying and had to take a guess, running through the list for a 'bingo'. From early childhood till I was about twelve, I often treated my hands like dangling attachments, often a compulsive source of self-amusement, and I was also often 'redis-covering' one side of my body or the other which had been 'left on hold'. At twelve I went through a tic-like phase where I could feel the physicality of my brain if I shook my head fiercely. In early childhood I experienced my throat as a way of enjoying the extremes of the sensation of screaming till it was raw. In infancy up till late childhood I experienced my eyes as a source of entertainment, compelled to push on them repeatedly to make colours. I compulsively used my flesh and muscles in early childhood up till I was about fifteen to give me sensation experiences as I was driven to bite, scratch and punch them.

My systems were actually *all* cohesive in there somewhere, but when they reached consciousness, they fragmented under the weight of an information-processing demand I couldn't keep up with. Gripped intermittently by the interruption of involuntary avoidance, diversion and retaliation responses, together with their effect on the supply of nutrients necessary to keep up with incoming information, I couldn't directly experience my own systems consciously as cohesive. But consciousness is not our only state. We can put ourselves into a self-hypnotic state to allow things out which consciousness might otherwise sabotage. I had to find other ways of getting that unknown knowing, that unprocessed cohesive sense of the world outside of me . It took me twenty-five years to really grasp a cohesive sense of my life and I experienced this through the typing out of my autobiography, *Nobody Nowhere*. It took me a few more years, till I was thirty, to actually be able to hold, walk around with, and live with that experience of self. I still felt, however, like a visitor who could never trust that this grip on a relatively cohesive sense of self would stay. Finally, thirteen years on, at thirty-eight, I do trust that sense of self as someone and think of it as 'me'. It can take a while to fill one's own shoes.

Body as mind

In the absence of being able to consciously and cohesively hold incoming information together there were still other systems which were usable. Acoustics was one – the sound of an object when tapped or how it reflects sound back to ascertain material and recognize its category from that. Touch was still available and this gave me shape and form when I body mapped everything like a blind person might. Impact when something was prodded gave me a sense of how solid and reliable or able to fall into something was. Dropping things from heights, holding a finger or stick outside of me; both gave me depth perception.

It was through a pictorial sentence dictionary when I was nine that I became able to fluently link incoming blah blah with meaning and experience. Unlike those people with 'autism' who 'think in pictures', as someone with severe visual perceptual problems, I thought more in felt out form and movement – kinesthetic sense and had to re-translate the pictures back into their related sensory experiences in order to link them to the words given. Chair was not a picture, it was a felt shape, slappable, which didn't bounce back, with one kind of acoustic for molded plastic, another for vinyl, another for cloth, another for wood. It had a certain movement when rocked which ball, cup, door don't have. These were my 'pictures'. Most important of all my senses was the ability to use my body as a tool of resonance (I wrote on this in *Autism and Sensing: The Unlost Instinct*).

This stops my body being used as 'me'. It isn't part of my sense of 'self' anymore than I identify my voice as my 'self' or my sense of touch as my 'self'. I found it absurd others actually feel they *are* their body and it is their 'self'. This is a great tickle for me. I do find it so humorous. Like most people with Asperger's I do now use body 'as self', but largely, like many people with autism, I still use body as a tool of resonance. When a child comes to see me, I map that child's systems. It is partially visual, partially auditory, but where I hold what I perceive is not in my head but in my body. I map the patterns of movement as though I had done them myself. I map the patterns of sounds, the use of acoustics, the use of texture and edges, as though it was me using these. Resonance is not mental, it is like a mathematical feeling of patterns via your own body. It is about using the body in place of mind. Resonance is logical, detached and like a computer printout waiting to be read. What distinguishes me from many people with autism is that I take this resonance and translate the experiecne of it to those who rely on mind for understanding. My job as a consultant is to clinically attempt to make sense of these patterns I have mapped. Resonance is non-mind empathy in a most pure form. I believe it is the same system some cats or dogs may use in familiarizing themselves with someone new whilst appearing to be doing nothing. Something shifts in their body in response to what they are mapping. Then they respond personally to that collection of patterns. I do respond personally to these but what always beats me to the personal is a 'read out' – pure information, devoid of much 'me-ness' because this stuff is not 'me', it is something external, not mine at all.

Relying so strongly on body as a tool of resonance in childhood also meant that I didn't consistently use body as self. This meant my sense of social–emotional development was severely altered. One must consistently use body as self to develop a sense of self-in-relation-to-other – a simultaneous awareness of self and other. Ironically, the very adaptation to severe sensory–perceptual problems cost me something far more important – my sense of myself as a coherent part of the world, to be not just at or in front of but to be with, the ability to simultaneously process self and other. This meant I swung between the assumption all others were 'normal' like me and were self-in-relation-to-self and that the world was bizarre and disturbed in its social–emotional self-in-relation-to-other invasive insistence on expecting I behave back in this alien, incomprehensible, (perceived as) distasteful way. I therefore had no desensitization to this social–emotional experience of self-in-relation-to-other.

Body as 'other'

My first responses of self-in-relation-to-other were not those of the outside world at all, but of my own body messages and emotions. I spent much of my very early childhood slapping, biting and trying to run away from my body to get rid of it following me with these annoyances and interruptions to resonance. It was like these sensations were 'blinding' me, cutting me off from the sense I used most to get a feeling of cohesion and understanding of the pattern, feel and nature of objects, people, situations and happenings. I was the absolute fly on the wall but it was a time of my greatest sense of awareness. Fragmentation was much harder to manage in joining the world than before I'd even tried.

My later experiences in mid to late childhood and into adulthood of self-in-relation-to-other involved attacking myself out of frustration and sense of invasion and overload. From late childhood this became 'a private thing' and I'd called these purges 'payback'. They progressed later into tearing and other obsessive compulsive rituals that made me feel I'd 'set things straight again' (until any reminder, mental or otherwise, triggered the same feeling).

In my early teens it took me a long time to not excitedly pre-empt the feeling of killing my body. I had a desperate compelling drive to let my body fall from a tall building and thereby leave the call of my body forever. I knew from the shock/withdrawal sensation that followed self-abuse that to kill my body would leave it even more 'shell-shocked'. I equated this release from the now satisfied addiction of my Exposure Anxiety with the belief my body would then leave me free from the invasion of self-in-relation-to-other approaches at the hands of other people and the trappedness and contortions of Exposure Anxiety in response not just to this but any level of my own emotion-evoking conscious awareness.

Exposure Anxiety caused an intense distaste and disrespect for the body others could reach me through and provoke emotions in. I saw my body as external and theirs, not mine. Only as a tool, a sensory tool, did I feel glad to have it. As part of having 'person-hood', I detested it following around my internal feeling of 'me-ness'. I wanted to move from room to room without it and saw it as heavy, visible and a provocation of the environment to approach me with the intent of directly-confrontational self-in-relation-to-other interaction.

In spite of an intensely disturbed emotional, perceptual and mental relationship to my body, Exposure Anxiety could still allow me to develop responsibility for this thing following me around. I learned in my mid to late twenties to be good to my body. I stopped siding with my Exposure Anxiety in starving it with intent to pay it back for getting sick or robbing me of control. I stopped siding with the drives of Exposure Anxiety to hurt it with intent. I stopped making it freeze out of feelings of vengeance against feeling invaded by uncomfortable feelings and resentment at it making me take action for it. I still do these things impulsively and subconsciously at times but I now ask for help and try to resolve the emotions that trigger Exposure Anxiety so badly as to cause such 'paybacks' on the only person it can – my body. I could close out the whole world and get Exposure Anxiety off my back, but this external other known as body, I could not.

My body sense, as much as it can experience terror, must have been terrified of me. I have felt this in my stomach when I hold myself back from Exposure Anxiety self-directed rage. I have made friends with my body now. We try to work as a team and I try to be good to it. It is sorry to me when it allows too much Exposure Anxiety provoking stuff come in. I am so terribly sorry to it when Exposure Anxiety stuff breaks through without me able to stop it from its effect on body as its enemy. I love my body. Me and body are working on Exposure Anxiety through managing life and what we take on and how we ask for help. It's a long process and those who live with or work with this in others, should not give up hope. It's a rocky ride but it's not impossible to come out the other end reasonably intact.

Body as the road to reaching self?

The idea that people approach my body with a view to reaching my 'self' is the antithesis of how it actually works in the hands of Exposure Anxiety. When others talk to themselves, give a feeling of being self-owning, self-in-relation-to-self, Exposure Anxiety senses no invasion and calms down, dormant. Questions addressed directly trigger Exposure Anxiety, statements made to oneself with no expectation of answer often trigger verbal responses because they don't demand consciousness so don't trigger Exposure Anxiety. Exposure Anxiety causes intense detachment and develops equally intense internal empathy. It is no coincidence that those with severe Exposure Anxiety who type-speak because other avenues are blocked or contorted are some of the most passionate and empathic people I've ever heard 'speak'.

We have to remember that Exposure Anxiety speaks through the body. Exposure Anxiety body language includes all kinds of expression.

This list can include:

○ Clenched jaws

○ Grimacing

○ Clenched fists

○ Arms pulled back into the torso

○ Neck arching

○ Intense hand flick-outs

○ Sharp warning-like clapping

○ Irritation and warning noises

○ Heightened excitability noises

○ Tuning out throat noises and sound patterns

○ Diversion behaviour finger-play

○ The use of peripheral looking and the 'blank' stare

○ Pull-back retaliation responses on initiation

○ Push out retaliation responses on sensed invasion

- ◦ Lip biting

- ◦ Inward feet and leg turning

- ◦ Rocking

- ◦ Backwards throwing

- ◦ Tearing

- ◦ Masturbation-related social control tuning out/self-calming/context removal tactics

- ◦ Masturbation/nose picking/saliva throwing as social revulsion/distancing tactics

- ◦ Ear covering/smacking

- ◦ Screaming fits

- ◦ Furniture throwing...

Exposure Anxiety's displays within 'autism' are many. As Exposure Anxiety causes chronic stress, exacerbating gut immune system and toxicity issues, it is easy to understand why sensory–perceptual problems so often co-occur with Exposure Anxiety. These make it harder to tell Exposure Anxiety-driven behaviours from those essentially relating to information-processing and sensory–perceptual problems. This is especially so for those parents or professionals without Exposure Anxiety who haven't experienced the internal drives for such behaviours. And the behaviours don't just stop with body language and sounds. There are people who can only speak to their shoes, in a put-on voice, speaking in the words of adverts or songs. Some of these communications are aversions, diversions, or retaliation communications. Others of them are intended; though they are indirectly-confrontational communications that can only emerge in self-directed dialogue. These may be people whose communication skills are suppressed or channelled differently because of the antimotivational force of Exposure Anxiety.

Then there are secondary behaviours. Such as those of passivity, involuntary mimicry and characterizations when Exposure Anxiety leaves people unable to do things as themselves. There's a misleading clinginess when Exposure Anxiety leaves people terrified to be left alone with

Exposure Anxiety responses or unable to feel safe doing anything on their own. There are also misleading responses of 'helpfulness', 'protectiveness' and 'eagerness to please' when Exposure Anxiety leaves people unable to do for themselves but still free to experience themselves as capable and whole when focused on doing for other as a diversion from self. Sometimes, even the helplessness is misleading when Exposure Anxiety insists on playing on it to force others to carry the responsibility for self-help skills and communication.

Somewhere in there is the person, each with his or her own personality and interests, expressed or unexpressed, known or unknown, triggered or still buried. The journey of someone with Exposure Anxiety to first lose selfhood to Exposure Anxiety and then fight for it back is an exhausting and costly one many never make or complete. Some identify self with their Exposure Anxiety and it becomes their face to the world. I have met many using adaptations to sneak around their own Exposure Anxiety and try to indirectly teach the environment how to stop triggering Exposure Anxiety. Unfortunately, Exposure Anxiety can be so terrifying and saddening for parents to watch, by its very nature, that it compels them to be desperate for contact. This desperation makes the very people who might otherwise help directly confrontational and very self-in-relation-to-other. They almost never speak/interact back with the same language of indirectness the Exposure Anxiety individual is modeling for them, and when they do they too often doubt themselves when professionals without Exposure Anxiety come up with another 'expert' idea on 'reaching' their child.

Exposure anxiety and social touch

Acute chronic Exposure Anxiety may affect the use of touch for closeness, though there are people who will use physical clinging almost as a tool via which to lose sense of self within submission to the sense of other. Some learn to do social touch as part of a characterization or role, remaining as isolated as ever in spite of a façade of inclusion.

As social connection, Exposure Anxiety can compel aversion, diversion, retaliation responses, and may leave the person unable to touch socially as themselves or for themselves. They may still be able to comply, performing touch 'as you' in effect, or do so as a characterization of someone non-self or according to rote learning 'for someone else'. They may even learn to feign enjoyment if this is part of what someone else needs and this will divert attention away from themselves and real connection.

Social touch is not necessarily blocked by Exposure Anxiety where it is between two people who are self-in-relation-to-self and where touch is not a social act but part of one's own sensuality. I found the idea of using touch socially bizarre. Sensuality made sense because it was primarily self-in-relation-to-self. Many environments discouraged it because they see it as 'too autistic', 'too bizarre', 'invasive or unwanted by others' or a potential avenue to social danger.

I did develop a pragmatic sense of physical contact. I could help someone if they were being hurt (can't do it for self, by self, as self). The use of touch for social convention, (to do so for self and as self) however, was generally beyond my ability to comprehend or stomach. But if I sensed others would exclude or control me, take power over my life by virtue of this difficulty, the self-protection instinct focused on the inability more than the touch.

I had extreme problems with touch and, later, sexuality. I couldn't bring myself to stand 'the defeat' of someone needing to take personal significance or gratification out of seeing what I felt or causing me to feel something (this was how it was then, it's quite different now). When someone enjoyed my own pleasurable response, not keeping this to themselves for their own sake but wanting to make me aware of their feeling, I froze.

A lecturer who once stalked me once gathered some photos of me performing in a play where, according to the script, I had learned, in character, to let another character swing his arm around my shoulder. He sold the photos to a tabloid magazine as supposed 'proof' that I did not have the problems with social touch I had written about. Whilst I had been able to handle this performance of social touch as a character in a play, in my personal life I dissociated continually from my own body in response to touch. I saw myself, at this time, as a 'domestic prostitute' who had traded being touched by those who lived with me (and in return for their function as 'caretakers'). Much as I harboured deep resentment at the trade off, however much I detested these circumstances, there was no one else to help me. There were no services at that time for someone considered 'high-functioning'. Without these men my severe attention problems, information overload, extreme emotional fluctuations and the diversion responses of my own involuntarily self-provoked Exposure Anxiety, I could not cook a meal, keep track of or pay bills, tell the week from the weekend, nor easily remember to wash. Without these men I so resented, I'd have had no map to follow and have struggled immensely with living both safely and independently. Nevertheless, many high-functioning people with autism-spectrum conditions live like this and although there are beginning to be better alternatives, the lessons are still important ones in understanding the mechanics of Exposure Anxiety under such circumstances.

Exposure anxiety and emotional expression

To know a want, to show a want

I would have to say that one of the ways we first know 'I' is through the experience of wanting. There are two aspects to wanting. One is to know a want – to feel wanting internally in one's own world, an inner concept of self-assertion. The other is to show a want – to experience expressed wanting in relation to the external world – an externalized concept of self-assertion, of 'I' in the world.

The threat of self-acknowledgement of an unexpressed want can be enough to trigger Exposure Anxiety in some people. The very having of it is linked to the emotional drives behind expression that might invite in the outside world. To have a want is to threaten Exposure Anxiety with becoming observable by the outside world, even if one keeps the want to oneself. I can remember a phase of such severe Exposure Anxiety that I would sit staring at the wall for hours, getting lost in the pattern of the wallpaper. At the same time, frustration came and went, intense boredom came and went, intense drive and desire to move, to activate, to do, came and went. Yet I couldn't even hold onto any awareness of these wants. They drifted by me like barely tangible clouds. It simply felt too threatening to want, for to want was to be committed to life and to the joining and connection and attachment that would entail.

To be aware of the want you have is to recognize you are trapped and that your Exposure Anxiety is not you. This is why Exposure Anxiety combats awareness of want, diverts and distracts at the first sign of such a 'threat' to its absolute power over suppressed and tightly controlled self-expression. To fight for a thought takes a lot of energy. To fight to hold it takes even more because it feels not as though you are fighting for your survival, but as though you are doing something emotionally dangerous which threatenes the security and sanctity of one's own world. It's like being a twig standing on the edge of Niagara Falls and trying not to get swept over the edge. Only anger ever got Exposure Anxiety off my back. Anger and utter raging rebellion gave it it's sought after adrenaline high and it would then release its victim until the next 'call'. For most people with severe Exposure Anxiety, the constant battle to fight back is like trying to hold back tidal waves. It is never worth the tiny rewards of snatched life and many drown in a sense of despair, futility and frustration, giving in to an absolute denial of any desire to be as oneself, for oneself or do by oneself, for however despairing, depriving or frustrating, it feels, ironically, 'safer'.

To be aware of the want you have doesn't give you the keys to body any more than wishing away a behavioural tic means it won't continue to burst throigh or govern expression through the body. In the grip of adrenaline, the body goes into fright or flight mode. You can end up feeling so much worse for the awareness if all it brings is involuntary self-sabotage or a kind of freezing which feels like being buried alive.

Why can't he just be himself? Why does she propel herself into characterizations? Why can he never let the topic go and have a flexible discussion? Why is she so compelled to divert from personal conversation and attention by constantly hiding in applauded self-analysis (guilty as charged. Your Honour). Why can't he talk in something other than TV adverts? These people, however apparently dysfunctional, are your success stories. With severe long-term Exposure Anxiety, there may be no absolute freedom, only a diversification of escape routes which make life broader, however committed or self-challenging the person may be. To turn around ten years of Exposure Anxiety-balanced adrenaline addiction and its fight/flight mechanisms is a great task. To turn around twenty years of these learned, constantly environmentally reinforced primarily chemical but also neurological responses and experiences is a work equivalent to the building of the pyramids.

When it comes to 'want' all one may have left is what Exposure Anxiety allows – all those activities that control the involvement of others or divert from the jolting realization one has committed to involvement. To me, these 'wants' are those of Exposure Anxiety, or an Exposure Anxiety compromise. They are not the free wants of self.

The grittiest should learn to laugh, to joke with the prison warder, to make light of their prison and snatch the keys when it's distracted. To model humour as self-in-relation-to-self was one of my father's greatest gifts. He modelled characterizations as a route to a form of freedom, a parody of the self one could have been had one got free. He modelled absolute surreal eccentricity, creating an environment in which Exposure Anxiety could never jump clearly in defence. It could never predict that when it pressed 'A' my father would go 'B'. He often went 'X' or 'T' or 'K'. These were valuable things to model. I used them in navigating my own hiding from the warder. I went on the run inside myself, a barrage of constant characterizations with surreal eccentric shifts just when Exposure Anxiety would preempt my own desires and seek to squash their expression, their acknowledgement, their internal existence. Since I was three, I have been able to escape almost anywhere. Stuck with imprisonment, I became obsessed with escape. I then became a master of escaping my own internal labyrinth created by the tic – like responses of Exposure Anxiety and my own involuntary but intense addiction to overload-induced adrenaline rushes.

Exposure Anxiety had a grip on my external self but never truly won in its absolutely suffocating 'protection' of my inner self. Whenever it found me, I changed. I became intensely diverse, surreal and able to befriend it and turn on it as it did with me. I learned from my own master how to play it back. Until the use of Risperidone 0.5 mgs, I was not over my Exposure Anxiety but had mastered as well as perhaps anyone could this wild horse which seeks to distinguish the life of the person it is driven to 'protect' to the point of that person's expressive extinction.

The problem with 'I'

Everyone wants people with Exposure Anxiety to say 'I' – but who would this be? If it is said in compliance to expectation, it is not felt, and the mind may be forced to trick itself out of identification with that 'I' or risk losing the abilities it is attached to. I rarely used 'I', finding myself diverting from it, talking in generalizations, in diversions into litanies about 'then he went... and then she said...and then they went...' I learned to address my shoes and mutter 'to myself' about 'when a person...' and 'then the person...' Through time with a psychiatrist, I got my first foundation in learning to discuss myself as a book, an object, a case. Through psychologists and journalists I learned to beat them to the exposure of analysis by analyzing my mechanics. At least I had now exposed so much there was little territory left for Exposure Anxiety to 'protect'. Besides, I know I am more than my mechanics.

I learned to think of myself in the third person but say 'I', crisp and detached, as a 'the world' translation for my third-person-felt concept. Throughout childhood, my father was Jackie Paper; a name from a song. My mother was nothing except in the third person in which she eventually had her full first name, or made up names that captured the feel of her at that time. My older brother had a name, just like Table is a name for table. I never felt personally jarred by using his name. It was always used in the third person to control his contact with me. Directly in relation to me, he, like most people throughout my childhood, didn't have a name. My younger brother had a name, again, mostly in the third person. Teachers had no names. Some 'friends' had names. The older I got, the more I dared myself in a teasing game with Exposure Anxiety to use names to see if 'we' (Exposure Anxiety and I) could stand it.

The problem with 'I' or the direct acknowledgment of a personal relationship to other, like 'Mum', is that it puts one in the social–emotional world of *with*. Exposure Anxiety is allergic to that because *with* equals *invasion* which equals *overload* which equals *loss of control* which equals *survival response.* You may as well say to someone prone to adrenaline highs, hey, would you like to use a term of reference which denotes the absolute right of others to rob you of control and overload you with information and emotional provocation all by virtue of your own perceived invitation to do so? Exposure Anxiety would answer quickly for you. Like hell, not without it being a rote-learned stored response borne of compliance rather than connected self-expression.

The 'I' is not just verbal. It is visual. For my entire childhood, teens and much of my twenties, I didn't see my reflection as being 'I'. I saw it as my twin, someone external whom I could relate to with a depth and empathy others could only scratch the surface of. I felt, too, she had a deep empathy for me, seen in her eyes, a deep respect for my secrets, which I saw her hold and keep to herself and an excitement for my excitement. Beyond her, the responses of the environment were secondary and external to our world. Without her, I'd not have developed an internal concept of 'social', a desire to be understood and to turn to anyone outside of my own body. Yet I could not conceive of her as 'I'. When I finally did so, it was a terrifying, deeply-challenging developmental move that went hand in hand with an intense despair and aloneness. I tore myself away from her by choice and readiness. Had someone else done this without my volition, I'd have experienced it as if they'd imprisoned me away from my twin. Many people with severe Exposure Anxiety love the person in the mirror. Predictable, safe, never overloading, the person in the mirror asks for nothing foreign to oneself, doesn't threaten to take things further than asked for and doesn't trigger overload. In that, the person in the mirror may be the only human being some people with Exposure Anxiety have experienced themselves in company with *as* themselves. Many parents, carers, teachers, try to join the person in the mirror. As people without Exposure Anxiety, they assume they are joining not with an image of external 'other' but with the image of the person's 'self'. They even go so far as to persistently point out the visual reality that the person is looking at 'themselves' in there, with comments like, 'Hey, that's you, see', and 'Oh, you like looking at yourself'. To the person who is only able to make this deep social connection as long as they don't see it as an exposed act of self-expression, this jolting force-feeding of self-consciousness triggers Exposure Anxiety where the mirror had otherwise been a 'safe realm' unaffected by it. The person goes into involuntary avoidance, diversion, retaliation responses, ignoring the mirror as the bridge via which the 'invasion' came, diverting from it suddenly into that pattern on the carpet which became suddenly interesting or a 'What's your name, where do you live', verbal diversion-response control scenario. The answer is so obvious that those without Exposure Anxiety can't see it. You don't try to join with the other person's reflection, you join with your own. More important you do so *in your own space* and as though *for your own sake,* doing so in small doses to avoid the person with

Exposure Anxiety finding the sense of audience a potential threat of invasion and being compelled to leave or sabotage the activity.

Contrary to what you might expect, mirrors can be used to heighten self-consciousness (and with it inhibition and raised Exposure Anxiety) or to decrease self-consciousness by altering the directly-confrontational nature of the sense of self-in-relation-to-other. In the bathroom, before mirrors, I felt alone in there but someone invaded by big expectations of 'Have you gone yet', 'Get back in there, you haven't been yet'. With the mirrors, the atmosphere of the bathroom now became one in which I felt reassured by the heightened sense of company with myself (to the exclusion of others) and it became comparatively safer to do what I most dreaded. This thing so dreaded was the loss of control involved in giving in to the needs of body and voluntarily applying myself to using my own body muscles, the result of which would be I'd fulfil the wishes and expectations of others worried I wouldn't use the toilet. Exposure Anxiety makes people so often really terrible at this, making it far more natural to just wait till things 'fall out of their own accord' (wasn't 'me', it just happened). Learning to use muscles actively to excrete was actually a very hard task to master. One has to say either 'This is my body' (to which concept Exposure Anxiety may be intensely allergic) or 'I am responsible for body and it needs to let this stuff out now. It's too full and has been in there too long'.

The use of the mirror was good for dressing. I could watch, not the act of me getting dressed, but my facilitation of her getting dressed. It was also good for play and she and I laughed a lot at the many different ways we could wear things: underpants worn as a hat, jumpers worn as trousers, socks on our hands. This humour was invaluable. To have someone, one person in the world with whom I could be free without the problems of Exposure Anxiety gave me a strong inner concept of my own identity and a desire to escape my own cage. Going back to my reflection with the despair of my own trappedness in the world and to be comforted by her as someone in whose eyes I could see she understood from the inside, was something no-one else could have given me. Left to my own devices to dress myself without the diversion of either doing so as someone else or in the company of my reflection was difficult to organize or follow through until as late as my thirties. Doing for myself, as myself or by myself, triggered such persistent avoidance, diversion and retaliation responses, it was difficult to get together the simple act of getting dressed, of making a meal, of running a bath or going to the toilet. All of these remained difficult until now if there was no one as a mirror and no mirror either.

This problem of feeling too much 'I', so much you can't stand the awareness and seek desperately to lose it in a distraction or self-hypnosis, is something which shapes life choices and the impression of one's own capabilities. I'm still unable to work out whether my particular reliance on a mirrored external 'me' was, to an extent something akin to the security of the guide dog to the blind person and signing to the deaf. I was meaning deaf and meaning blind yet, unlike those without hearing and vision, I was bombarded with stimuli I could not make meaning out of. I was both intensely isolated and bombarded, triggering a massive innate instinct to comfort and protect myself whatever my social circumstance.

The 'I' was also auditory. I couldn't stand the impact of my name. I didn't mind being called by my surname, my category, a made up name or in the second or third person, but to be called directly in the first person threw me instantly into involuntary aversion, diversion and retaliation responses. It was the fact people could scream and scream my name without any response (together with meaning-deaf incomprehension behaviour and hands-over-ears overload behaviour shouting 'can't hear you', 'can't hear you'), that I, age nine, was identified as deaf.

When assured that I was not deaf the insistence I respond was severe. In her intense frustration my mother brutalized me for not responding and I was made, under threat of violence, compliantly not only to acknowledge my name but to respond, albeit in a choked voice full of hatred, with 'Yes, Mum'.

By the age of ten, this compliance had caused such severe feelings of emotional disturbance in the hands of Exposure Anxiety that I remind myself of something from 'The Exorcist'. I would respond to being called, enter as taught, smile and then punch myself hard in the face or drag my fingernails down my face. This was the price I paid for her conquest.

I understand the despair that may have driven my mother to try a compliance model, but with severe Exposure Anxiety, the short-term compliance wasn't worth the long-term payback. All she'd had to do was to enter my room and try to start up a conversation with me. I'd have diverted into going down the stairs and she'd have achieved her goal. She could have put the emphasis on the object/issue, not on me the person, calling out, 'There's a dinner plate here that is looking for Ms Williams immediately'. She could have put the emphasis on someone else: 'Tom needs some help down here immediately'. She could have brought a small mirror up, pretended to have caught my reflection and taken it downstairs, causing me to have to follow it to save it. She could have called me as a character from the TV, enabling me to respond also in character. She could have called 'the cleaner', 'the dinner person', 'the shopper' and I could have come down in a role. Instead, she defied her own instincts and brought a sense of 'I' crashingly into my perception, progressively triggering Exposure Anxiety in its most severe and disturbed presentations.

The crime and punishment of want and need

'Give me a hug' is a request aimed at 'I'. 'Put those arms here' is not about the 'I', it's about the arms. 'That body needs a hug' is about the body, not the 'I'. 'Let me give you a hug' is about the 'I' and Exposure Anxiety might stand the invasion only so long as it is processed as a 'disappearing' act of submitting to compliance. There is a sinister feeling in submitting to compliance. It is not an act of expression or empowerment. In fact, the very disappearance of the inner self and its own volition can be like a secret punishment to the person seeking the contact. There are those who will wish they didn't have Exposure Anxiety, who welcome the opportunity to comply as they feel a sense of achievement. The problem is, they may then equally feel despair when left to their own devices to initiate – they can't find the internal connection to the action, a connection they won't find because, stemming from compliance, emotional connection to the action was never 'theirs'. There are those who welcome the relief of compliance as a way around the internal struggles and frustration, even self-directed violence posed by Exposure Anxiety. Whilst appearing to be interacting with the world, they are interacting with their Exposure Anxiety, simply on the run, haunted by an invisible monster waiting to claim them should they try to initiate as self, by self or for self.

Exposure Anxiety makes it a punishment to have a want or need. Awareness of want or need can itself jolt self-consciousness, plunging the person into 'disassembly' and 'denial rituals'. From late childhood into my teens I used to shred paper into tiny confetti, contain it in a small ball and set it alight to make it disappear, after which I felt relieved to have disintegrated and disposed of that which had made or threatened to make connection. It can propel the person into a retaliation response in which they display indifference where they felt concern, rejection where they had felt want. It can propel the person into projecting the want or need onto someone else, compulsively distracting from self, even giving away that which was wanted or needed so badly. Eventually, Exposure Anxiety conditions the person to experience want and need as a source of extreme frustration, self-sabotage and loss of control over self-expression. The result is the person becomes conditioned by this internal invisible prison-warder/parent to experience want and need as a bad experience. Eventually, the person can only use those mirrored wants and needs of others or appear to have none – so easy-going, so easily pleased. This leaves the person appearing functional but too often deeply disturbed. Their trappedness is now successfully hidden, even socially applauded by those who see the person as something far removed from the extremely frustrated, invisible, disconnected or buried person they may feel themselves to be.

Aversion, diversion, retaliation responses: the 'me' in one's expression

Exposure Anxiety is like a vulture – watching, waiting. The more I wanted to say or show something, the more my own Exposure Anxiety was tuned in, hanging on my every expression. My body, my facial expression, my voice and my words were pulled about by some wild horse inside of me. I'd want to say I was sad, my face would be beaming. I'd want to sit calm and still and enjoy a sense of company, my body would be propelled into wild diversion responses demonstrating discomfort and hyperactivity. I'd try to tell someone I liked them and swear at them, try to show caring and be compelled to do something to repel them. This happened on a daily basis until my mid-twenties and I describe two of the clearest examples of this at my conferences.

One was when I was seventeen and someone would knock at the door. I'd go to open it, open, calm, ready to be human with whoever was on the other side of the door. Exposure Anxiety would jump in and not open the door but defensively wrench it open. I'd go to say 'Hi, can I help you?'

Exposure Anxiety would jump in with an obnoxious distancing 'Hiya woman, how's your hormones', after which the door would involuntarily be slammed in the person's face. Back inside, Exposure Anxiety would be relieved and lightened, almost as though it were laughing at the naughtiness and power of distance it had created. I'd be shocked, embarrassed and gripped by dread and despair. Then, now freed from its grip (having reassured itself we now had social distance from the poor recipient on the other side of the door), I was free to open it as myself. This happened for years and I had no choice but to laugh it off as though I was being a clown. The other choice, an impossible one, was to disclose I was not in control of my body and mouth, one that Exposure Anxiety would never have allowed to be expressed. Even going near such a disclosure was a sensed threat of utter self-sabotage aimed at whoever I had taken into confidence.

Another such example of Exposure Anxiety in control in such a complex way is exemplified by something that happened when I was in my early twenties. A friend of my father's who had known me all my life announced he was getting married, indicating with pointing that he wanted a congratulatory kiss on the cheek. I went to move forward, Exposure Anxiety lunged, grabbing for this man's arm. I tried to tone it down into a compromise of a gentleman-like kiss on the hand. It was too late, Exposure Anxiety had taken the arm up to my face and bitten into the man's arm like a dog biting into a bone. We both jumped back shocked. I felt the rising panic of imminent impending face-slapping self-abuse as a result of the raised adrenaline from internal struggle and counter-struggle. I managed to contain this display…just, digging my fingernails into my palms surreptitiously instead. Ah…the joys of socializing when you have Exposure Anxiety!

Exposure Anxiety also cashes in on expectations, diverting from my own independent and personal stance by compulsively echoing expectation. I had been in therapy in my teens for two years. It had taken almost a year to get me to speak more than one or two non-obscure sentences during sessions. I was feeling the topics welling up to the surface, almost able, almost able to start talking about the inner struggles I was having with impulse and severely challenged identity because of the constant internal battle between freed sterile intellect and crippled emotion. Instead, a last minute diversion became an obsession that went on week after week. Instead of discussing what was most relevant and helpful, one of my Exposure Anxiety diversion characterizations blah blahed away to this Freudian psychiatrist about issues which were not the real issues. What I really wanted immediate help with was in understanding the invisible cage I was tackling. As always, the most important discussion had to wait years and years until all the diversions from it had been exhausted. Then, and only then, would it allow me to address it as an issue. Mostly, I ended up doing so not verbally, but in writing, not to others, but to myself. Such is the nature of Exposure Anxiety that it so restricts the ability to get outside help. To own up to the full horror and frustration of what it is like to live, consciously aware, in the grip of Exposure Anxiety, is almost psychologically and emotionally intolerable. It is easier to try not to acknowledge it.

A world within a world of worlds: implications for social–emotional dialogue

The social–emotional reality of someone with information-processing delay is different from that of someone who can adequately keep up with the rate of incoming information. Some people are more mildly affected, able to have the simultaneous sense of self and other necessary to the experience of 'with', but still very literal, unable really to process information in the context in which it immediately occurs, at the level of relative or personal significance. Some people are moderately affected by information-processing delay to the extent that they compensate by keeping up with one channel at a time. This means they fluctuate between a simultaneous sense of self and other and the overload state in which they experience one or the other but not both. A sense of all self/no other leaves them still seemingly involved but cut off, somehow 'in their own world'. A sense of all other/no self is like switching to a sense of accumulation about other but with little processing of what one personally thinks, feels or wants in relation to the other person. Here the world of self doesn't retreat, it just ceases to be experienced.

This social–emotional state can fluctuate if the underlying physiological problems affecting information-processing fluctuate. Or, if the underlying physiological problems are extreme and constant this can be a fixed state. Under extreme chronic stress due to Exposure Anxiety, someone who might be literal yet who has a simultaneous sense of self and other may slip back to swinging between a simultaneous sense of self and other, and a state of all self/no other or all other/no self, and no longer experiences him or herself as being 'in the world'. They experience, along Aspergerian lines, the feeling they may not exist except as an information accumulation database (all other/no self) or the more 'autistic' route of someone who is like a world within the world (all self/no other).

In both cases, there is a loss of self-consciousness and a threat of invasion. In the case of all other/no self, the sense of invasion is felt when the walking 'database' is asked what they think, feel, want. The question calls up a simultaneous sense of self they do not have on line or use in social contact. It is like addressing Spock about emotion. The question does not compute. The question itself is alienating and draws attention to a gulf of experience due to a compensation for processing problems in a state of overload. In the case of all self/no other, the invasion is felt when the external world seeks directly-confrontational social contact.

Where someone is not on the autistic spectrum but has, for social–emotional developmental reasons, been in a chronic state of Exposure Anxiety from a young age, such a person would be likely to have a poorly developed sense of simultaneous self and other. This is simply because a developed simultaneous sense of self and other is not just a matter of processing but also of being part of the world rather than self-protectively in a world unto oneself. From the chronic self-protective stance of investing all one's security in being a world unto oneself, it becomes seemingly self-defeating, provoking of intense insecurity, to try to identify with a simultaneous sense of self and other. Security and identity may be invested in keeping the worlds of self and other distant and distinctly separated. This makes behaviour management and counselling quite a challenge with such a person, but the same rules apply as for any case of working with Exposure Anxiety.

The implications of the system of self and other with regard to social–emotional dialogue are different for each group. Even more complex is the case of someone who has adapted neither in one direction, nor the other, but in both at different times. In this sense, the person with autism and the person with Asperger Syndrome may have the same degree of difficulty manifested in two completely different ways. But, although the professional world distinguishes between the two conditions, there are those who fluctuate between the two states, being thus 'Aspie-Auties'.

To remove sense of self from social interaction is to remove processing for social affect – a huge level of information-processing. To remove sense of other in relation to self is to remove intellectual awareness and cognitive processing of these dynamics in favour of focusing on one's own sensory and emotional experience – again the removal of a huge demand on information-processing. If this is the consequence of accommodating the impact of Exposure Anxiety in order to continue some level of functioning, this is a big price to pay.

Simply being and new ways of socially relating

Living with someone in a state of all self, no other or all other, no self, doesn't have to be the end of the world. There are ways to help such people, though they may be ways that don't come naturally to most people.

Speaking through objects as though for one's own sake sets up the topic, not between two people, but as a conversation of one, interacting through an intermediary – the object. By addressing the object or issue that is physically out there and observable, sense of self and sense of other become irrelevant, incidental. So in directing all the communication to the object, two people can interact indirectly with each other by sharing the topic. Other techniques such as going walking together and talking out loud to oneself, running about, exploring the environment for one's own benefit whilst allowing the other to do the same, is a way of relating socially which I called 'Simply Being'. In inspiring the other person through your own lack of self-consciousness and strong boundaries as a world unto yourself, the other person becomes free to be expressively in their own world in your company, and an incidental sense of simultaneous self and other is the result. This can include playing video games together, focusing on a game of chess, shredding leaves in the garden, rolling down a hill, watching a TV show... there are all kinds of areas of interaction which allow parallel interaction not directed at the other person.

Counselling on the issue of social–emotional expression in 'the world'

One of the biggest gaps in services in the field is the complete absence of translators for the incomprehensible behaviour of those who don't have Exposure Anxiety. Why, for example, would someone keep saying they love you when they can see it shuts you down? Why would someone insist on eye contact when it cuts you off from connection with your face? Why would someone want to shake hands when they haven't even mapped out or felt who you are within? Why are people so obsessed with wanting you to tell them what you think, want, like and why can't they sense it? Why do people seem to want feedback and then when you give them a repertoire of what's going on for yourself, they seem put off? And, why, oh why, is it so different for them?

When I counsel people about Exposure Anxiety or about sensory flooding, or about information overload and shutdown, sense of self-in-relation-to-other or sensing versus interpretation, I make sure I do so without breaking the rules. I counsel people by playing out patterns of interaction through objects and characterizations. I bring the experiences to life in a visual and concrete way where comparisons are observable in direct relation to each other and the examples kept so small as to remain visually cohesive for those who experience visual perceptual fragmentation when visual information is too big. I make sure that I direct my discussion to myself, as though for my own benefit, and I make this so in how I sit, in my body, tone and volume. I do not look for confirmation. It is not mine to own, it is theirs. If an answer is useful, I'll pose myself a dilemma and ask, not for an answer, but for help. I'll be consistent in my use of body, tone and volume that the need for help is mine and about me, not about the other person.

Exposure Anxiety and sense of self

Self without awareness

Most people think of having a self as being a matter of awareness. The irony of Exposure Anxiety is that being aware cuts you off from the experience, the feedback, of sense of self. Many adults who have learned to function in spite of severe Exposure Anxiety, have told me they felt dead, plastic, not real, disconnected. Yet those who remain lower functioning seem to have a good deal of self, albeit at the expense of being able to dare or manage to hold any consistent sense of other.

My earliest baby photo, at only months old, shows one eye turned in, fists clenched, feet contorting inwards – what I recognize as an Exposure Anxiety response. I have memories from around three to six months old of the coloured patterns amongst whiteness, which I was unable then to conceive of as the Noddy cartoon wallpaper on my wall. I remember the feel of tassels on the pram and the view of wire within frosted glass, the pattern on the garage door, looking at the world from under the fine yellow mesh of the netting over my cot. I remember the movement of a blanket blowing in the breeze over a window of broken glass, the intermittent light sneaking into the room, the feel of people's voices and movements. So awareness, albeit devoid of interpretation, was there, awareness of perception and feelings, mostly absorption into sensory experiences. It is this, this absorption into experiences, this resonance with pattern and form that gives me a memory of self. I was someone simply being. I accepted everything without question and assumed everything, just like me, simply was.

At the age of three and a half I was sent to a nursery which took special needs children. I remember it was a structured, patterned day and I remember feeling much less Exposure Anxiety when I could give will over to the structure of the setting, becoming, in effect, part of the rhythm and pattern of the surroundings. Something changed in the photos. I stopped avoiding the camera, was no longer so obviously 'blind', looking through what was in front of me. I appeared progressively to realize the world was out there, not just me in my world. My eye contact became shy, nervous, but relatively directed.

Then at four and a half, my grandparents, who lived with us and cared for me, were gone forever and within six months I started primary school and the photos changed again. The smile was no longer mine, almost pasted on. The eyes not looking but looking through in spite of the projected pencil smile. By six the postures got cockier, by seven, back to shy but now bewildered. Then there are no more photos. What I know is that by nine, interpretation had begun with the help of vitamin C, zinc and multi-vitamin/minerals and I was beginning to be no longer utterly meaning deaf. The words began to become interpreted and I could understand simple sentences if there were not too many in a row. But my memory of the experiences of this time, was a distinct, sharp, intolerably acute sense of self. It was as though I was much too me. In the progressive awakening of the conscious awareness of interpretive information processing I felt exposed. I felt raw and utterly naked. My dreams reflected this. I fell into a deep depression that lasted two years in which the problems of OCD became progressively more dominant, and more obvious Tourette-like tics such as compulsive blinking, flinching, sniffing, throat-clearing and slapping, as well as hand weaving, became far more frequent. When I emerged from this depression, at about the age of twelve, I began to make a bridge from my own particular speaking through advertisements, songs and jingles, to speaking using interpretive language addressed to my shoes. I began to make a shift from speaking in feel and theme, to using interpretive meaning.

I found, at this time more than ever before, that in order to make any progress, I had to tune out awareness of self, and of other. Anything that caused awareness, triggered Exposure Anxiety and shut down the ability to process information. This included becoming meaning deaf to the processing of my own words. I could not understand my own speech, merely being struck by the experience of hearing it. It's a bit like hearing yourself on a tape and reeling back in embarrassment and shame that you 'sound like that'. I had two choices; keep going whether I could understand myself or not, continue to invite reply whether I could process it or not, or close off and be stuck with the consequences and helplessness. There was nobody who was interested or prepared to take over for me, carry me, do everything for me. Giving up and closing off was not an option. To do this meant institutionalization and I was shown where this was and what it was and I knew that, if I ended up there, I would not go back to my room, my structure, my predictability.

I learned that in order to not shut off from all meaning coming in, including the processing of my own actions and speech, I had to tune out awareness. I did this through a huge repertoire of tricks. I made myself feel I was only talking to my shoes, only talking as someone not me, not really talking, only singing, that I wasn't able to be understood by others so it didn't matter. I made myself feel I was only doing something because I'd been made to or because it was for someone else's benefit, not for my own.

I made myself feel I was only doing something involuntarily as a shadow of someone else or that my actions were just part of getting someone out of my face. I spoke the language of Exposure Anxiety back at itself. I was the prisoner who was learning to play the warden.

My very functioning relied not on getting sense of self but on fighting awareness of sense of self. At the same time, like anyone, sense of self is a source of stability, of home, of distinction from others. Having a lack of it or an inability to assert it or defend it made me vulnerable. But to be vulnerable was so much the better option than being frozen, helpless and, in my case, liable to being institutionalized.

Now consider the force-feeding of praise as part of the educational system. The praise is so often done by drawing a sense of audience toward the child, sticking its achievements glaringly in its own face and behaving as though this is a valued and enjoyable experience. How many people, particularing hyper-sensitive teenagers, have played down or lost their abilities because the praise itself feels like a gut-wrenching imposition or because the constant reinforced awareness it triggers, feeds Exposure Anxiety responses until the demonstration of anything which could lead to being joined, applauded or celebrated becomes taboo? Yet Applied Behavioural Analysis (Behaviour Modification Approach) is said, by its supporters, to 'work' with fifty per cent of people with autism. Compliance is co-opted by Exposure Anxiety and this is not the same as *self*-expression. What if what works is merely the sense of pattern and structure, rather than the invasion of praise – yet we attribute success, perhaps to our later detriment, to the misassumption that praise works? Furthermore, what happens when the child is big enough to get a biscuit for itself? Will Exposure Anxiety still allow the defeat of performance when the reward is no longer in the hands of the audience? Also, what of the effect of rewards high in gluten, dairy, sugar or salicylates, which ultimately build the adrenaline highs and reinforce the dietary patterns which feed these in so many children on the autistic spectrum?

Self buried alive

The experience of one's self being under glass, behind an invisible wall, in an invisible cage, buried alive, is a very distinct experience of self. It can be one of both the sanctuary, in which you feel contained, protected, untouchable; it can also be one of the prison in which you feel dominated, bullied, bossed about, robbed of control and excluded from life. In *Nobody Nowhere*, I opened my autobiography with the statement, 'This is the story of two battles, the battle to join the world and the battle to keep the world out'.

The experience of self as protected, contained, untouchable, was, a Buddhist-like state. I felt the world outside of me was like a waking dream: removed, not personally relevant. It was to my emotional reality like Renoir is to vision. I felt the world was something beautiful I was moving through but that was outside of me, not joined to or affecting my own world. On emerging from this state perceptually and cognitively but mostly psychologically and emotionally, I found this was actually true. It was as though I'd lived my life under a rock. Although I'd accumulated a huge repertoire of actions in the external world, information, mapped patterns of 'the world' and the 'the worlders' in it, I had performed, yet not experienced, self-in-relation-to-other. Mine had been an all self, no other and all other, no self world in which the awareness of one barely impacted on or shared the other directly.

This experience of Exposure Anxiety as the sanctuary is one of feeling utterly in control, powerful, a god in one's own world. I was able to take anything I wanted, leave and return to the house whenever the impulse took me, use objects however their sensory nature dictated, play with language however the entertainment factor moved me. This was, for me, largely a time of great depth of emotional experience in becoming one with objects, losing myself utterly in ritual, pattern and symmetry and feeling the freedom of beingness without consciousness.

When I was nine, this changed dramatically. When I was nine, I began to watch the world from my own world under glass. I began to be moved by how free and interactive, how flowing people were with each other, how different I was from my TV characterizations. I began to be jolted by awareness that I was not protected in my own world, I was vulnerable. I began to sense ridicule, impatience, and disgust. I began to realize the helplessness of being unable to run or scream in relation to the actions of another person. Only in relation to self, within my own world, were such things possible. In relation to the world, I was frozen and helpless. I could help myself to food, dress myself as I pleased, climb into my bed and pull the covers up, go the toilet wherever the experience seemed less challenging, more interesting. Yet I was unable to eat among others, to sit still at a table, to answer whether I'd like a coat, to ask for something else, to ask for comforting, to conform to rules which would make me part of 'the world', eaten up by the themness of them.

As meaning began to step in, I began to feel torn between two worlds. I have seen this same awakening in children aged three to five who have started on dietary intervention, supplementation, detoxification programs and treatment for digestive system and/or immune system disorders. Waking up at three or five is hard enough. To do so at nine is a major identity jolt and challenge in reconciliation. It is as though you've arrived in a new world that isn't 'you'. You can't mesh it with the old world, and you are not quite sure which to keep – the one that isn't you but is the majority of the world, or the one attached to your history, your experience, your emotion, your structure, the sense of self.

So the shift in beginning to identify selfhood with a place in the world, instead of in your own world, signals the start of being buried alive. No longer is this the Buddhist sanctuary. It is now something which holds you back, cuts you off, in spite of, and even because of your own intense drive to join the world.

This experience of self, self the prisoner, is a moody, despairing, often resentful, bitter sense of self. It is one which becomes angry at the world for being there, and for being shown the carrot it can never reach, the dream it can never hold. The world becomes a place of the privileged who are free to move and be flexible, to respond without façade or strategy and you cannot help feeling resentment for their lack of appreciation of what they have and how easily they have and hold it. Respecting the environment becomes difficult. On the one hand, you can now identify with it. On the other hand, because you are still trapped, often now even more so because of awareness and consciousness, you become defensively aloof or openly resentful of the very people you now have begun to identify with. It is as though, emotionally, you have turned against one version of self, only to find yourself now allergic to the very image of the new version of self as well. This is the point between the rock and the hard place. It takes great grace, self-calming and an indirectly-confrontational approach on the part of the environment to rescue people who get trapped at this point.

Non-autistic people romanticize about the great rescue, that moment when the person gets out of his or her own world and realizes he or she is part of the world. But images like that of the Kaufman boy in Son Rise (Option Program) are, in my experience, not the norm. One must keep in mind that there is a small percentage of children who, however severely affected, do spontaneously overcome the digestive system/immune system disturbances underlying their autism, whatever the program used. Nobody is to say whether the case of the Kaufman boy was a coincidental quirk of fate or whether his success was a direct product of the approach used with him. Raun Kaufman came through his autism at such an early stage of childhood that it would perhaps be unreliable to go by even his sayso of why this approach worked for him. Yet every year families pay thousands for the promise of the same success, as though love were a magic wand.

I wished a magic wand could remove Exposure Anxiety, the physiological problems driving it or its impact on gut, immune and toxicity issues. However, off nutrirional support for even short periods and my receptive understanding made me feel meaning deaf, isolated, in a state of all self, no other all other no self. My vision returned to being fragmented, fluctuating and overwhelming, in a state of sensory flooding. Before long, the Exposure Anxiety crept back, claiming territory and in the chaos and isolation, in spite of all my struggles, I sided with it. Twenty minutes after consuming dairy products and I was in this state.

For many there is no romantic rescue. Instead there is a tough, committed, consistent and realistic approach which requires tough love, detachment, playing hard to get and breaking cycles of co-dependency and learned helplessness in order to drive people to seize their own life. In a majority of cases, the approach to Exposure Anxiety is half the battle. The other half must address physiology in order to make fertile the ground not just for the reduction of sensory chaos and processing-related anxiety, but so you are reducing Exposure Anxiety in circumstances where the processing burden has already been removed.

What's in a name?

Who is self without a name? What is the concept of self if you are compelled to reject the very sound associated with the invasive connection being sought by others via that name?

I was unable to respond to my name and was tested for deafness at two and a half and again at nine for not responding to spoken language as expected or coming downstairs when called. I remember my mother in total despair and desperation bashing me as a last desperate measure to teach me to respond when called by my name. She had been screaming and screaming my name and I was unable to respond, stopped by Exposure Anxiety. I was unable to explain this to her then (and her own difficulties would have made it futile to do so), nor even have I explained it now I'm an adult. Once I came to associate not responding to my name with being bashed for it, I eventually began to be gripped with far greater fear at not responding than the dread which gripped me when I was expect to respond.

Her strategy did get the result she sought, however much terror and damage and chronic stress it caused in other areas. It would have been a much easier strategy for her to have got something I loved the sound of and used it downstairs. Rather than compelled to tune it out, I'd have been compelled to reclaim what was so mine, so me, and wander, fly-on-the-wall style, downstairs.

Far from being deaf, I had very acute hearing, finely tuned to what was 'my world', and highly organized to tune out what was not, such as my name. Sometimes we have to look at what we want to achieve and not the symbol. The goal was to get me to respond, not to acknowledge my name. But then, in the seventies, there were all kinds of apparent magic 'cures'; get me to cry and I'll be cured, get me to face my reflection and I'll be cured, get me to answer to my name and I will be part of the world.

My name became associated with trauma on two levels, one caused by Exposure Anxiety and the freezing which happened when I was expected to respond. The other was associated with fear of what would come after me if I didn't acknowledge it. My mother was a mistress of the indirectly-confrontational approach, but countering Exposure Anxiety day in day out is an exhausting feat and by the age of nine or so, parents can reach a point of desperation and despair. They want the problem to be cured and go away, and that, for once, their autistic child would just respond 'normally' – just for a change, just for a break. These days, there are at least parent support groups at the end of a phone, if nothing else.

The problem of responding externally to my own name was only part of the problem. Internally, I couldn't connect to the name and spent hours searching my eyes for connection to the word, mouthing it and whispering it over and over, trying to call up some personal connection with it. It took me until my twenties to begin to really feel the connection between the me inside and this name and to feel it with some compassion and empathy.

So who did I think I was in the absence of connection with or acceptance of my name as me? I was unable to stomach the connectedness of acknowledging other people (my parents; my teachers) in relation to me. To push towards such daring gripped me with such dread I felt instantly the compulsion to attack and this compulsion was usually addressed at myself. It was simply easier to avoid the name-ness of people. Yet referring to people in the third person was far less blocked. I could chatter to myself about them, particularly internally. So who were my parents or teachers in the absence of any titles or names spoken directly at them?

I had little idea of self and when I began to get any element of it, the inability to hold ideas over from one context over into the other meant it couldn't accumulate or gain continuity. Perhaps this, also, was a self-protective function of Exposure Anxiety in that it protects from self-consciousness. Still, my experiential sense of self was whole and relatively consistent, much as the ingredients in a cake mix remain relatively constant whoever mixes it or however much it sits before being mixed a little again. And my sense of others was similar. Ideas of the other person were hard to hold on to, hold over or join up to form a whole picture or understanding. What was left was the mapped feel of others, something I referred to as the 'music of their beingness'. Eventually, with the same kind of force used to get me to respond to my own name, my mother succeeded in getting me to comply in calling her 'mother' in response to prompt. By the age of about eleven, I eventually progressed, by choice, to calling her by her first name. My father I continued only to refer to in the third person. I finally called him 'Dad' in the two weeks he had left to live. I was by then thirty years old and it was six years after treatment for the physiological problems underlying the Exposure Anxiety. My mother is now referred to half the time by her first name, still in the third person but also in the second person. She is also referred to as 'my mother', but only in the third person. This is the progress by the age of thirty-seven. I have never named professionals and helpful people who I have liked, except in the third person. By my twenties I was able to refer to them by their full name (first name and surname). By my thirties, I had mastered daring the informality of leaving out their surname by saying that part internally, silently to myself, and since the use of Risperidone 0.5 mgs, on top of the effects of a nutritional approach, it is as though it had never been a problem. It is still the norm, however, to leave people mostly without names. Yet to me, my sense of them was as whole, perhaps more so, than conceiving of them in terms of their names.

Compliments that hurt

Compliments spoken out loud by someone, as though to him or herself, were generally undisturbing. These were taken as people simply saying things about their own feelings about something to do with me. When the compliments were directed at me, I didn't feel like this. I felt like I was being force fed, forced to take, to accept. It compelled a sort of emotional vomit reaction in me, and I was compelled to spit the invasion back out at the giver. When people used my name as part of the compliment they compounded difficulty accepting the experience of the name associated with myself. My experience personally, and in the field, is that the person with Exposure Anxiety stops cringing, avoiding, diverting, and retaliating, when a compliment is aimed at something external rather than at oneself. I suggested such a change in one of the schools I was consultant to. I instructed that compliments should be directed at the photo of the person, not at the person themselves. I showed that this could be done, not for the in-their-face benefit of the person being complimented, not as an act of giving (sensed as invasion) but instead to the complimenter, as though for their own sake. This seemed to make the children physically relax more with the session, and, I think, not feel compelled to reject the very abilities which lead to such force-fed, non-asked-for, giving.

Behaviour modification and the concept of 'rewards'

This has direct bearing on the Applied Behaviour Analysis (ABA) concept of rewards. If someone with Exposure Anxiety is playing down or losing skills after six months of ABA and directly-confrontational praise or 'reward', then the environment should listen. Six months of damage is not too much to undo and some children without severe Exposure Anxiety respond well to conventional Behaviour Modification approaches such as ABA. The problem is that for those who don't respond well, some have actually progressively lost skills when given more attention than they can stomach emotionally and this should not be ignored. Conventional Behaviour Modification approaches can be adapted so as to be used in an indirectly-confrontational way. Being provided with the activity required and given the clear sign that if they complete it they will be rewarded not with applause or attention but with simply being provided with something else, may facilitate activity without inhibiting it through triggered Exposure Anxiety. It is a matter of how one understands the motivations and anti-motivations of the person with Exposure Anxiety and incorporates this into a system of 'rewards' according to that reality.

An indirectly-confrontational approach to developing tolerance to having a self

The first step in developing tolerance to having a self is in avoiding taking over at the first sign of helplessness. It is also about not applauding or drawing attention to the person when he achieves something so that he does not become inhibited from repeating the action in order to avoid the sense of audience. Providing the environment with the media through which the person can 'incidentally' 'discover' for himself a way of exploring self, is the second step. Mirrors are an example of this, so is a typewriter, a record player and records, a radio, art materials – anything through which someone can progressively explore and experience a sense of her own expression and taste. These things should just 'appear'. They should have no attention drawn to them. They should be provided in their own space, away from observation and left without explanation and without the person seeing you leave them. Their discovery of such things should be as an act of taking from the environment rather than receiving in a social situation. Progressively as they explore interests and self, then, they may begin to explore people as objects but this is only likely if such people are not waiting, wishing to make directly-confrontational connection. The first step is a sense of self within one's own discovery and exploration and control. From there, sense of other as object becomes possible as an expansion of one's own world. Then, exploring sense of other as something pursuable with one's own volition becomes possible and unthreatening to Exposure Anxiety. Finally, building up from small doses, directly-confrontational interaction can go gradually to larger, seemingly tolerated doses of social contact. This form of interacting and providing opportunities and modelling for people with extreme Exposure Anxiety runs counter, I am told to the social–emotional nature of most non-autistic people. It also leaves people open to social criticism, something families of people with severe Exposure Anxiety are particularly likely to be sensitive to and overly influenced by. The approach I'm talking of here, though on the surface seemingly similar to the Option Approach, it is in fact nothing at all like it. With Option, the desire on the part of the family is to 'break through' by mirroring the child and the emphasis is often on how much the environment has to give. An indirectly-confrontational approach is about the desire of the child. It is about stimulating the child's pursuit of the environment which is not co-dependently waiting outside to give but is getting on with its own beingness – in doing so it is still a facilitator and inspiration rather than teacher.

Counselling on the issue of self

People with Exposure Anxiety need counselling about what the adrenaline addiction behind Exposure Anxiety is, what causes it, what makes it worse, what reinforces it, how to calm oneself down in the grip of it. The need for counselling is also about how the environment does understand and is trying its best and why having Exposure Anxiety isn't the end of being part of the world or claiming a place in life. They also need counselling about who they are, who is the self, the very issue Exposure Anxiety will not allow them easily to explore socially, especially through verbal communication. Question is, with all this need for counselling, what do you do if directly-confrontational counselling is not going to work? Even worse, directly-confrontational counselling, because it triggers a highly reactive, defensive state, is not taken as caring, but as invasion of one's own world, and as abuse, however well intentioned.

There are ways of counselling people without doing so directly. Leaving notes addressed to them isn't the answer because it is too direct, and they may then only suppress their own expression even further so you have even less to address or comment on. You can, however, writing yourself notes about 'someone' you care about or worry about. You don't have to mentioning the person by name. 'Absentmindedly' leaving the letter seemingly half written as you 'suddenly remember' something you had to go and do is a way of providing an opportunity for someone with Exposure Anxiety to take this indirectly-confrontational counselling.

Many people with severe Exposure Anxiety, like a lot of people with dyslexia, have trouble reading things word by word but can scan-read in an instant, as though photographing the page. Although consciously they may not realize what they've scanned, on a preconscious level the brain continues to try to decipher such peripheral information. Many such people can read but are not aware they can read because when they try, it is like jumble. Yet the same people will seem to 'pick up' knowledge as if from out of nowhere, finding the indicators of this sneaking through the cracks of their behaviour without even realizing that the knowledge is in there but behind conscious awareness.

Influence and change happens on that very subconscious level. On a conscious level, we challenge it, block it, but subconsciously only internal logic is left to decipher it and weigh it up. I had great difficulty reading anything with conscious meaning, yet I could scan huge volumes of writing, able to go to the exact place on a page in my mind where I'd seen a certain sentence or word (a pattern). I scanned around twenty books a day during my return to education, simply knowing that even if I didn't under-stand a word of what I was seeing, as I slept, my brain gradually deciphered this flood of jumbled information. All that was then left to do was to be in situations which did not ask me about it (for without conscious awareness I would not know I knew) but which would trigger the information by people's expressions and questions posed not to me, but to each other. Answers were jumping up out of nowhere, much to my own terror and, later, acceptance and amusement.

Self-directed diary letters can be left screwed up and discarded for 'discovery'. Exposure Anxiety can be such a sneak when 'no' equals 'yes' and 'yes' equals 'no'. They can be left on post-it notes 'to oneself' on the fridge. They can be left lying on the basin in the bathroom. They don't need to be expressed in words. Feelings, experiences, connections, even issues can be conveyed not in words but in diagrammatic form. I'd still recommend including the words beneath the diagrams as many apparently non-verbal people who are seemingly unable to read have later demonstrated that they could map words (common with dyslexic people learning to 'read') and had a huge repertoire of mapped-word patterns, equivalent to reading. With a Camcorder you could make a video-diary to 'yourself' about your feelings and slip the video into the the video recorder left on 'play' as you strategically become 'interrupted' to go make yourself a cup of tea. Will it seem 'normal' to someone with Exposure Anxiety for you to be so controlling or obsessed with communication from you to yourself? This relationship is second nature to many people with Exposure Anxiety.

Other techniques of indirectly-confrontational counselling, involve characterizations done at the counsellor's own reflection, even spoken whisperingly, privately (playing hard to get works wonderfully to inspire Exposure Anxiety-driven 'curiosity') into the curve of a soup-spoon or ladle. But keep it small doses, keep it in the third person, about a person, never named, focus on the issue, not the person and always cut the self-discussion short, leaving the fly-on-the-wall audience pondering annoyedly what the ending was. Nothing sticks more than the story that left the ending off.

Counselling can be played out through playful characterizations through small objects, but always done as though for the counsellor's own benefit. The body language should be kept as though this is a private discussion with oneself, the volume kept low at times, compelling the fly-on-the-wall audience to listen in even harder to hear what they are obviously 'not meant to hear'.

Counselling can be done drama style through humourous characterizations and character shifts played out to oneself and projected at an invisible 'other'. The counsellor can play alternate roles, but as though the counsellor is resolving an issue for him or herself. Again, use small doses, leave the 'audience' wanting more and however confrontational the audience then becomes, be half-hearted about their initiation, as though the counselling wasn't for their benefit, it was for yours, but you'll allow them a moment's participation. Remember, being allowed the privilege of a moment's involvement of something not for or about you is a far greater honour than being given something for you that you did not ask for, simply because someone else wanted to give it.

For those with severe information-processing problems, you can keep your characterizations at a reasonably slow pace and leave processing breaks, as though you just stopped momentarily to ponder something to yourself before continuing. But remember, even if the fly-on-the-wall audience didn't keep up, the brain still accumulates all the patterns, visual, auditory, kinesthetic and continues to process these, albeit beyond conscious awareness. This still has progressive emotional effect as it begins to cause change from the inside. And characterizations don't have to be verbal. Gestural signing is very different to Makaton and much more easily interpreted in the moment in the case of information-processing delay. Yet gestural signing can speak the content just as well, if not better than words. Best still is that you can combine gestural signing with the verbal language in your seemingly self-directed characterizations which address the issues of Exposure Anxiety and the self.

You are best focusing on the feel of the person being conveyed in your self-dialogue, rather than clearly identifying specific expressions of self. Otherwise, the self-consciousness this can cause may make Exposure Anxiety then suppress these very expressions. So the art of indirectly-confrontational counselling is a very subtle one. If you think 'this person has learning difficulties, I have to be big, bold, loud, and blatant', you have got it wrong. People with learning difficulties, however much they may have difficulty taking in knowledge, are very often extremely sensitive to pattern and can pick up very subtle shifts. Counselling isn't always about changing knowledge and understanding, especially when Exposure Anxiety cannot be reasoned with and it is always listening in to mind, co-opting every piece of new understanding with a counter move. You actually don't want the conscious mind to be too aware if what that means is that Exposure Anxiety simply co-opts and contorts that awareness. What you do want is to work on affecting the person on the emotional level, in terms of mapped pattern of that very subtle dialogue you are having 'with yourself' about similar issues or about having experienced 'a person' with these issues.

Developmental programs for desensitization

Anything that allows the person to lose self-consciousness in order to just let go and 'be' are good programs for desensitization to this 'allergy to self-expression'. Drama, dressing up, free movement together with music and the use of colour and form help one to experience 'the feel' of oneself whilst having no sense of directly-confrontational audience to this because everyone else is off in their own world anyway. Huge sheets of paper on the walls which one can run past, using creative movement to draw, write, create pattern on them to the music or whilst chasing lights on the wall – these are activities that allow the experience of self without the self noticing. These don't have to involve using conventional tools. One can use water on wet hands to make disappearing imprints of self. One can use, purely, movement impacting on this surface in the external world – intangible, instantaneous, then gone, like self in people with Exposure Anxiety. Drawing a block over a surface may be more user friendly and indirectly-confrontational than using a pencil (which is being wanted, noticed and clearly part of the external world and taken as a sign of conceding to join it). Using the drum to play the stick may be more possible than using the stick to play the drum.

Jumping from heights, jumping into depths, throwing things into large boxes from up a ladder, daring to stomp and then slide, to scream and then whisper, to make large steps, then tiny over objects on the floor, to jump over small obstacles on a floor representing the world. These are activities that exercise the challenge to the boundaries of Exposure Anxiety without drawing direct attention to it. They address the Exposure Anxiety on a body level and an emotional level, not an intellectual level and this is where therapy is most effective and most likely to cause flow in other forms of expression.

Desensitization to Exposure Anxiety is about daring to let go control, to feel modulation, to explore boundaries, but it has to be done without making the person consciously aware they are doing so. Rewards and praise may counter the productivity of the entire thing, increasing sense of audience and destroying the good work by making as many steps backwards as the person is making forwards. Next time the session doesn't progress, and you have to start from scratch. The best reward and encouragement is to sense the environment is not focused on you. In between, of course there is subtle, consistent but indirectly-confrontational direction where it is important that the therapist appears involved not for the sake of the person with Exposure Anxiety, but as though the activity is wholeheartedly simply a buzz in itself. Fun is contagious when it's not being stuck in your face. But being half-hearted in this therapist role, being too much of a hero, a martyr, waiting in desperate hope with deep desire to save the person with Exposure Anxiety will make this technique a burned bridge, because the carer could not find the self-ownership, detachment and love of self to become truly inspirational to the person with Exposure Anxiety whilst demonstrating the safety of freedom and wild creative self-expression.

Words can swim and spin and line themselves up into wild surreal sentences, played out to yourself through movement and gestural signing. Numerical patterns can become hopscotch – take numerical turns in going down a slide in groups or being posted into cut-out boxes in groups of four or eight or seven. Objects, words, numbers can be thrown up to the chant of 'gravity'. Objects can be spun on a lazy Susan (you can get these cheaply) to the chant of 'inertia' as they fly off. You can chase your own spot on the wall to the chant of 'reflection'. You can wobble objects to the chant of 'reverberation'. In doing so, you model indirectly-confrontational physics. You can draw a huge body on the floor, fill it with representational organs and go on a tour through the body, or make a dummy and stuff it full of representational organs, unzipping its front to expose, go through, name, explore, explain and put back each one. Here you are modelling indirectly-confrontational anatomy.

You can cover the entire curriculum. Just because you didn't get the person with Exposure Anxiety to comply and be put through the same activities as everyone else doesn't mean the lesson wasn't successful. Most people with Exposure Anxiety will map the happenings around them which then come out later in their own space, their own time, their own privacy. Progressively, the Exposure Anxiety becomes convinced that however much expression is let out before others, it is never pounced upon excitedly (impactingly, invasively) because the environment is too busy simply being and having a buzz for its own sake. Then the person begins to 'steal' the objects of involvement to test whether the environment will then pounce. Find new objects and let the 'thief' take these – or steal them back, they are 'yours', and so raise the motivation for inclusion even higher. Progressively, you 'give in', allowing them to be involved and progressively move into an intermittent interplay between parallel 'play' and self-in-relation-to-other interaction. Keep it clear that both are valid, that the person has not been tricked, they have not been trapped into everything now being self-in-relation-to-other – a non-autistic social reality. Sometimes only by knowing we are free to be socially free do we choose to stay involved. Compliance and pleasing others isn't everybody's thing. Some people close off in protecting themselves against what seems, otherwise, a lack of choice about interaction. Take the heat off. The best flowers don't always grow in a hot house.

Exposure Anxiety and detachment

Detachment, depersonalization, performing and other useful tools and their saboteurs

When I have seen parents with verbal children, one of their main focuses seems to be on whether or not their child uses 'I'. This seems utterly bizarre to me as someone with Exposure Anxiety, for why on earth would a child with Exposure Anxiety be motivated to sabotage his or her own freed-up communication by jolting awareness with a conscious sense of self-ownership of what is flowing out? This is actually what the pronoun 'I' does. In many non-autistic people, in situations of extreme exposure, the saying of the pronoun 'I' is something sharply committal and they will often speak this word quieter and a little further back in their throat than the rest of what they say. It always amazes me they are so unaware of this that they can't use this experience to understand the same thing with the volume turned up in the Exposure Anxiety-provoking everyday situations faced by their child. Some will even say, 'I don't understand it. He/she is obviously capable of using it when prompted (when not said as self) and sometimes uses 'I'' (probably in situations where Exposure Anxiety is at bay or the interaction is not being waited for or wanted).

Privately, I never thought of me as 'I'. The thought seemed bizarre. Even though I used it intermittently with third person referral to myself as Donna, the pronoun 'I', still seemed an empty word. It felt, to me, a convention used by the outside world, something with no more specific association with the feel of me than if I referred to myself as 'he', 'she', 'a person'. The only difference was that it carried associations with compliance, forced recognition and a forced sense of self-in-relation-to-other – something I was unable to experience until I was thirty. To satisfy this highly-revered marker of social normality was not only to admit defeat in defending the boundaries between my own world and the world, but also to lie about my capacity for the social relativity inherent in using the word. It's like using the word 'glumph' convincingly when you have no real capacity to experience it. Although I could conceive of the 'I' inherent in my Donna-ness, I was unable to conceive of the beingness and personhood in the term 'I', perhaps especially because when I perceived 'you', I lost its beingness in the context of 'I' and vice-versa.

Referring to self as 'you', or 'she' (or 'Donna' for that matter in my case), is also about one's relationship to verbal language. If you experience it as self, then you are not detached from the use of it as personal, spontaneous expression. If you use verbal language as something taken on with a clear sense that it is not as your own system but someone else's, it simply feels more meaningful to speak it as if it is an external describer of what is going on within and on the outside.

The issue of being mono is a major aspect of sense of self-in-relation-to-other, central to avoidance of the use of 'I'. How ludicrous to force people in a mono state of all self, no other/all other, no self, to only use what they may be unable to perceive in a simultaneous context. It seems to me equally ludicrous to feel satisfied when we have taught a blind person to use directed looking or getting a deaf person to speak clearly enough to not be identified as deaf. The sense of ritually-reinforced failure and alienation is one thing, but the heightening of the sense of Exposure Anxiety now surrounding this desperately sought after symbol of normality turns the use of 'I' into a control issue.

Detachment is not just a product of Exposure Anxiety but one of the most important keys to getting Exposure Anxiety to relax as though there is no threat. I was extremely frustrated by the fact that I was always so blocked, particularly when I had a desperate need or desire. This meant in a situation of danger, I would freeze and could not scream. Having stepped into a bath that was too hot, the desperation to get out quickly would trigger Exposure Anxiety responses and freeze me there. Desperation to go to the toilet was guaranteed to trigger one diversion after the other. I learned, eventually, that every time I gave up in despair, Exposure Anxiety would let my body and voice go. I learned, by the age of eleven or twelve or so, to convince myself of a flippancy, indifference and detachment that allowed me to free up and move or express myself. I had the fear always that my Exposure Anxiety was watching me, ready, waiting to stop me at any move. So once I'd sneaked expression I'd often rush it maniacally, as though it would be cut off, disappear at any moment. Often it was, but by then I'd got my expression out. The result was that I appeared very all or nothing, very hit and run. In my late twenties and thirties I discovered a much better strategy. Announcing the impending block seemed almost to guarantee the Exposure Anxiety would leave me alone. I had learned to expose the Exposure Anxiety. It pulled back instinctually to prove my expectation futile and incorrect. Though this embarrassed me, it achieved what I needed so, in my bloody-mindedness, I didn't care what it took as long as I got the expression out. But it has been a long hard road to know this enemy, side with it, study it and progressively play it at its own game. It used to be my parent. My primary relationship in life is, by necessity, the relationship with this mechanism in the bargaining for life. I do play my hand well and as much as I was still fifty per cent in a very hidden prison, it was nothing like the times in my life where I was almost completely buried for long periods of time.

In schools and homes where this detachment is not allowed, where the emphasis is on constant recognition, proof and acknowledgement of ownership, this freeing mechanism of being able to play one's own Exposure Anxiety would not develop. The person would be so caught up in the persistent reactiveness that so constantly justifies the Exposure Anxiety payback that there would be little or no personal space to develop the needed strategies to live, in independence, in spite of Exposure Anxiety.

Using objects as prompts

When I needed the toilet, a drink, a jacket, I was propelled into avoidance, diversion and retaliation responses. I found a solution by diverting to the mess in the room. The clearing up of the mess meant I could put things about as triggers. In my twenties I learned to put things on the stairs that needed putting away. Next time I would pass I'd be compelled to put this away. On the way to putting this away I'd divert away from the diversion itself, heading into the toilet. Then I'd go as a way of putting off the self-expectation to put the object away. Though the process would take up to two hours to go the toilet, it was so much of an achievement. Usually, I'd have held on for six hours or much more. I couldn't grab a jacket, but I could grab someone else's for them. With someone I was very close to, I could sometimes also put theirs on as part of reactively robbing them of the control of having it. I couldn't have a drink of water very easily, but I could water the plants and then take a sip, in defiance of giving the drink to the plant. In my twenties I was able to speak when it was useful to others or as a diversion from what I wanted or needed to say. To say something personal and emotional, without clinical detachment and externalization, I was generally only able to do in non-verbal dialogue with my own reflection. At twenty-four I progressed from being able to type poetry and song as personal expression to writing to myself my entire autobiography. After the exposure of this having become internationally known and read, I was then free to type openly to myself as a way of replying personally to others within myself, then giving them these words.

As I have said earlier, a typewriter appeared in my room when I was nine. After my initial distaste for this new addition in my territory and with no pressure or observation to use this seemingly abandoned item, I began to press the keys. After letter patterns and word lists, a page of paper one day appeared in it. I began to type on the page and this progressed, by the age of thirteen to typing poetry. Had this not become my personal self-dialogue, I doubt that typed communication would ever have become friendly with Exposure Anxiety, and all the books and interviews and lectures that eventually followed would never have happened. I never felt it was me typing. I managed to type because I merely pressed the keys, and the keys, not me, then put the letters on the page. Some people with severe Exposure Anxiety have used others to type through, needing to attribute their expression to their facilitator in order to get the communication out. Some have progressed to independent typing, but this is a long hard battle with their own Exposure Anxiety in daring the eventual ownership of this ability to communicate. Others, perhaps because they have been watched, manoeuvred, been the object of too much external hope or need, forced to prove ownership of their communication, or gave up or failed to progress from fully-prompted, fully-supported typed communication. Perhaps the understanding of the mechanics of Exposure Anxiety and the need to attribute expression to the control or volition of something non-self, will help to change this state of things for non-verbal people with the potential to communicate through other media.

Anyone familiar with my autobiography will also know that I used my characters as a means of daring expression and attributing it to something external. Although these characterizations came through my body, I saw them as external to self, as add-ons. Though a majority of their actions and communications were the avoidance, diversion and retaliation flight and fight responses of Exposure Anxiety, some of this communication and expression was from me, channelled through their freedom to express as non-me. The result was a very confused environment, never sure who was in there. From my side, it was despair in waiting to break through as me, being sometimes amused, sometimes disturbed by where the avoidance, diversion, retaliation responses of these characterizations would take me. If nothing else, life was not as frozen as it was without them. Communicating through these characterizations as external objects was sometimes the only freedom I had in the external world. I could be free in my own world, but interacting as myself was far more bizarre and incomprehensible most of the time to the environment.

Carrying objects was also very important in being able to take action or use self-expression. Being able to address these special objects, tell myself I was taking them to places, accepting things because the object wanted it, was an important avenue for facilitating connection. Later, speaking to my shoes, telling them where we were going, helped to initiate, and after that it would involve more Exposure Anxiety to dare the expressive choice of stopping than to keep going.

Getting purpose: the freedom and the trap

With Exposure Anxiety, the compulsion to push away from self is extreme and fighting it is exhausting. The isolation, though, in accepting it and where it might otherwise keep you is a source of utter despair. I believe in giving people jobs. When you get someone with Exposure Anxiety to do for self, they freeze. When you get them to do for you, they may comply but it is just that, compliance basically done as you. This is different from the environment playing helpless and absent minded. 'Max can't reach that, pass it to him will you', said with the focus on the object not the person and said from a true feeling of this being not about them but about Max, is far more likely to get the object handed to someone than simply asking for the object. Asking for something on behalf of someone else puts that person in the middle as an object, severing the sense of the direct contact between asker and giver (because Max did not ask). People with Exposure Anxiety in conjunction with severe information-processing problems are often highly sensing and will feel whether this is a test that silently wonders, 'Will she, won't she'. Exposure Anxiety will flare and you'll get nothing – can't get a response if the person suddenly appears deaf. So it is important that these are not 'set up' situations but situations which reflect real needs. If it fails to get you the help, a comment which exposes Exposure Anxiety's ownership of the person such as 'Oh, sorry, how silly of me, of course you're unable to dare, I forgot' will probably infuriate Exposure Anxiety. which may seek to prove you wrong next time.

People with Exposure Anxiety can sometimes become compulsive helpers even though they will not do anything for their own direct benefit. They may help the shopping to go home to its right place on the shelf. They may help the washing to find its way into the washing machine, help the smelly sheets to go for a wash, help the rubbish to go for a walk to the bin ... but asking someone to do this for their own needs may meet a brick wall. In late childhood, my mother did ask me to do things for other people and this felt different from direct requests. It didn't involve a connection with the asker so Exposure Anxiety generally didn't flare as badly. This was especially so if she seemed indifferent, or flippant about the request because this promoted a sense of non-audience, a neutral situation in which I either did or I didn't... there was nothing for Exposure Anxiety to defy.

Of course this makes people unable to stop themselves because once this is the route to freedom, all volition has been given up to the needs of the environment. But having sat in the same place eight hours a day frozen by Exposure Anxiety, I always found being frozen and inactive much worse than being compelled and unable to stop. You can always learn to self-limit, but it's much harder to get someone started from nothing.

It is especially so that when Exposure Anxiety freezes social connection, what is still left is purpose in relation to objects. Most importantly though, is that this can't be overplayed because that makes it blatant, too obvious, and Exposure Anxiety is relentless and incredibly sensing and perceptive of the feel of situations. It will smell a trap when you are barely even conscious you are setting one. Setting enabling, empowering 'traps' for Exposure Anxiety-crippled people is something you would have to do from a strong place of detachment and self-ownership and helping the environment develop that is often a bigger battle than the Exposure Anxiety itself.

The problem in doing 'for self'

The problem in doing for self has many parts to it. One aspect is associated with the long-term association that doing for self means the environment has won. The environment needs, therefore, to model surrealism so that what is 'normal', 'expected', 'wanted' becomes blurred. The sense of what the environment wants becomes less clear and the avoidance of that far less focused. One can't get extreme stress about the rules, either breaking them or complying with them, if the rules are not crystal clear.

Another part is about feeling the desire too strongly, triggering self-protection. The solutions here include tapping, finger clicking, singing to oneself, having the radio available; whatever it takes to tune out to what you 'allowed to slip through'. Of course a nonchalant environment which is getting on with its own thing in respectful self-ownership without breaking into applause probably helps get the heat off.

A third aspect is that in doing for self, the gut reaction is one of vulnerability in leaving oneself open to the possibility that others now have something to attach to in holding a connection with you. When environment is aloof, self-owning, warmly playing hard to get, always leaving the person wanting more, there is progressively no fear of the environment co-opting or pouncing on one's own expression.

Another part of the problem in doing for self is of commitment. If you have fluctuating sensory–perceptual or information-processing problems it grips your gut to have the environment see what you can do because you may be completely unable to make the connections to do it again tomorrow, but it will still be assumed and expected that you can. Further-more, if in the doing you had to cut off from awareness to let the action out, you can't take pride in your actions, for to do so triggers self-consciousness and that means it becomes twice as hard to do these same things next time. Removing the directly-confrontational praise can be a big help here. Con-ventional Behaviour Modification approach does a disservice to people with Exposure Anxiety in convincing the environment we all need love or thrive on the directly-confrontational expression of praise. Ask yourself how you feel about having attention drawn to you, your slightest compli-ance or achievement applauded gaudily in your own face. Having asked audiences about this in workshops, many non-autistic adults have reported that they did not thrive on attention but quite the opposite. Quite a number reported embarrassment and discomfort, some to the point they played down their ability or sought to undo the sell out with heightening unwanted or 'rebellious' behaviour to compensate and re-establish a sense of self-ownership.

When you are not used to doing for self before a sense of audience and with a sense of conscious awareness, the effect is like hearing yourself on tape. The individuality of self can appear so stark, so gratingly real, awkward, imperfect, out of control, that you become phobic about seeing it again. The result is you never desensitize to this extreme heightened sense of self. Being self-in-relation-to-self in the company of someone with Exposure Anxiety and not forcing conscious awareness of their actions back in their face means they have a better chance of experiencing their own behaviour silently, internally without having already rejected it in pushing away the attention.

Issues of independence

After running away with a stranger I'd met the week before and returning battered and bruised and twice as defiant and uncontrollable, I was put into a flat. I was fifteen years old. I could not cook. I had no idea how to pay a utility bill. I had no idea how to pay rent. I had, as I can recall, rarely or never run a bath for myself (always got in after others). I had never taken washing to a launderette. I had never had responsibility for the key to my own residence. I had little sense of time and a poor sense of how many days there were between the weekends. I was left with a sofa, a bed, a lamp, a toaster, a kettle, a pot, a frying pan, a bowl, a plate and some cutlery, plus a set of sheets and a towel. This was 1979 and my mother's alternatives at this time would have been things like a psychiatric placement, make me a ward of the state and put me in a children's home, or let me take my chances on the street. At home the violence between my older brother and I was dangerous (I'd thrown a frozen chicken at his head and chased him with a knife. He'd trapped my head in the ironing board stand and tried to burn my face with the iron). I was out of control and aside from going to work in a department store, I came and went without the slightest courtesy or consideration for others and my behaviour indicated I'd become more disturbing and disturbed at the family home than elsewhere. However unsafe or out of self-interest what my mother did was ultimately humane. She was at the end of the line. So was I.

In my flat I flooded the bath every week. I burned half a loaf of bread each time I tried to make toast. I lost the keys every week and locked myself out continually. The clothes and sheets didn't get washed. I didn't wash myself properly. I ate out of tins. The electricity got cut off. The landlord knocked on the door for the rent. I often got my clothes on inside out and usually wore clothes for the wrong weather. I sometimes left for work on the weekend. I never flushed the toilet. I always forgot what time it was. I was extremely socially vulnerable. I survived. The result is someone with reasonable ability who can ask for help with what she can't conquer, someone with great empathy for the experiences of others, who has deep pride in her independence and feels she owns her life. When I was fifteen I did not have that.

If you wait for proof, you may never see independence from someone with severe Exposure Anxiety and information-processing problems. I don't believe in prompting and cajoling. It reminds me of my weaknesses and I have many of them. I resonated with the fear and worry of others and I started to fear standing alone. I believe in tough love with a safety net. It either takes great detachment or great guts to be tough with a terrified, confused and chaotic adrenaline addict, especially if it's your own child. Society and its judgements shouldn't make that job harder. So many more people could achieve independence through being forced into situations where they have to, for survival, teach themselves. The only question is how to do that safely, from a distance and hold back enough until you are asked for help. I've been to that point, and even the toughest nuts crack. One can come to rely on patterning in spite of severe infromation- processing problems. Neither life nor labels are a black-and-white reality. There are many greys in between if we dare to look beyond the self-futility prophecies of our own pre-conceived assumptions.

Exposure Anxiety and empathy

Alienation and the world of 'the appear'

I could have coped with the Exposure Anxiety, had I not also had severe information-processing problems and, to an extent, visa-versa. The processing problems constantly reinforced and justified the usefulness, the need for Exposure Anxiety as protector just as the involuntary avoidance, diversion and retaliation responses severely interferred with information-processing and certainly taxed the nutrient supply otherwise used to cohesively keep up with incoming information. Throughout childhood, being largely meaning deaf and meaning blind, dealing with severely fluc- tuating sensory–perceptual messages due to food intolerance, toxicity and nutritional issues (in spite of adequate diet and probably partly due to the impact of severe chronic stress on the gut and immune system) meant I felt utterly robbed of control all the time. Exposure Anxiety, quite simply, enticed me with the reassurance of closing off, going in, and feeling in control. Perhaps I could even have coped with this, but one of the byprod- ucts of these severe information-processing problems was that I compen- sated for interpretation problems by being extremely acute in mapping pattern. This meant that whilst I couldn't interpret, I was, nevertheless, highly sensing. The byproduct of this was I could feel intensely when the world was focused on the 'appear' and not the 'be'. If ever I needed yet another justification for siding with Exposure Anxiety, here it was. Drop the façades. Drop the role playing. Get connected. I can smell dissonance like a snake senses heat and it triggers self-protection all the time. For me, 'autism' is not one state but three, which combine in a multi-directional way to create the impression of what gets called 'autism'. For me, these three faces are 1. The involuntary self-protection responses of Exposure Anxiety, 2. Information-processing delay and the adaptation of being mono-tracked in a multi-tracking and multi-tracked world, and 3. Having left–right hemisphere integration problems leading to being either reliant on sensing but devoid of much conscious interpretive processing ('autism'), or reliant on at least literal interpretive processing at the cost of its integration with the sensing of 'theme' or 'feel' ('Asperger Syndrome') or a fluctuation between either state, yet having a limited ability to combine them (the split-brain state of the 'Autie–Aspie').

The mistrust and envy of those who can 'hide'

I have been told so many times, by adults with autism spectrum conditions, that they feel too raw, too naked, too exposed before others. Whilst they may hide within the behaviours of others, they have great difficulty hiding from themselves. The saying, 'You can run, but you can't hide', seems to sum this up. Some of them run very well and are utterly convincing in their role-play as 'non-autistic'. This is something I know very well and it amuses me these days more than it traps or terrifies me, how well I can pass, using their way as a kind of language of behaviour, albeit often discon-nected. One thing I find it almost impossible to do is to get lost in ideas of myself – to build up an image of myself and then confine myself to it. Though I'm a wonderful mimic, this is all it is. I can merge with a pattern, but I can't convince myself utterly of the me-ness of it, nor does anything I do transfer well or stick in a way likely to build up ideas of myself. The result is that I'm like chewing gum. Much as losing control is a huge chal-lenge, I'm extremely adaptable when it comes to the bottom line. The kind of crashing loss of an idea of self doesn't happen much to me because I have very little ability to hold those ideas in the first place. I am the 'Autie–Aspie'. I swing between the sensing and the interpretive, with all of its consequences in a world where most people use them in an integrated way.

Yet I felt deep envy of those capable of holding an idea of self, of being closed minded, of being more than either an involuntary, driven buzz junkie or an information machine. I loved their cardboard two-dimensional simplicity and envied them the safety of being convinced of their roles as self. I wished many times I could live in the mind concept of self-image like them and lose the open boundaries which come from using body as a tool of resonance in knowing the world through sensing rather than interpretation. Unlike the more purely interpretive Aspergian social reality, I go into a take away and map the patterns of the cashier and undress her from her surface politeness like a computer with a huge database of pattern. In the thirty-second dialogue in taking my order, I map that the patterns of suppressed hints of behaviour which if expressed, would be consistent with phrases like 'I heard you the first time you know' and 'Are you stupid or something'. Sensing to this degree is not the blessing you might imagine. It hurts. It's a pain in the neck. My gut senses sadness in smiling façades, satisfaction in people portraying drama and distress in their lives, strength and independence in those who see themselves as weak, and nastiness within polite friendliness. Sometimes, in Tourette-like fashion, their patterns trigger sentences that sum up the sensed pattern or spontaneous involuntary mimicry of the inner reality, much to the shock of those around. Mostly, I manage to suppress this involuntary attempt to purge the mapped pattern but it makes it hard to hold my own world when I feel that of others so sharply. So much worse is when I am judged as having no empathy when I sit, blank or smiling as someone pours out the drama they are not actually feeling. The dissonance of what's expressed and its disconnectedness from any flow and connection to the whole seems shamefully, even laughably evident to me through the way my body resonates with the mapped pattern. I feel so often as if I'm seeing people's ghosts. The German for soul, is 'Geist', and it is this I feel my body maps.

But being highly sensing is not a necessary connection with extreme Exposure Anxiety, just an added compounding factor in many people diagnosed with autism rather than Asperger Syndrome. Many people with Exposure Anxiety but who are primarily interpretive, rather than sensing (left side of the brain rather than right) lack apparent empathy because of delayed processing or having little simultaneous sense of self and other. If they do not rely on sensing then, in the absence of good cohesive visual or auditory-processing they will wait to understand what they have seen or heard in order to respond (I'll respond and have no idea why). Yet when this processing is delayed, there may be no response. They may be asked for help and just stand there hearing sound, watching movement. I'd have stood, not understanding the words or actions but unlike many people with Asperger Syndrome, I have still resonated with the person's felt desperation (if I was not actively in a defensive Exposure Anxiety state at the time). When I was younger, I'd have taken this on in my own body, getting into a panic as though the feeling were mine. The adrenaline addict will be highly queued for this. Having lived in extreme, often violent family circumstances, with what, in my view, were two challenged parents on the autistic spectrum themselves, I did learn what helping meant and the actions needed that followed from the feeling sensed. I was the one who put the dangerous cutlery away, knew when to save my younger brother and eventually taught myself to call the emergency services.

Particularly when put on the spot, the interpretive Aspergian is likely either to continue with his or her track in spite of the needs of the other person, or to appear to freeze whilst taking in the information from the other person, as a database might. This too can look like a lack of empathy but it is not and such people may care very deeply about their special people or people in general, even if this doesn't easily transfer functionally.

Another problem is that when in a heightened state of emotion, agitation or stress, Exposure Anxiety can flare up, displaying avoidance, diversion or retaliation responses that get taken as self-expression. The person themselves may be quite empathic but the behaviour blocks or contorts the expression of this when needed. When the Exposure Anxiety is reduced, the person may do something to demonstrate caring but by then the context has passed. The likely response of the environment is, 'Oh, so you want attention now. What about when I needed it?' In fact what is seen as taking may, at this point, be an act of reassurance or giving but in this context isn't understood as such.

Exposure Anxiety is a tic-like response to the feeling of robbed control, fearing being exposed, fearing the glaring attention to individuality and humanness inherent in failure, in not being perfect, in having lost, in failing, in breaking something, in making mistakes. It is often instantaneous when Exposure Anxiety responses to someone else's misfortune jump in before the person herself is able to. I had often found myself highly amused by people slipping over, nearly getting hit by a bus or breaking something accidentally. At the same time, there was another me, which was not governed by these responses and which felt the happening as the other person and I did feel sympathy. It was a matter of which response got to the body first: Exposure Anxiety or me. Simply, as a tic-response, it is usually connected more instantaneously, blocking the self from the body. I was deeply confusing to live with because I never knew which response was going to get there first. I may not have liked it, but it's how it was. I didn't care, but the Exposure Anxiety part of me didn't care a damn. It was utterly self-interested and only focused on the 'buzz'. Both fortunately and unfortunately, I was very deeply, passionately, strongly in there too. Just sometimes I was the first one connected to the body, sometimes I was second to get there. The percentages depended on the severity of the Exposure Anxiety in that particular phase of my life. It's like the tide and the undercurrent. We are each both of these and what is one minute tide, is undercurrent the next, and then switched back in the next blink of an eye. It may depend on the food colourings, the sugar, the flood of attention received yesterday or the build up of toxicity issues, all imbalancing dopamine, seratonin and noradrenalin in the brain, which underlie the flight–fight defence responses. We are each this chaos, this buriedness, just some of us more than others. This broken switch is a hard thing to live with, but it has made me deeply appreciative of life, of acceptance and of my personhood as well.

Exposure Anxiety and insight

Unknown knowing

Insight is elusive with Exposure Anxiety. Exposure Anxiety can make information-processing harder, making the person more mono, making it more difficult to get from the sensory to the literal, or from the literal to the significant, and that is where insight lives. It will also make it extremely difficult to allow, with conscious awareness, the joining of the two worlds, of self and of other, necessary to most experiences of insight. Even if insight is gleaned, it will be lost in the next instant into the depths of a labyrinth where information is protectively compartmentalized to avoid the jolt of realisation and inevitable change and there is little fusion. Then of course, further processing resources have to be diverted to keep this stuff in its separated and contained compartments. I used to say repeatedly 'no muddy water'. It felt 'against the law' to allow or seek to open the doors within that labyrinth and cause 'muddy water'. It was through art, music, typed poetry, and later books, that these doors were naively, unconsciously opened within my own world, muddying the waters until they eventually cleared.

Trying to teach people with severe Exposure Anxiety insight is possible but they have to reach for it. It is an art to present the issue in such a way as to stimulate the person to do so. One approach is through unknown knowing, although if the person is unable to access his or her own knowledge or insight, how does this work? The answer is triggering. Triggering is not about expectation or compliance but is about provocation and inspiration.

In response to the environment, delayed processing, fragmented visual perception and intermittent auditory comprehension together with the freezing up and out-of-control behaviour of Exposure Anxiety, I looked as if I lacked insight or 'common sense'. In fact, consciously, it was absolutely so. I completely lacked sense. But there was always, running parallel, the meta-self of the me I might have been had I not had these difficulties. This was a preconscious state but I caught glimpses of it. It was like being monitored by a you who is a step behind you and whom you cannot hold. It was this preconscious self which typed *Nobody Nowhere* and which progressively made its way to the surface.

Impressions can, without any expressive avenue, become self-perpetuating. It was first through poetry, music, art, song that I discovered there was someone else in there, far more passionate, cohesive and insightful, and I came to adore and value her, striving for her as I had once for joining my reflection in the mirror. This insight would not have been there to tap had I not been subject to a great richness of experience. I was a child of the city, rather feral and (mostly because of my parents' own challenges) free to roam the streets, people's houses and gardens, to take myself on excursions into people's workplaces, car washes, behind shop counters, into other schools, jumping on and off trams, exploring cemeteries, playing in the back of flats and running through the market. I was mapping a huge range

of patterns around me and delayed processing meant I held them and processed the information beyond awareness. So many children and adults
with autism brought up by more neuro-typical parents are kept away from
society and broad experiences for fear of what people might think.
Nobody could keep me inside. Nobody could control me. I ran in front of
traffic with the timing of a musician and I'm still here. I fell and I got
shouted at, I got chased and I climbed up to great heights, but I am still
here and the environment survived and we were all the more colourful for
it. In those days 'autism' was not known. I was, quite simply, feral and
there is something about that that meant like me or lump me, I'm here.

The other sources of insight were the stories and characterizations
done around me, which conveyed feelings and connections between
things.

Detachment, 'mathematical structuralism', and the concept of 'insight'

The ability to map pattern is like feeling the mathematics of life. It's like
feeling musical intervals between notes except that each note is divided
into ever finer distinctions within those usually 'heard' as the same note.
Struggling for what to call this 'mapping', how to describe how it works, I
came up with the term 'mathematical structuralism' – my equivalent of
lived 'insight'.

For those not so capable of shifting their behaviour or hiding within
the mimicry of others, 'autism' means that their version of insight is neither
credited nor given equal credibility with that of non-autistic people. In a
world of proof, those who merely demonstrate insight in an indirectly-confrontational way, to the directly-confrontational observer, are
not considered to have it.

Those who use typed communication are perhaps some of the best
examples here. If able to attribute responsibility for their communication
to the assistance of someone else, some functionally 'non-verbal' people
can communicate. In fact what drew such criticism to this technique was
that some such people had, in spite of their social–emotional retardation
being mistaken for mental retardation, not only picked up how the written
word corresponds to concepts, but sometimes expressed profound and
moving observations and experiences. Often their typed communications

were cast aside either because it was considered impossible that they indicated a normal intelligence or because the person's own surprise at what
emerged through typing gave the impression that the communication was
done without any real self-awareness.

There is an extreme cultural bias here. Insight in the non-autistic world
may, by definition, be worth so much because it comes from
self-awareness. But by autistic definition, insight may slip out to one's own
surprise and is often much more profound than anything the person may
have done, created, expressed with conscious self-awareness, because it
was done with a profound depth of beingness. And beingness is something
may non-autistic people struggle to rediscover and, however endearing it
is to watch, seem often to do so with an abundance of clumsiness and with
little grace. But there is a far more institutionalized reason why the slipped
'autistic' expression of beingness-associated insight is not given credibility. This is because, were that to be so, it would shatter almost every stereotype about these people and challenge the credibility of so many educational programs and psychological approaches based on the assumed correctness of those stereotypes.

Exposure Anxiety and personality

The appear versus the be 'self'

Drug addiction is known to alter personality. Exposure Anxiety is a condition driven by addiction to one's own adrenaline highs. There is no doubt
that Exposure Anxiety alters personality. Whilst Exposure Anxiety shows
itself differently in different personalities, personality itself doesn't
directly alter the metabolic causes which underlie the level of Exposure
Anxiety.

I always felt my main interaction throughout my life has been in being
taken over by, siding with, submitting to, diverting around, tuning out
from and rebelling against my own Exposure Anxiety. I see it sometimes as
my jailer watching, waiting for the world to try to get it. I see it at other
times as being on my side, like a strict social worker with its probation case.
Exposure Anxiety shapes personality through constant reaffirmation of
imprisonment and the individual's own behaviour in inviting the involvement of the environment is the trigger for this. Imagine you have been kid-

napped at birth or shortly after and you get this reinforcement every day. You initiate eye contact that brings involvement from the environment, and Exposure Anxiety jumps in and trains you that you have done something requiring you to be protected against invasion. You eat something and the environment is pleased and comments on it or offers you more. Exposure Anxiety may sadistically allow you to comply, only to later vomit up this external invasion. You are informed this behaviour is unwanted, even life-threatening, and your Exposure Anxiety is thrilled and rewarded with the adrenaline high of risk taking. Imagine you go to speak and you know by now this will be futile. It will be futile because as soon as you start to try, Exposure Anxiety will either freeze you out of processing what's coming back or you will be compelled to tune out to the very act or meaning of your own expression. You know you may be compelled to behave as though it's not even happening, in order to get it out without triggering the shutdown by Exposure Anxiety. It is at this point that Exposure Anxiety claims the throne of internal parenthood. Imagine that when you are out of line it will trigger such an adrenaline rush that the only thing which helps Exposure Anxiety feel vindicated and 'come down' is that it has triggered intense self-abuse. Furthermore, it may have now mapped your own 'inability to learn this lesson', mapped your constant 'defiance' of the rules of 'self-protection' from external invasion. In its stance as 'protector' this may mean it may pay you back with self-abuse so over the top that you are now utterly withdrawn and internally promise never to dare what caused this again. The next offer from the environment to 'join them', has an obvious future translation – back off. It is at this point that Exposure Anxiety claims the throne of internal parenthood. Imagine all this and you cannot ask for help, nor even accept comfort, for to do so triggers even worse 'self-protective' payback from your 'protector', your captor.

Prisoners of war have their personalities affected by such circumstances, as do people who are kept highly institutionalized, those who have been constantly watched and controlled in 'therapeutic' settings, and those kept in solitary confinement, unable to face or reason with their captors.

Some constantly plot escape or in their minds or emotions live who they'd be if they weren't 'in here'. They build a colourful, free, bold, meta-self. But if the guard is in there with you, monitoring your feelings and desires with a compulsive hypersensitive self-protection mechanism which can shut you down even on this level, you may have times when you may not be free to imagine this as yourself. Instead you may be compelled to externalize it, to convince yourself this is not what you wish, no, not ever, but this is what someone once was, somewhere, once, out there. I created Carol, the girl in the mirror who lived in a free world under glass (where the environment could not affect her – in other words, what I could not dare even think, 'where Exposure Anxiety could not protect her'). I convinced myself (and thereby Exposure Anxiety) that this was not me. It lasted as long as I did not have a personal emotion about anything Carol 'enjoyed' or 'achieved'. To do so meant imprisonment. I created Willie, who was also not me, but something that had taken up space in my room, outside of me. Because Willie had the role of protecting me, Donna, from the external environment, Exposure Anxiety was not against the actions of this 'involuntary' characterization. The fact that the character of Willie did not have a body of its own was never taken as an invasive challenge to Exposure Anxiety. Anything that severed me from the direct connection with body, through which I'd connect or invite connection with the environment as self, was welcomed. What pushed these characterizations into existence was not just the extreme imprisonment, despair and frustration caused by the Exposure Anxiety alone, but the demands for survival triggered by a disturbed and violent environment in the home. This is often taken to cancel out the relevance of my experiences in the field of 'autism'. After all, I must surely then be 'an abuse case'. It is also equally possible to view the challenges of my parents as being at least partly due to their own developmental 'difference' on the spectrum.

Whilst the characterizations may have been a product of the extremely challenging home environment, the Exposure Anxiety had its own metabolic causes and was at least largely exacerbated by severe magnesium deficiency, reactive hypoglycemia and digestive disorders affecting food allergy and intolerance. It is too easy to cast aside what may be useful information on the basis one is not a 'pure case'. If you look closely, there are actually no pure cases, only aspects which are overlooked because they are assumed, by virtue of a label, not to exist. In fact many able people on the

autism spectrum have blown apart an encyclopedic collection of stereotypes about 'autism-spectrum' labels.

The physiological problems I live with which underlie the intensity of
my own chronic Exposure Anxiety responses have been found to be
common in up to eighty per cent of people on the autism spectrum, in
contrast to society in general. Most of these people are not from such an
extreme home environment as I came from. Unlike me, most of them were
not pushed into extreme survival situations and did not develop characters
to answer the need to survive. Some, however, did, and much of what we
know about the mechanisms of Exposure Anxiety have come from those
who have found a voice, even if it is not directly their own. It is not the
characterizations that teach us about Exposure Anxiety and personality, so
much as the labyrinth of depersonalization involved in creating these in
order for them to escape the extinguishing effect of Exposure Anxiety.

Others in a state of internal imprisonment submit and become passive,
puppet like. I was at times like a doll and extremely passive once cornered.
But mine was not the passivity of active compliance. It was one of almost
absolute abandonment of volition and in these situations my eyes appeared
blind, as though I had gone very far inside, disconnected from my actions.

Some people in a state of imprisonment cope by being constantly busy
and seem to hop compulsively from anything and everything as though
something is chasing them, about to stop or control them and they are
heading it off. When it has taken me three hours to get a drink for myself
and I finally manage, nobody sees the three hours I have waited, they only
see the fact I guzzle the drink down as if someone is watching, waiting to
take it, or take me away from it. When I have been compelled all day to
avoid my need for the toilet and someone else goes to use it, thereby
freeing me up, all the other person sees is someone copying, competing.
They don't see someone desperately co-opting, for my own need, the
Exposure Anxiety compulsion to take this opportunity from the other
person. It is as if there are always two selves in there, the free one, watching
the captor and looking for a break, and the captor on the defensive.

Exposure Anxiety made me a bigger person than I'd probably have
been. Like anyone held back, it increases passion, it increases depth, as
much as it builds passivity, frustration and despair. Yet as it builds this
passion and depth, this in turn only serves to justify the existence of this

protector even more. After all, such a driving force would surely, if let free, invite the world in wholesale. For me, one of the only ways to let this passion and depth out was first convincing myself this would never be shown or seen by anyone. Almost all my art, poetry and songs stayed underground, hidden, never shown, for years. In the case of my autobiography, *Nobody Nowhere*, I convinced myself this book, just dared only for self, would now be seen by just one person, just to get an opinion before Exposure Anxiety saved me from the despair of my imprisonment by jumping in front of a train in the London Underground. The child psychiatrist who read it saved my life. He passed it on to the person who had taught him. This went to her publisher, then to a literary agent whence it became an international bestseller. I had, in the meantime, abandoned the book, but I was now so exposed out that there Exposure Anxiety could not do me such a favour as killing the body because it would be noticed. Conveniently, the demand of the public in being so useful to them meant I could spend the next thirteen years without the Exposure Anxiety struggle of doing for self by doing, instead, for the world. I still dreamt of a farm with smiling goats and freedom just to be. Exposure Anxiety was so much less than it ever was. I could do so much. Still, asking for a drink, going to the toilet, grabbing a jumper for myself, were still very challenging when I noticed the need, and a farm with smiling goats was a much bigger challenge of giving directly to self.

Of all the personality characteristics, the most useful ones with Exposure Anxiety are sneakiness and humour. Ask any prisoner and they'll tell you the same. Yet the environment, faced with 'autism', often loses its humour or fears daring it, and sneakiness is not modelled nor promoted. So I am glad I lived in such a surreal and eccentric environment in which both parents modelled some of the most useful traits I could have. The final aspect of personality directly related to Exposure Anxiety is that of 'buzz junkie', for not only does the adrenalin addiction provoke involuntary self-protection responses but it also drives 'thrill seeking' behaviours and the adrenaline rush that goes with them. It is no accident that the mania of an excitable buzz such as that I got staring at pink street lights, chandalier crystals or listening to the ringing of the front door bell over and over, went hand-in-hand with a sudden onslaught of involuntary defence responses. Further, where Exposure Anxiety as a defence response causes

such feelings of entrapment, getting a manic, euphoric high is the equivalent of jumping from heights (I did a lot of that too) and becomes the lure
into the cycle of adrenalin addiction. My milk allergy, causing LSD-like
sensing highs and lows fed into this and as a personality I had to address
my nature as a thrill-seeking 'buzz junkie' in order to stop reinforcing and
heightening the same biochemical mechanisms underlying the defence
responses. Hence, treatments to address Exposure Anxiety effectively must
address it on all its fronts, its metabolic, biochemical and nutritional bases,
the environmental approach and the self-induced highs which reinforce
the addiction.

The consequences of an expanding internal social world

The ever-increasing complexity of an internal labyrinth creates someone
who may develop many islands of ability, but equally many buttons, all
capable of triggering Exposure Anxiety. Blocked from relating directly to
the external world with any consistency, one's own world seems, by comparison, more cohesive. Add to this severe information-processing delay
due to nutrient deficiencies and the person not only can't stand the world,
but can't easily understand it in the moment of each happening either.
Nothing sinks in til it has past – five minutes, an hour, a week or months
later.

   This cohesion and 'safety' of one's own world makes it harder and
harder for the external world to compete. The emphasis on proving ability
and getting people to comply, whether connected inside or not, means the
external world can appear unforgiving, uncaring, geared only for appearances, unconcerned with the person's internal reality. Why bother wanting
to connect with those you progressively see as unable to see the 'you'
inside? This is especially so when, although you might be staring into
space and humming a tune to yourself, your sense of cohesion and belonging within your own world can be, at times, as much a lulling sanctuary as a
tormenting prison.

Exposure Anxiety and self-hatred

If someone has fallen in love with someone else, you cannot compete,
because they become tuned out to you, merely tolerant. Only when you

make your world incredibly appealing, and user friendly, and play hard to get about it, does it begin to stir curiosity or any sense that in one's self-absorption one may be missing out. Pursue the person in love with their own sense of entity and you are a gate crasher, an annoyance, an invader, who neither appreciates nor understands. This is a hard reality and one the environment, doesn't deserve, but it needs to be told as it is.

Self-hatred works two ways. On the one hand, there can be intense despair, frustration and self-attack when the extremely frustrated self distinguishes itself from Exposure Anxiety. It may, even in experiencing self, still see Exposure Anxiety as another version of self – one which is holding it back, denying it opportunity and life, embarrassing it before others, denying it a place of belonging among others. Self-hatred also happens on the part of Exposure Anxiety when the self rebels against it, breaking the rules, or when the self is free on the condition it is whitewashed, perfect, devoid of self, but messes up in being undeniably individual, fallible, human. Where the person is full of self-hatred because of frustration in being held back or the pressure caused by the dissonance between the intellectual or able self and the social–emotional self, this requires good indirectly-confrontational modelling of self-calming strategies. It also requires modelling of a sense of silliness and play to let go expectations, realistic modelling of achievable goals which take account of Exposure Anxiety but are not dictated by it and modelling of indirectly-confrontational ways of giving, communicating, building friendships, making choices etc.

Where the person is full of self-hatred because of the internal pressure or payback caused by Exposure Anxiety, it is important not to behave co-dependently. Exposure Anxiety will co-opt attempts to run to the rescue, which rewards it for taking control, reminding it that it is in the position of power over the person and over the environment. I always found that sympathy and eagerness to help only strengthened the grip Exposure Anxiety had on me and made me weaker and more in despair. It was as though the environment said to Exposure Anxiety, 'No', and sadistically it said inside, 'Now I know how to pay the environment back for invading. Their no is my YES.' Exposure Anxiety has no conscience. When it makes the individual starve and then eat rotten food, or hold on till they wet themselves, or swear at people they are trying to say 'hi' to, it has no conscience. Perhaps it is the internal psychopath within us all and the only difference between the clinical psychopath, the person with autism and the neurotypical is a matter of percentages in the balance of Exposure Anxiety as 'self' versus the real self. The best strategies that were ever used with me in the face of self-hatred behaviour was to draw attention to what Exposure Anxiety was making me do, not in a derogatory way, but drawing a sense of audience about it. My mother's public announcement of 'Look, here she goes, watch, she'll throw that chair in a minute', was bound to have Exposure Anxiety defy this environmental expectation. Telling me not to hurt myself would guarantee the behaviour would become even more extreme. Nonchalantly making the observation it was happening and telling me to do that gently, left Exposure Anxiety in a dither. To continue meant to do what I was being told to do. The attack on the self would turn to a response to the invasion of the environment, and the behaviour was extinguished as though in spite. I have found this again and again in schools. Where a child is told not to bite itself, the arm pulled away, the child is compelled twice as hard 'to win'. Where the worker has pushed the arm actually towards the child saying, 'gentle biting', either then or later the child is compelled to reject this apparent invitation, social invasion, to do as she is told and often either tones down the biting or rejects it.

Dealing with self-hatred is also a matter of counselling and this is about modelling in an indirectly-confrontational way. The magic book is a book with blank pages that can contain any Social Story told, without using names, about an issue. The invisible or battery-less mobile phone is a strategy for addressing these things in an emergency situation. Communicating your own feelings through objects about the issue as though it were happening not to them but to you and responding with the solution or resolution is the most effective way of tackling the information. Done directly, you may well be counselling Exposure Anxiety and it is not hearing you as you expect, with your values. Even worse, the person is listening, and Exposure Anxiety is defensively plotting the sabotage. Model the issues externally about the object or issue, not the person, and doing so in an indirectly-confrontational way as though not for the client's benefit, but as though you are resolving your own experiences with these issues in yourself. This way Exposure Anxiety is not on guard. It is just 'information' out there, which plays within the listener like an unresolved puzzle.

Exposure Anxiety and the impact of 'war' on personality

Some people cling to the environment, terrified of being eaten up, taken away again. Others feel they have been through so much they have little tolerance for indulgence in minor melodramas taken so seriously or indulged in by those without Exposure Anxiety. Some are like war veterans, shell shocked and traumatized in the face of any reminder of loss of control or imprisonment, including that of being needed or loved too much. Some are so weary of the struggles that, once free, instead of joining the world, they sit more peacefully in their own. Some are like starving beasts suddenly set free, almost overloading the environment as though each minute will be the last. Some watch and wait for the captor to sneak up on them, certain after years of reinforcement that it could never just leave. Living with an internal war, swinging between a state of war and truce, or recovering from years of having been in a state of war or alternation, all has an impact on personality.

Social misunderstanding, labelling, and the impact on personality

Exposure Anxiety can give the appearance of being aloof, indifferent, flippant, lacking empathy, selfish, contrary, disturbed, robotic, defiant or spoilt. The impact of having a social judgement constantly reinforced becomes a self-fulfilling prophecy. I was judged disturbed and I could sense people's fear. This gave me free rein to live up to low expectations of self-control, and promoted in me a feeling that the environment was impotent and had weak boundaries. At the same time, the expectation that I was disturbed and could not control myself worked in my favour. Exposure Anxiety thereby compelled me to counter these accusations, being defiant by 'acting normal' and, thereby, proving the environment and its expectations wrong.

Social misunderstanding and social judgement can, on the one hand, convince the self it is everything the environment says it is, especially when all social–emotional contact, insight and reflection is so governed by

Exposure Anxiety. On the other hand social misunderstanding and social judgements can trigger Exposure Anxiety to either hide within such claims as an excuse and way out of expression of self or it can outright counter the expectations of the environment.

Those who say he or she can't help it because of the 'autism' and jump in to take over at every turn may well be giving Exposure Anxiety the perfect excuse to laugh at the environment for providing the excuse which has the self give up fighting for expression. Those who explain the person doesn't care, can't control themselves or doesn't have any friends, may trigger such a sense of injustice and shame on the part of the self and compulsion to prove the environment wrong that this produces positive results. If, however, the environment then seems pleased with the results, Exposure Anxiety can compel the person to abandon attempts to show caring, control behaviour positively or attempt social contact.

This strategy, this reverse psychology, was used extensively with me. It resulted, ironically, in my abandoning violent behaviour midstream, going out of my way to do things for others in the absence of any connection to why or to caring and attempting to gather the appearance of 'friendships' in spite of a gut aversion. In short, although I was a caring and social person, Exposure Anxiety, could compel me to go through the motions as an act of defensive control and spite. This often meant there was a massive division between the social–emotional presentation of me as self to the social–emotional presentation of Exposure Anxiety.

Those I felt safe with and would choose as 'friends' in my own way, were never the ones set upon out of defensiveness to prove the capacity for 'friendship'. The way of showing caring was quite different from that which came from my own emotions and feelings. This adaptation, much as it made me appear far higher functioning than I could actually live up to, compounded the sense of imprisonment and contributed to a deep depression and frustration. This lasted until I was twenty-four when altering diet and addressing digestive system problems reduced the fire and drive behind compulsive Exposure Anxiety. It then took another fourteen years until I tried Risperidone 0.5 mgs before I knew life without Exposure Anxiety.

Though Exposure Anxiety was still the undercurrent which made itself the tide, addressing these chemical and processing issues was enough for me to get a grip on communication and actions as a connected emotional self, and not just the stand-in, retaliative performance of one.

Exposure Anxiety and identity

The battle to join the world and the battle to close it out:
the prison–sanctuary

As a person moves from the battle to keep the world out into the battle to join the world, it is like being torn between divorcing parents, not knowing which side to trust – the one that offers freedom and expression or the one that offers protection and sanctuary and has always been there. That's a lot for mere human parents in the external world to compete with. Sometimes dietary and nutritional intervention is not enough on its own to turn around this intense relationship with one's own self-protective defense mechanisms especially if the person continues behaviourally to try to hype themselves back up into the same addictive state. Sometimes the use of an indirectly-confrontational approach can be relatively flexible and shifting. At other times what is required is a very tight ship, which would show absolute consistency and commitment to the technique, not just until the results are achieved on the surface, but until identification against one's own Exposure Anxiety has been more globally achieved.

If you give up being strategically indirectly-confrontational too early, Exposure Anxiety catches on, digs its heels in, recovers its territory and you have a much bigger battle to be convincing next time. I have spoken with many teenagers and adults who 'came out of their own world' and later realized they'd lost this (or been driven by their own self-protection responses to lament this loss and the vulnerability, touchability it now meant in the world) and tried to go back. Because they'd been out in the world for a while, it was too late to return to the encapsulation of before and the only way they could do so was out of choice. I have met individuals who have lamented this loss and romanticised their earlier encapsulation. As someone who knew it as both sanctuary and prison, however desperately mono I was, I could never remember it as one without feeling the utter dread of the other.

Once someone is swinging between the battle to join the world and the battle to keep the world out, the battle plan of an indirectly-confrontational approach has to be consistent. If Exposure Anxiety is sharp, it will catch on and undermine the pattern and the environment may need to add the surreal, eccentric and fluid to its indirectly-confrontational arsenal. Above all, don't be conned. Performance is not self. To appear is not to be. And as you applaud compliance, Exposure Anxiety may well be watching and mapping your every strategy.

How to own up when you're hiding and how to give in when you've won

Introducing an indirectly-confrontational technique of communication is absolutely a matter of timing. Being without communication is one of the frustrations that can drive the self to fight Exposure Anxiety and ask the environment for help to do the communication for it. This can be a positive thing in that it is an acknowledgement that the environment is needed and valued. This can also create an absolute dependency and feeling of owner-ship over those who meet the person's needs, as though they are the person's external, functional, selves. It's important, therefore, to become progressively sloppier, less complete in the help offered. Turn on the tap, but only so it's dribbling. Put the jumper over the head but leave the person's head half covered, half uncovered. Brush the hair, but only half of it. Brush the teeth, but only a few. Nothing annoys a compulsive so much as a job half done and this digs at the person like fleas on a dog. You can only avoid scratching for so long. Only by becoming gradually more unable yourself can you indirectly trigger the person into taking over, not for your sake or your desire, but in order to correct the discomfort and annoyance.

It is harder when someone will neither indicate, nor prompt, nor whine, nor ask for anything. With people in this situation, you cannot hold things back because they will go to great, even masochistic lengths, to avoid humility and 'defeat'. You can, however, provoke the development of self-help skills by placing things in difficult-to-access places, requiring complex actions to be undertaken to get to what is needed.

It is extremely difficult for a family to relax socially among others with a child with severe behavioural problems or who is very unpredictable. Whilst close associates of the family or those in the community may be used to the child, this is not so easy in new situations. When I was nine I used to get locked into my room when my behaviour was utterly out of control. This would have worked had I been the one to lock myself in, but as it was beyond my control, I became obsessive about escape.

When my family was out one day, I took wooden planks from the back yard and took them upstairs to my room. I took them into the roof void and laid them out, as they'd been outside, to make a platform. I took a torch I liked and had seen my brother with and took it into the roof void. Now, when I was locked in, I could defeat this external control by retaliatively locking myself even further in. Since I couldn't be found in the locked room, my room was explored when I was out and my platform was discovered. I'd been defeated again.

I took the next opportunity when they were out to go to the hardware store. They had bells, and toilets, and keys on a board. They were quite used to me enjoying myself in there. I knew I wanted a key, the one to get out whenever I'd been locked in. I tried to take a key and was stopped, asked what I wanted. 'A key', I declared defiantly, demanding the key. 'Which one?', I was asked. 'A key', I insisted. I defensively saw myself demanding rather than being offered assistance. The man asked, 'Do you have the old key?' He said, 'Come back with the old key and I'll give you the right one. If you haven't got a key, you'll have to bring the lock in. You'll have to take a screwdriver and remove it from the door,' He showed the actions of unscrewing the lock from the door and removing it as he spoke. I left and returned home, sought something to unscrew the screws in the lock. After lots of tears and attack on the handle I found the screws to it and found out how to remove them from the lock after which I prized the lock out.

I returned to the shop with the lock and put it on the counter, saying 'I want the key now'. The man found the key from his board of keys and it made the lock work. I didn't have any money and he wouldn't give it to me. He told me to leave and bring back some money. I was intensely frustrated but absolutely determined. I went back, put the lock back but could feel in my body the time had gone long enough now and my family would be back.

I waited till my family was out again and took some collector's coins from a jar up high in our pantry belonging to my brother. I removed the lock again and returned to the shop, slapping the coins on the counter. The man commented on the coins, which were legitimate currency, but special edition collector's coins, and gave me my key, upon which I left, returned home, put the lock back and hid my key.

I have known of non-verbal children, seemingly incapable of learning, who, step by step, will through pure defiant obsessive drive, manage to get what they have seen or need without asking for help. When things are kept far out of reach, some such children have demonstrated, to their own surprise, amazing self-help capabilities they'd never have found or dared before an audience. Most of these children are considered 'destructive' to objects and kept away from anything they might disassemble or any tools they might use. Such children, because they cannot be taught directly, are often not left to be around the modelling of such abilities either, because they might 'get in the way'.

Getting someone to communicate may be a matter of providing an indirectly-confrontational form of communication through which the person can communicate, not with you, but out loud to him or herself. A storyboard of objects could be the medium as long as it is not associated with attempts to invade through directly-confrontational interaction. A typewriter or letter board are other alternatives. But in the end, if the person can progressively come to disclose what Exposure Anxiety is compelling them to do or avoid doing, it can mean that Exposure Anxiety may well defy the individual's disclosure, proving the thing disclosed invalid and, incidentally, achieving the individual's goal for freedom. I have used this many times, being compelled to leave a room or feeling driven to the verge of a retaliation response. If I then disclosed, through speaking out loud to myself or, more likely, through typing, that I am being bossed around inside, compelled in a direction which is not 'me', I have generally found the grip on my expression to disappear. I call this strategy turning Exposure Anxiety on itself – exposing the Exposure Anxiety to trigger its own implosion. I have used this to say, 'If I wasn't so controlled by Exposure Anxiety, I might be able to say thank you', or 'I'm feeling sad because I'm compelled to close you out right now', or 'I want to go out but Exposure Anxiety won't let me admit it and is compelling me to avoid the question, divert in my responses or retaliate against the idea so I'm sorry I'm being so confusing'. I have found, certainly since my mid-twenties, this was the most wonderful and useful strategy I had found to get my personal social–emotional communication and actions free. I was fine on stored topics, such as the topic of autism and a handful of other topics, but this was different from simply talking about what I liked or wanted to do. Free as I had become, this remained quite a challenge, until recently.

Developmental programs for working with identity as a key to motivation

Told to oneself out loud, Social Stories and fairy tales involving themes of imprisonment, escape and resolution could be valuable tools in helping people understand the difference between self and Exposure Anxiety. Unlike existing stories in which the dragon, the evil captor, the nasty step-sisters are beaten and the victim freed into a welcoming self-in-relation-to-other directly-confrontational world, these stories need to involve a different theme. Rather than the world waiting, hoping, desperate to save the victim (which in Exposure Anxiety would justify the 'protection' of the captor), the outside world should be full of self-owning people. These people should be portrayed not as waiting, watching, interacting with each other, but being self-owning, and having a wonderful time, uninterrupted by others. The imprisoned victim is unable to get free to do the same. The victim has to miss out again and again until, one day, she saves herself. She invites Exposure Anxiety out with her, but it refused to come (if you try to abandon Exposure Anxiety it ups the odds and increases the self-justifying anxiety which makes you feel unsafe and unsure in reaching out). I have created similar stories about how the dog escaped its fleas or how the camel got the straws off its back. Storylines can incorporate special interests such as 'how Thomas the Tank Engine got derailed and back on his track, how the wheel learned to roll further, how the pink street light got its sparkle back, or how the rusty pipes got repaired'.

Such stories can be played out through objects, or told through a 'magic book' full of blank pages. It can be overheard as told to someone non-existent on a dead mobile phone. It can just be spoken out loud to oneself whilst staring out of the window, putting on one's shoes or busy doing something 'much more important'.

CHAPTER 3

Relationship to Others

Exposure Anxiety and the world 'being normal'

In mainstream schools, the person with Exposure Anxiety can be the weirdo, the freak. However excruciatingly hard that is, it is intensely motivating because the only way to get the attention off you is, ultimately, to act like others. There is far less reward for siding with Exposure Anxiety. What's more, when you do dare expression, there is no special education teacher and one-to-one assistant all breaking into the kind of applause that is bound to compel you not to do that again. Most likely, there's an overworked teacher with thirty-five or more pupils who doesn't notice or make a point of it when you finally co-operate.

In special schools there is often a mixture of children, but as a consultant working in them, I have almost always seen that children with severe Exposure Anxiety are never the only one in their class. Most often there are at least three or more in the class with the same problem; in some cases two thirds of the class has severe Exposure Anxiety. In 'autistic' classrooms, it is unusual to find one or two who are not severely affected by chronic Exposure Anxiety. The environment here puts incredible pressure on the child to side with his Exposure Anxiety.

Not only is attention being focused on the slightest achievement and expression (thereby inhibiting from non-prompted repetition) but there is a silent unspoken empathy and loyalty with others who also suffer with the same Exposure Anxiety. Though, respectfully, these children do not generally invade each other with directly-confrontational self-in-relation-to-other play, there is a wonderful silent dialogue going on. A number of children with extreme Exposure Anxiety at a special school I visited were made to sit around a table where they were to be forced to demonstrate by pointing what they wanted in order to get a biscuit. One boy was using his peripheral vision to watch the other, who was being cornered into compliance, and it was clear he was being directly affected, even controlling the boy on the spot through his behaviour. The boy being made to comply, after much insistence on the part of the staff, started to point. The other boy went wild in his seat, diverting attention. The attention was then put on him, at which point he escaped his chair and scurried into a corner where he was retrieved and forced to come back into the circle of chairs.

I saw this kind of behaviour, this silent indirectly-confrontational social–emotional dialogue between peers in one class after another and I knew I was seeing a loyalty game being played out between these children. It was as though there was a silent, instinctual conspiracy between them to stick to the rules according to Exposure Anxiety and that it was incredibly important that one person letting down the side would let the others down too. Exposure Anxiety watching a child 'give in', would jump in to divert or cause retaliation on behalf of the person being confronted.

I saw this in adult care homes many times too. The most poignant example was one I wrote about in *Somebody Somewhere* where three adults were all interacting in an absolutely indirectly-confrontational social–emotional dialogue with each other and then with me. One man was being patronized by a worker who was being very much in his face, discussing his lack of intelligence in a mocking, provoking, pseudo-kindness tone. The man at the back of the room began to agitate, muttering to himself compulsively, building up in a phobic crescendo. The non-verbal woman at the back of the room began to pace. I confronted the staff member, who was doing the patronizing, challenged her and diverted her from her quest. The non-verbal woman breezed through the room and, on her way out, briefly placed her hand reassuringly on my shoulder as though in a comment of thanks.

I have seen this silent indirectly-confrontational dialogue and conspiracy again and again from one establishment to another. Having grown up as the only child like me in mainstream schools in the sixties and seventies, there was nobody to reinforce such loyalty or the 'normality' of Exposure

Anxiety-related communicative suppression. Though these adults, and so many children with severe Exposure Anxiety, have treated me as though I'm on their side, I have never been on the side of their Exposure Anxiety, however much they sense it in me. I am a double agent. I sold out and I have no shame about that because I know self from my own prison warder. Many of them do not and those who do need all the informed help they can get.

I put one such boy into a position of having to take action to re-join the class of his own volition. I had always kept the secret with him, speaking the silent language of indirectness, resonating a deep empathy for his identification with his Exposure Anxiety. But this time I encouraged everybody to walk off, as did I, maintaining peripheral vision out of sight of the boy. Now abandoned in the playground, he had nobody to prompt into taking responsibility on his behalf. He continued to stay in his self-protective mode for a while and then, realizing nobody was taking the hint, he dropped the defensiveness and headed back towards the class. I met him back inside the door, refusing to lead him back to class. He made his way back, as best he could against the resistance of his Exposure Anxiety to admit he even knew what to do or gave a damn. I followed eventually. At first he began to stare at me as though I had done something incomprehensible. Then he began to search my eyes, as though asking me something. Then, having made up his mind he'd been sold out and I was not on the side of the Exposure Anxiety he identified with as self, he lashed out wildly at me, eventually breaking down in tears. He had broken his own rules, he had given a damn. He had trusted me. I had spoken the language. I knew the rules. Yet knowingly, I had sold him out. Of course I had. It may be easier to live as a baby or a puppet or a robot or a characterization, but I could see the wasted potential of his ability to live life as a self. My only regret is that this was merely one day in this boy's life and his life in a special school with constant one-to-one attention, ever willing to prompt and help and take over, will never challenge him to be capable as himself.

Get a grip: the difference between Exposure Anxiety and 'playing your violin'

Learned helplessness and the compulsions to play on self-pity are prompts to blackmail the environment into taking over the responsibility for self-expression and self-sufficiency. I have seen this particularly in teenagers and adults who have dropped the behaviours they'd once been 'taught' to do. Cooing and cajoling doesn't work in these cases because Exposure Anxiety is a hungry beast. The more inches you give, the more miles it wants. Instead of 'encouragement' leading to greater ability, it leads to greater learned helplessness and indulged self-pity.

I have gone so far as to suggest that an older child who is capable of taking what she wants or needs but who doesn't dress herself, eat her breakfast or put her shoes on to leave the house in the morning, should be treated as having made choices and bundled into the car in a dressing gown with shoes and breakfast in a bag. By comparison with learned helplessness, being treated and respected as having made informed choice makes self-sufficiency seem far more appealing. The same is true of toiletting. How much easier to tune out and let things just fall out into a disposable nappy (and the moist warmth and texture can actually be very much 'one's own world' and part of closing out moment-by-moment awareness of the external world). When left to deal with this annoyance in towelling or in the stickiness of urine-soaked trousers sticking to one's body, the tolerance is quite different. Rarely do people with 'autism' seem to cope well with stickiness. Warmth and moisture we can all handle, even squidgy sensations can be amusing. But cold clammy stickiness doesn't cut it.

Combine this with a mirror on the door of the toilet to tune out the awareness of the world, easy music to tune out responsibility to and an assistant who is not watching but reading a book and never breaks into applause over using the toilet, and you may have a recipe for toiletting in people with Exposure Anxiety. If the drama is about using the same toilet as everyone else, then the bath, even the basin may be a better option than a twelve-year-old in nappies. Remember that severe social–emotional retardation has no necessary relationship with mental retardation. 'I can't bring myself to acknowledge', doesn't necessarily mean the same as 'I can't grasp the concept'. But, let's face it, convincing oneself and the environment one does not understand is the greatest hiding place if severe social–emotional retardation holds you back from being able to dare taking responsibility for your own life.

If the drama is about the jolt of conscious awareness and responsibility involved in acknowledging the act by pulling up trousers, pulling them up unevenly might well do the trick as the person is compelled to correct this sloppiness and imperfection. If it is about the jolt of conscious awareness and responsibility triggered by expectation to flush, or wash one's hands, the flushing can become part of something removed from the toiletting, such as sprinkling salt into the toilet afterwards and flushing it goodbye. The washing can be about washing an object rather than one's hands after using the toilet and many children with 'autism' carry these everywhere at all times. In washing the object after the toilet, the act is not about them, it is about caring for the object. In the process, they happen to have to use their own hands to wash the object.

The problem with 'I'll teach you'

Some people wish to teach people with Exposure Anxiety how to perform relationships and touch as though they did not have the problem. This is futile and can lead to a deep internalized depression and deeper dissociation from body as well as being a potential danger to the other person, should the person with Exposure Anxiety suddenly drop the learned facade. There are programs which can help people build up a relationship to their body and to physical contact, but the emotional self is not something which can be pushed. A program which helps people enjoy body or seek physical contact is one in which an indirectly-confrontational approach involves modelling a caring, sensuous, physical relationship with oneself. Here I am not talking about modeling sexuality. Sensuality can grow from something as simple as enjoying brushing your own hair.

Feelings of autosexuality, as a matter of freedom and of choice, naturally spring from sensuality and don't require modelling. Obviously this is open to exploitation so it needs to be made clear that sensuality can be involved in something as simple as learning to enjoy music and being moved by coloured lights. It could involve playing with the sensuousness of made-up words that have no mental associations and simply involve wonderful shapes and textures in their form. It could involve creative movement and the use of ribbon to create exciting, sensual flow to the music being played. It could involve fabric textures, play with sand or water, cushions and modelling using one's body to explore the physical surroundings. Multi-sensory rooms with their dim lighting and sensual atmosphere have helped some people to let go and use their bodies to explore the sensuousness of the environment.

Many people are attracted by the enigmatic nature of Exposure Anxiety and very often it attracts 'heroes' who want to 'save' the person. Occasionally people are motivated by self-importance and their interest may be based on morbid curiosity or a feeling of being made impotent by the Exposure Anxiety 'beating them' rather than true caring. The concept of caring is usually associated with someone wanting to 'teach you'. In my experience caring takes many forms and unselfish caring is empowering, and it seeks to understand and inspire, rather than seeking to 'save'.

Adults with Exposure Anxiety have found themselves in compromising situations where people have become aroused by their aloofness or their enigmatic nature, so difficult to fathom and pin down in front of others. This becomes an object of potential conquest to such individuals and I have personally been the object of obsession for this reason. These people might start out with just an innocent curiosity but someone who appears to wish to 'teach' the person with Exposure Anxiety, especially regarding trust of touch or intimate disclosure, may say they are a friend when they are not. This might be a supervisor, a lecturer, a supervisor, a visitor to the home, a shopkeeper – almost anyone.

People with Exposure Anxiety can be tortured by their inability to connect to their body. This may be especially so when it involves touch and intimacy in social–emotional relationships, and they often want desperately to be like others but don't have the understanding of what they are being prompted into. This makes them especially vulnerable to exploitation. A good teacher has a public involvement with their pupil; their actions are not exclusively behind a closed and private office door. If people genuinely want to help and are not out to exploit, they can leave the door open, choose times when others are in the building, allow you to tape the sessions and take that tape home where you are free to ask others for an opinion.

Teaching which involves a feeling of entrapment is not healthy. People with Exposure Anxiety may be in particularly trouble here. For them, almost everything may feel like entrapment. Because of their anxiety state, they are liable, also, to being blamed for their own exploitation at the hands of others.

The other problem with being a magnet for the 'I'll teach you' types is that when they are unable to 'get through to you' because Exposure Anxiety keeps answering the door, they lose interest. Whether as friendships or relationships, when these connections are actually wanted by the person with Exposure Anxiety, this cycle can be extremely disheartening and confusing. The person with Exposure Anxiety is better off learning that when someone says 'I'll teach you', they should correct them with 'I'm good at teaching myself when I'm inspired by what I experience'.

Taking solace

What's hard about Exposure Anxiety is that the more diverse its appearance, the more functionally able one appears, the more one is expected to be grateful for not being as affected as those functionally less able. I have met many very able teenagers and adults who have become anorexic or suicidal because they are trapped within their own functional adaptations. They may be so trapped that they may prefer to abandon everything they have taken on which hides them as they are independent of these adaptations.

Being cut off from experience or identification with your body as your own can be an alienating and trapping experience. Being able only to speak with someone else's voice or to use your own but be able to understand barely a word you say, is isolating and a source of great frustration and despair. To be able to perform a reality you are unable to experience can be frightening and this is a position of extreme vulnerability. There are many able people in this situation who are as disabled as those termed 'low functioning' and although their lives may appear fuller, without the ability to experience that life as your own, you might well envy some so-called 'low-functioning' people their cohesion, however chaotic.

Many parents have envied families with high-functioning people with 'autism'. They are sometimes so set on waiting for the appearance of ability, they forget that that appearance doesn't matter if the person is unable to experience or identify at all with that façade of apparent ability. What may lie beneath it may be an abyss, whilst their so-called 'low-functioning' child may at least be standing on solid ground. I was one of these so called 'high-functioning' people. I fell into this abyss. I became, at different times, frighteningly self-abusive, anorexic at times, bulimic at others, masochistic generally, ceasing to speak for weeks or months, unable to speak in comprehensible language generally, eating non-food stuffs, depriving myself of sleep, walking into the path of oncoming traffic, leaving my body in dangerous and vulnerable social situations like something I wished to discard. Whilst some 'high-functioning' people are connected and able to experience their level of functioning, some have, defensively and self-protectively, learned to portray 'high functioning'. Underneath, there may not be as much difference between the 'high-functioning' and 'low-functioning' person as might be assumed.

Exposure Anxiety and respect

There are three types of respect when living with Exposure Anxiety. There is the respect demanded by Exposure Anxiety. This is associated with an authoritarian, tight, controlling, tyrant-like version of 'respect', however indirectly it is imposed on the environment. Second, there is the respect required by the person independent of the Exposure Anxiety who is realistic about its ability to exert control, chaos and domination over this person's life. This might involve hinting to the environment to back off, be more self-owning, stop watching, waiting, drawing attention to the person or continually provoking self-consciousness, however good the intentions. This type of respect leads to freedom from Exposure Anxiety by disarming it of the justification to defend the self from 'invasion'. The third type of respect is that of the meta-self. This is the version of the self that the person might have been had they not had Exposure Anxiety. This self might be utterly free inside but severely blocked from letting this out and is, therefore, imprisoned. This self may desire the respect of being treated 'just like anyone else'. Sometimes it can give rise to such a feeling of anonymity it actually works to provide a functional façade in which the self can hide. Sometimes this results in the self feeling angry at this same 'respect' being shown, as though the environment has deliberately set the person up for disappointment and frustration.

The respect demanded by Exposure Anxiety should be met with surrealism, aloofness and an enigmatic response. Exposure Anxiety is like a climber looking for a footing. Don't give it one. Respecting the ways of reducing Exposure Anxiety involves understanding on the part of the environment and the realization there are different ways of loving those you wish to help through facilitating their ability to help themselves where nobody else can. Respecting the meta self means remembering not to view the person wholly in terms of their Exposure Anxiety nor their relationship to it. Sometimes, this kind of respect yields some wild surprises, as long as you don't let the person with Exposure Anxiety notice you are noticing.

Why Exposure Anxiety can be seen as 'rudeness'

The avoidance, diversion and retaliation responses of Exposure Anxiety can be seen as 'rudeness'. So can the indirectly-confrontational self-in-relation-to-self nature of expression, communication and contact the person with Exposure Anxiety is forced into as the only functional adaptation to being otherwise 'low functioning'.

I had flippant stored lines that so often came out reactively because of Exposure Anxiety. Opening the front door persistently with 'Hiya woman, how's your hormones' and then the door slammed can look pretty rude. It took me forever to get to the point where I could stand silently and just open the door, and even then, because the pattern continued privately inside, I just burst out laughing as if I was observing what hadn't got out. Swearing with every stored piece of verbal abuse may be the only way Exposure Anxiety would allow me to initiate social contact. Anything more user-friendly may have been far too directly inviting to an 'outsider'. When complimented I spat. It was involuntary, compulsive and instant, as though I was removing the connection. When said hello to, I was compelled to look away and avoid contact (unless I dared the initiation). When asked what I liked or wanted, I was compelled to glare as though being insulted. When asked to come out of my room and greet guests, I responded with a grimace followed by punching myself in front of them. In my teens, when asked a question, I responded with a two-hour litany and never asked a question in return.

Inside, I felt I wasn't like this person. Inside, I was in control of my behaviour. I was like anyone else. Sure, I adored colour and sounds and smells and textures and patterns and certain kinds of movement. This stuff was me. But the Exposure Anxiety responses I didn't see as me, at least not as I got older.

Counselling and other people's needs

People with Exposure Anxiety are suffering from a physiological problem and should not live in shame. They should be able to introduce their needs to the community and this can be done with a simple business card. Their name on one side and on the other an explanation of Exposure Anxiety would be useful. Something like:

> 'I'm a person with metabolic problems which cause Exposure Anxiety. Exposure Anxiety means I have an involuntary self-protection mechanism that gets control of my communication and responses. I'm intelligent and far more capable if you talk out loud to yourself rather than to me and simply make things available rather than trying too hard to 'help' me. Thank you for your understanding.'

People living with those who have chronic Exposure Anxiety need somewhere to let their hair down and be directly-confrontational, even a counsellor on the end of a phone, or someone they phone not to discuss the issues, but just let go and have a laugh.

The person with Exposure Anxiety might try to control the environment from making or inviting in such outside contacts. Don't coo and cajole, it gives the power to Exposure Anxiety. At the same time, you cannot openly defy or this is taken as fuel. What is left is to blame it on something other than your own volition. 'Damn phone, wish it wouldn't make me use it like this.' You can also make it clear in a definite, even self-defensive stance that your actions about your own life and are nothing to do with the person with Exposure Anxiety. Declare your space as your space but show this is a mutual matter of respect. There is no logic in declaring your own space when you are persistently seen as invasion in someone else's. That simply looks like unfair play.

Exposure Anxiety and trust

Trust and the alienness of those without Exposure Anxiety

Arrive on another planet where their ways seem utterly inhuman and you'll find it difficult to relax and trust such a foreign system. In the world, there are differences between cultures to do with manners and introductions and what impresses and what causes insult. One thing all human cultures supposedly have in common is a simultaneous sense of self and other, a reliance on the system of interpretation and a social–emotional drive toward directly–confrontational communication. Whether such people are with or without verbal speech, this is still so, unless, perhaps, they have information-processing differences or severe chronic Exposure Anxiety.

People with Exposure Anxiety can usually learn to adapt to living in this very foreign reality. Some actually use communication to prevent others from joining with them personally or causing affect or overload. The majority, however, of those who can 'do' this, may be unable to sustain the effort or contact without exhaustion or escape.

To the adrenaline addict, being on the receiving end of directly-confrontational interaction may not only be seen as unfriendly, but as threatening, invasive, disturbed or insensitive and disrespectful behaviour on the part of the environment. The suggestion that one should speak with others when one cannot simultaneously process a sense of self and other (and therefore cannot imagine how others can) can seem a disturbing social contortion. To the defensive self it can seem a game about proof, a conspiracy to perform an experiential reality that must surely be known not really to exist in spite of the ability to perform as though it does. The offer of a handshake can seem a matter of being pushed into contact. That one is expected to speak to, listen to or look at someone sensed as very directly-confrontational, very self-in-relation-to-other or, worse, very dissonant in their appearance and their being, may seem a sadistic expectation for no obvious purpose. Those who learn to do these things may have no idea why they do so. They may just see this as how the world is. The person with Exposure Anxiety may feel that provided they are free to escape, they get less attention in playing along than in insisting on their own ways and standing out as well as being utterly isolated.

Trust in relation to the external world, in spite of its foreign system of relating, is only half of the problem. Compelled to hide from yourself in order to get out any actions or communication, you become unable to trust *yourself.* Where you cannot trust yourself you might place all your trust in someone else, but this is not true trust. It is dependency. It can be parasitic and one sided, promoting a co-dependent relationship in the hero who is the focus of this dependency.

To truly trust you have to first own up that you do not trust, perhaps cannot trust. From there you need to get to know your own space, find at the very least the feel of who you are and decide whether you like it or not. If you don't like the feel of the person you are, explore why and how to change that. If you can't do that in your head (and I can't), find out who you are through typing, through writing, through music, through art, through movement, through making or building things, through some external expression of you in your own space, even thinking it through using representational objects. From knowing the feel of the person you are and whether or not you feel safe and trusting in your own world, in your own space, then you have half a chance to hear others and to trust out of choice and decision.

When you trust anyone who doesn't trigger Exposure Anxiety

A person with Exposure Anxiety may decide he or she 'trusts' someone simply because the 'trust' behaviour takes their focus off him or herself and stops others trying to 'break through'. This has bad consequences because the environment takes this as a green light. This is encouraged in behaviour modification programs and openly praised. Yet it is the same empty 'trust' that led to years of sexual exploitation. It took me until well into my adult years to make any self-initiated choices. Yet it was pretty much guaranteed that if you pursued me (which others think of as flirting) I would play dead by going along, puppet-like, with whatever was being asked of me. When, later, I'd become progressively disturbed, withdrawn and then run away, this was always seen as me being 'crazy'. I also feared that one day I'd lash out, being a danger to those who had exploited me or those who came to symbolise them. I could not talk about the problem. By its very nature, discussing Exposure Anxiety was impossible.

I was especially vulnerable because I would often give empty 'trust' to get people off my case and focused back on themselves. More than this, when I found those who, because of their aloof or distant nature, did not trigger Exposure Anxiety, I felt what I perceived as real trust. I came from quite a rough suburb. I met people I eventually understood were involved in some areas of life which meant they either totally disrespected themselves or others. I gave absolute trust to some of the most detached and sociopathic people you could dread your child to meet and all because they were utterly detached from their attempts to connect and I sensed them as totally focused on themselves – hence, by the definition of Exposure Anxiety, 'safe people'. As my mother once commented, 'anybody could run off with you'. If they behaved as if they didn't give much of a damn, it was true, I'd sense no fear and without any other reason not to follow, I'd follow.

There's a saying that the greatest risk in life is to take no risks at all. I believe that. I didn't learn the first time, or the second, or the third. But I do have a whole life, a colourful life and an independent life. Being wrapped up protectively in a mountain of cotton wool would not have enriched my life. It could have used a safety net, but at the end of the day, even in tightly controlled residential settings, people with severe Exposure Anxiety have been abused sometimes and often for the very reason that potential abusers get into the establishment. The person in tightly-controlled residential care, unlike me, is not free to escape from the next attack, is even sometimes prescribed psychiatric drugs if she persists in trying and becomes 'a behaviour management problem'. This is a hard reality, but it is one, I think, technology may be able to help with. I foresee that people with severe Exposure Anxiety could have both space and protection in situations of relative independence where they are no more preyed on than they are trapped with an assailant who is meant to 'care for and control them'.

There is also the wonderful and beautiful side of people who trust so blindly, even emptily. In a world where mistrust is everywhere, such 'trust' can be wonderful, and uplifting. I spent the first seven years of my life entering everyone's backyard to explore their gardens, play in their fishpond, make showers out of their shredded flowers, humming or singing away to myself. The neighbours all knew me. Nobody took offence. At nine I did the same in the Chinese Cafe down the road, going behind the counter, racing up the stairs to their kitchen. I explored car washes this way, caravan show rooms, people's offices, public transport. In my teens I explored factories and walked into other schools, taking a seat in new classrooms. These were good learning experiences and the neigh-bourhood coped better than most people would imagine when they saw a skinny little freckle-faced kid with curly hair and a cheeky aloofness. There is no reason why such a person has to be constantly stopped or con-trolled, but with communication technology as it is today, someone trained in using an indirectly-confrontational approach strategically could safely shadow them. With severe auditory and visual processing problems as well as Exposure Anxiety, the world was my classroom and I learned and remembered more cohesive experiences from these excursions than I got from years of sitting in classrooms expected to learn with 'mind'. I also think I gave a lot to the neighbourhood, and I challenged them. A business card given out by 'a shadow', would have done no harm at all, especially one letting them know that all they'd have to do to get me to leave would be to try to strike up a directly-confrontational conversation with me.

Counselling, support people and social safety

In secondary school my responses were almost utterly governed by Exposure Anxiety reactions or sensory buzzing and disorientation caused by food-related chemical highs. I'd like to say that directly-confrontational counselling works but I'd be lieing. It might work with some people but with others, indirectly-confrontational story telling may well carry over better from one context to another. I never forgot a jingle or TV commer-cial and the theme of these came up in appropriate situations. Yet lessons I'd been taught never came up. The answer is to present the lessons in the same form as the jingle or TV advertisement – short, concise, summing up the situation and what to do and always done as though for the carer's own benefit or entertainment. 'You knew the job was dangerous when you took it, Super Chicken', won't get you very far if you are trying to tell someone you feel pressured and don't feel right about what's being asked, but jingles can be modified, co-opted to carry important communications and only the environment modelling such a use as though for their own benefit provides such an example. Children who love repetitively watching videos might be able to learn to emulate solutions portrayed by their favourite characters. A camcorder and the toys based on these characters can produce Social Stories including purpose-made jingles sung by the charac-ters. The videos, left for discovery among those used, is your indirectly-confrontational classroom; just don't hover in the doorway waiting and watching for a reaction or Exposure Anxiety will surely give you one and probably discard or throw the video.

Exposure Anxiety and love

Allergic to love

As Exposure Anxiety protects the individual against invasion, this means it protects the individual from social–emotional connection. In severe cases, it can look as if the person is allergic to love.

Love is an act of giving and connection. Giving is a wonderful thing if you don't experience it as invasion. I found it gut-wrenching to ask, so I either simply took, ignored the appeal or desire or left the interest on hold until nobody was present to trigger the Exposure Anxiety surrounding the object of desire. I found it impossible to accept what was given directly, so generally I was compelled to shun it. The degree of respect involved in how indirectly-confrontational the giving was, was usually far more important than what was being given. You could present me with the most wonderful present and I'd be reasonably likely to ignore it and (as a diversion response) discover a wonderful piece of carpet fluff by your foot and then spend the next few hours exploring its structure intently. Had you apparently forgotten something obviously yours, left it discarded as though its value held no trigger of potential connection, and it was possible I'd feel I had 'discovered' this wonderful thing. If you followed this with a blasé statement that you'd found it and were going to throw it out, it would have been more likely I'd have taken it.

The hardest thing to give me was personal closeness. You could, using an indirectly-confrontational approach, reach me through the appeal of objects; their colours, textures, sounds, tastes or smells, but connecting with me directly and personally was Exposure Anxiety's greatest taboo. Yet I craved involvement and closeness. I watched the world and its closeness like a poor child with its face pressed to the window of the sweet shop. But where you cannot give, you can inspire to snatch and take. So many parents could reach those allergic to love if they learnt to be warm but aloof and very much in their own world. This can take the heat off so much, the bars of the invisible cage become thinner and thinner, with nothing left to protect and the natural desire to connect is free to come out. Unfortunately this runs so counter to the usual directly-confrontational instinct in the expression of love.

When almost everything is a 'secret love'

In the absence of the ability to dare direct loving connection as myself with people in the world, I did so by proxy, via my characterizations, watching what love and connection might have been had I not had severe Exposure Anxiety; and via my reflection, the only person I expressed open, direct unconditional closeness and love towards was the girl in the mirror. When I broke from this sustaining connection I mourned her and for some years felt the addictive call to return to this solace; I have strong love in the world now and I never stay long with my own reflection any more. I can't say that will always be so. If I lost Chris I'd probably spend a lot of time with my reflection again. Though my reflection is only a play of light on glass, in my social–emotional reality, I experienced a level of non-verbal connection and understanding with her that is extremely hard to match in the people world. I feel I'd never have become the loving person I am without my relationship to her on which to model all I sought in the world in connection with others.

It is very hard for the environment to know what does appeal to the person with severe Exposure Anxiety although, approached indirectly, it is possible to gather a lot of information about what attracts, compels and provides security and a sense of belonging or inclusion for someone with 'autism'. It may be she loves becoming one with colour, feels in company with rhythm or finds her freedom in movement patterns. Giving a clear sign you are doing so for your own sake, you can, in your own time and space, explore for yourself these things, perhaps allowing her now to be the 'fly on the wall'. When you co-opt such types of interests in a way clearly not focused on them or watching their response, this becomes a matter of 'What have you got there? That's my buzz.'

The choice between 'freedom of expression as self' and 'having love'

Some people with severe Exposure Anxiety have freedom of expression as long as they cut themselves off from emotional hypersensitivity. Emotion for these people can be an utterly all or nothing state. This is a kind of emotional suicide in order to ensure functioning and many such people will fight you like crazy if you try to bring flexibility and feelings into their world.

These people may feel afraid others will discover they are 'empty', so they become even more isolated inside, however much they compensate on the surface in 'performing' emotion. I tried to do this when I was in my teens. I managed for about six months to numb myself against affect in this way. But the despair I felt made me feel I was dying and I couldn't bear it. I failed to be like my mother. However much it sabotaged control over my self-expression or behaviour, I felt more whole living connected to my emotions than dead inside, cut off from them. Many do not have a strong emotional self screaming out against such a sell out. I have counselled adults who 'killed off' their emotional self in early childhood and for them the struggle and fear involved in reconnecting is awesome.

It is one thing to be an adult with retarded social–emotional development. It is another to be such an adult who has mastered a place in the world at the expense of the death of the emotional self, whose retarded social–emotional development is now no longer seen or breaking through the cracks. Helping people in this schizoid state can mean terror not just in letting go of the functional façade, but in teaching the emotional self to trust the functional, intellectual self, which may see as its persecutor, its abandoner, its murderer. It is difficult to build trust between two halves of the self, one which has made functioning and fitting in its god and the other which has no love nor trust of the functional self nor any hope for an integrated self in the social reality created by that functional self. Yet, in the absence of such integration are the makings of the everyday psychopath. Had I got meaning before the age of nine, perhaps I'd have identified self with mind, killed off my emotional self and gone down this path. I tried to push myself down it but couldn't. I cursed myself for that failure for if this were not the answer, then all I had left was a life sentence in the dance with Exposure Anxiety. Yet, I am a deeply artistic person with a great depth of passion and perhaps this too made it much harder for me than most to succeed in suicide of the soul. This death without a corpse is one where the murder goes undetected and unseen and the murderer is rewarded with inclusion.

Emotional suicide is also one form of a total systems shutdown that has been used to help people deal with information-processing. Given the choice between giving up visual and auditory interpretation and giving up the emotional self as a way of compensating for information overload and processing delay, I'd rather be functionally deaf blind and still be moved, if only by what I sense rather than interpret. Yet irrationally, this society, and especially behaviour modification programmes, have the power to convince the individual that functioning is everything and experience is secondary to compliance, for compliance is inclusion. This is not to say a flexible, creative, inspiring behaviour modification programme couldn't incorporate an indirectly-confrontational approach which might promote the experience and reaching out of the self, but presently such programmes do not.

Why choosing 'wrong' people is so much 'easier'

It can become so much easier to choose the 'wrong' people as these people often don't trigger Exposure Anxiety. Why? Because the 'wrong' people can be sensed as so self-interested they don't trigger a feeling of invasiveness as easily. This means that even though the person with Exposure Anxiety, more than anyone else, needs personal space to express themselves and develop, they also need a team which is good at being 'fly on the wall' and watching out for social danger without being seen to be saying 'no'. Saying 'no' to someone with Exposure Anxiety is often the best way to have them run straight into the fire you are warning them about. Being blase but open about the nature of what they are heading for, whilst treating it as a matter of choice, is much more useful, though the last thing you'd think to do. If you really need the person to reject the source of this social danger, you may, with no other course of action, need to make it clear and public that you expect, of course, they'll head in this direction. This may well be the best way to guarantee the person with Exposure Anxiety will defy your expectation and lose interest in this dangerous attraction. Remember, just as you learn to work the language of Exposure

Anxiety for the benefit of the person with the condition, so too may an abuser make use of the same tactics to entrap the person and alienate them from those who might otherwise help.

CHAPTER 4

The Development of a Social Face

Being 'social' – and the nature of 'Simply Being'

The value and beauty of 'simply being'

Since the sixties society has been becoming progressively more blatant, more 'in your face', yet no more 'real'. In the seventies and eighties, although people let go of convention, they still pursued image. Even in the apparent pursuit of individuality, they seemed conformistly non-conformist and in every decade there are definitions of being uncool, bogus, naff…in other words, not conformistly con-conformist enough, too starkly, nakedly, individual without enough impressive, dramatic or captivating trimmings. In such a society, impression and image continue to matter. In the media and advertising, sit-coms and magazines, impression and image matter more, not less than ever before. This pressure faces us all. In a world that is becoming more confrontational, blatant, busy and imposing of expected social image (and equally expected prescriptive conformist rebellion against such images) the reality of Exposure Anxiety has never been more challenging.

Where the person with Exposure Anxiety would cope better with being indirectly-confrontational, the world is so much more 'in their face'. Where they would cope better being left to teach themselves, they now live in a proof-driven society which pays direct attention to those who appear to be 'failing', the very tactic bound to amplify the freezing effect of Exposure Anxiety and its impact on ability. Where people with develop-

mental differences may take a different route to get to the same destina-
tion, the routes are now prescriptively limited by the revered opinions of
'experts' and the faceless yet all powerful grip of one size fits all delivery of
the national curriculum in its strangulation of creativity and differentness.

There are, however, some aspects of society today which improve
things for people with Exposure Anxiety. The ability to walk around
talking to oneself as long as one has a hands-free mobile phone inadvertently sets the good example for people with Exposure Anxiety that it's
OK to talk from self, to self, with no obvious audience to provoke and raise
self-consciousness. The ability to communicate, shop, even work via the
internet and through computer technology, where a voice is not necessary
and communication can be 'through the object', provides communicative,
social, educational and employment possibilities for people challenged by
Exposure Anxiety.

What is needed is the right and ability to 'simply be' without being
watched, studied, worked on, pursued, to allow the person a social existence outside the grip of Exposure Anxiety among others who have also
learned to 'simply be'. Whilst many people find this ability through
drug-induced experiences, it would be wonderful if, without drugs,
people stopped fearing so much the starkness of their own individuality so
that they might start to explore who they are in their own 'simply be'
space.

Exploring sound for the beauty of sound, form for the wonder of
seeing through touch, movement for the adventure of feeling space, redis-
covering smell and texture in the world around you is part of 'simply
being'. Moving away from the constant pressure to always think and know
and use mind is an adventure for any person. By getting back to sensing,
the sense of self-consciousness is off and the processing burden is off, and
the self-protection instinct so triggered by both of these is dramatically
reduced.

'Simply being' is no waste of time. Those so bent on filling up space
with learning might try to remember that mathematics, language, literacy
or science are not pieces of knowledge. They are mapped patterns of experience and they are everywhere. These mapped patterns of experience
make their way not just into knowledge but into life and they don't have to
be conscious to be useful. Knowledge does not exist only via pen and

paper, in classrooms or found sitting at a desk. Knowledge comes from reflection upon those mapped patterns of experience. Here we do not 'know' for the first time, but rediscover as 'knowledge' that which we already knew in what was once our 'unknown knowing'. Knowledge for knowledge's sake is useless except as pedantic self-entertainment (although this is worth something). It is only when we discover for ourselves a need for knowing that we draw it up from pattern and use it. Nobody can give that to you. It is something you can do out of compliance, but it is not yours until you, yourself, need it.

Making learning an objective process

Teachers are so focused on seeing whether the individual has understood that they can freeze the understanding by raising self-consciousness in the process. I have taken over directly-confrontational lessons and grabbed representational objects and brought the lesson to life in the centre of the table, working as though I am doing the lesson for my own benefit. The shift in attention when not being watched is remarkable. I have had the opposite reaction, with children seeking to take over the lesson. In which case, I simply brought them into it, not as pupil, but as teacher, focused, like I had been, on the topic itself, not on others. This is about empowerment.

A topic about self-in-relation-to-other can be represented through objects, and the smaller the objects, the more visually cohesive these are for those with fragmented visual perception. The more someone has to struggle to tune into a small object, the less they are compelled to reject being overwhelmed by visual information which seems too much 'in bits' and too 'in their face'. Representing a self-in-relation-to-other situation through representational objects is easier to memorize as serial memory, as if it had been seen in a video. This has a better chance of carrying from one context to another. Instead of this being a fragmented learning of all self, no other, then topic; no self, then other, no topic etc, it now becomes a cohesive experience in which the series is remembered cohesively. Speaking through objects also models a technique of communicating that does not involve the daring of directly-confrontational connection. This makes breaking out of the communicative block of Exposure Anxiety easier and, because the topic is kept tangible, visual, concrete, it doesn't tumble in one's head like mere unanchored, unsequenced blah blah.

Looking for feedback and pokes in the eye

If you asked me a question, you'd have been very unlikely to get an answer if it wasn't related to my 'special topic'. But make a statement, especially a wrong one, and I'd have been more likely to respond. This works the same with verbal and 'non-verbal' people. The sense of invasion triggered by a self-in-relation-to-other question causes a freezing, triggering aversion, diversion and retaliation responses. Make a self-in-relation-to-self state-ment and it does not, leaving emotional expression, however repressed, to answer you if nothing else. Looking for feedback is like being watched whilst someone waits for you to use the toilet. It is like being asked to watch but then poked in the eye. My expression is just that. It is mine. What you get out of things is not up to me. It is not my responsibility. Why do you have to make it so by looking so openly for feedback? If you don't get it, does it have to be the end of the world? Have you no life, no existence beyond my reply? Could you not merely get on with things and know, from my pursuit or lack of it what my response is? Yet this incidental replying is rarely considered. Even when it is received it is often not trusted unless it is confirmed, somehow proven.

Exposure Anxiety and the mixed messages of aversion, diversion and retaliation responses

The friendly person caught up in involuntary avoidance responses appears uninterested, cold, and unfriendly. The person capable of intense interest and focus who gets caught up in diversion responses can seem like a clown who never takes anything seriously. The accepting, empathic person caught up in retaliation responses can appear insensitive and selfish. Then, because people are attracted to others like themselves and repelled by those they can't relate to, the person's Exposure Anxiety responses shape their social world. I used to attract a lot of people I didn't want to be around. In my teens and adulthood, I attracted people who found my avoidance mysterious and alluring, when in fact I was very aware of their every move.

By typing, you can override what others see. I always find that whatever comes out verbally, Exposure Anxiety seems to have much less control over the less expressive movements of my fingers pointing to keys in typing. Perhaps it's confused. This skill has been discovered in those who have taught themselves to read from signs and advertising labels and should never have been assumed not present or unattainable on the basis of what Exposure Anxiety presents. This has been poorly understood in the field, leading to testing which is so directly-confrontational that it is set up to fail by its very definition.

For those who do not use a letter board or typing, there is also expression through music, art, by creative movement; all can express a personality very different from the one expressed through the grip of avoidance, diversion or retaliation responses caused by Exposure Anxiety.

Giving yourself permission to use your own system

What is most important socially for people with Exposure Anxiety is that they should give themselves permission to use their own system of working with their condition. So often the teaching of manners and expectation gets in the way of people's ability to help themselves.

I remember a client who came to see me feeling detached and dead inside and on the verge of suicide. This person was unable to give self-ownership 'maybe' rather than 'yes' or 'no', and then felt utterly trapped in social situations, unable to leave or protect himself when he had self-protectively shut down. Not only was he communicatively frozen in these situations, but he was only able to mimic others. This left him incredibly vulnerable and full of fear and self-loathing. His family saw only someone very good looking and talented who had given up. I told him he had a right to be a mystery, to not commit, to say 'maybe'. I explained that when we feel free to leave, we are able to stay. I told him he doesn't have to sit down. He doesn't have to stay for the duration of a visit or a dinner or a party. He can pop in for a minute, for five minutes and leave without excuse, leaving others to cope or not. I told him he could re-ask any question asked of him, turn it around and make it his, then answer himself out loud to himself in order to keep conversation flowing without being frozen. I explained that Exposure Anxiety is about feeling robbed of control and that if he seized control and steered social situations, being always free to leave, being non-committal, the Exposure Anxiety would come down and he'd be more connected, more part of his own actions. I explained it was not failure to find a place in life where functioning level and social–emotional capacity were more in sync, whatever the world might think. I may have been seen to be promoting bad manners, but I felt I was restoring hope, putting self-ownership back into life and helping someone feel part of the world where it most matters – inside. A dead success is not a success at all.

I have had many such contacts with adults who have reached this point and, in a world geared for appearances and achievement, my type of advice is seen as the opposite to teaching good social skills: the politeness, the handshake, the ability to stay for the duration. But what I build are the ingredients which empower the person so there becomes a point, a desire, in challenging themselves progressively forward as whole, connected human beings. So many 'able' people with severe Exposure Anxiety have 'made friends' who have never seen the real them, been to parties where they have never felt connected to the voice they use to chat. Some have slept with 'partners' with no connection to the body going through the motions, or have expressed the expected emotions although opposite or absent ones are the inside reality. These people have created pedestals so far beyond their capacity to connect on a social–emotional level, they have one prison on top of another. When they try to disassemble their own social entrapment, they are seen as regressing, somehow failing, in need of help to rebuild their socially-valued prison.

Some of the lucky ones find someone who can really see them and has the patience and humanity to support them in becoming a whole person, with what is often a new and rather different life from the one they spent in hiding. Some even manage to dare to write in discussion with friends, family, partners, explaining their dilemma. Some are listened to, those who know and care about them relieved to finally understand what they had felt but hadn't really seen. Some are not so lucky and are either ridiculed, pressured into remaining how they are (which sometimes has suited the needs of the environment) or forced to start all over again somewhere else. If 'alone' means having a chance to create a life chosen by self, being able to identify with and connect with one's own doing, or a chance to be proud however seemingly less the achievements, then alone is not always the regression it may seem. Alone may simply be the first step in an accumulation of steps on a path you've never walked before.

Exposure Anxiety and behaviour

Some speak freely with stored characterizations or feel safe in special topics. Some people with Exposure Anxiety speak with voice, direction, and topics driven by Exposure Anxiety. Some use speech to control others and avoid the self-consciousness of spaces or of being asked anything. Some speak in wooden, unemotive tone, terrified of loss of control, of daring emotion before others, unable to combine mind and emotion fluently into one expression. Some are freed through typing or pointed communication using a letter board. Some speak in theme and not the language of interpretation, others in sound and emotion without words. Some speak with their body, with their eyes, self slipping through the spaces between the invisible bars of Exposure Anxiety.

It is a myth, a well-perpetuated myth, that people with autism as a group are not social. However aloof they are compelled to be, however diverting or outright retaliative they are in response to feelings of 'invasion' and loss of control, these are the same people who will be 'fly on the wall', hovering in your space without being able to own up to the choice. And to own up to that choice so often means that daring inclusion becomes twice as hard when they are forced to be consciously aware of having chosen. These are the same people who will snatch and sneak what you have for yourself, sometimes discreetly when the heat of potential attention is off, sometimes outright and publicly in seizing control. In any case, it is connection. These are the people who will know you intimately through your objects, unable to own up consciously that it is you they visit, not your house or your things and yet, did they not like you, your house and your objects would be nothing to them.

The children with Exposure Anxiety, labelled autistic, whom I have met, have the same spectrum of sociability I have found in any children. Some are naturally quiet people in spite of wild diversion responses. Some are bubbly and mischievous in spite of compulsion to hide in a stored mask of presentability and 'right' responses. Some are melodramatic and tend towards self-pity, however aloof and indifferent they may be compelled to appear. Some are kind and empathic, however retaliative and defensive their behaviour. Of course, as in any mix, there will always be one or two who are, by nature rather than condition, socially cold or utterly self-interested, but that doesn't make the archaic and outdated stereotype correct. With Exposure Anxiety, you have to look at the contradictions, the impression given by the bars versus the impression through the gaps between the bars. What you think may be the Exposure Anxiety may in fact be the self; what you think might be the self turns out to be part of the Exposure Anxiety.

What I have found with adults, however, is that whilst some are aware of strong social desires, others have become hurt or disillusioned with what social involvement means. Some have rejected it as a place of falsity that doesn't care about the person inside, can't see them, or is seemingly incapable of helping in a way which works. Some have rejected it in 'self-protection', defensive spite and sometimes in a controlling prompt to force the environment to 'make them' so they don't have to take the responsibility for their own initiations.

Some high-functioning adults on the autistic spectrum seem to define themselves as 'truly' autistic on the basis that they have no desire to be social. Whilst this may be more true of psychopathy, it is important to distinguish this from autism in general. Some of the most severely affected children and adults with autism whom I've met are tortured by the fact they have a very strong desire to be social but their behaviour and communication contorts and alters all social involvement, opportunity and appearance of that desire.

Some non-autistic 'experts' have helped perpetuate certain stereotypes and some able adults have identified themselves by laying claim to what is becoming known as 'autistic culture'. Personally, I believe culture is everywhere and people, autistic or not, find places within the various elements of it, in their own ways.

Rituals and Exposure Anxiety

Though a lot of my rituals were about sensory fascinations, at least two thirds were about Exposure Anxiety. Reassurance rituals dominated everything. Symmetry compulsions were about the loss of control caused by acute chronic anxiety. Number compulsions were about symmetry and restoring balance. Placement rituals were about symmetry and losing myself in the oneness with an object or experience in a desperate need to lose self-consciousness in order to feel free. Dropping rituals were about visual–perceptual problems but also about reassurance of freedom from intense chronic feelings of constraint and internal imprisonment. Tearing and shredding rituals were about the reassurance of severing and disintegrating in order to appease the emotional discomfort, distaste and Exposure Anxiety-driven self-disgust, even rage, caused by having dared or allowed direct social connection as self. Spitting and forced vomiting were the same – proof of getting 'them' and their connection with me back out, into 'their world'. Urinating in my room was about reassurance and strengthening the walls between my world and theirs, surrounding me and all that is 'mine' with something very 'me' – territory.

Sorting and ordering was about the reassurance of control in response to intense feelings of loss of control, both in siding with Exposure Anxiety and feeling the world as invasive, but also in feeling imprisoned by Exposure Anxiety, suffocated and robbed of freedom. Repetition was about getting lost, caught up in the experience and the same as rocking in losing the grating experience of self-consciousness which made me feel like a person made of inward-facing pins that irritated and provoked me at every expressive turn.

Refusal to eat or demonstrate being 'part of things' was about appeasing Exposure Anxiety to feel more at peace, untormented, but it was also about controlling the environment to please Exposure Anxiety so it wouldn't retaliate against me. Ironically, the compulsion only to copy others was done with exactly the same purpose. This disarmed Exposure Anxiety in what was like a private inner joke of being undercover, in apparent compliance, whilst they would have no idea I wasn't in there; I was unconnected to the surface that pleased them. Compulsive singing and verbal repetitions controlled the environment, robbing it of the capacity to make an impact and reassuring me that in my aloneness, meaning deafness and meaning blindness, I was not alone; I was with me.

Completing circuits was about reassurance of perfection and control and demonstrated to Exposure Anxiety that I had the power and ability to keep the walls intact and absolute. Rituals of choking myself, holding my breath and tensing my stomach muscles to make myself faint were about reassuring myself that I could escape at any time. I had hand movement rituals involving holding my fingers rigid as though nothing could get in, or weaving my hands back and forth in front of others, or making a cage with my fingers in order to look at people through or put over their face. All of these involved reassurance of control or putting something between myself and them which made it safer to dare initiation or involvement. Hand weaving made me feel relieved, somehow 'rebalanced'.

Holding my breath was not just about anxiety in general but was also the reassurance that I was not 'receiving'. There were rituals of jumping which allowed me not only to tune out but to allow learning in, in a way that I might otherwise have found impossible. There were tapping rituals which were not just about meaning blindness and understanding through acoustics, but were also a reminder I was not as invaded as I felt; I was with my reflection, with my special objects, with the table.

There were also obsessive compulsive disorder patterns that involved primarily reassurance in undoing a feeling of connection or reassuring myself the pattern would somehow ensure the maintaining of 'control'. No matter how much I sought to control these, they seemed merely to go 'underground', becoming more internal – breath holding, involuntary noise making, clicking my inner ear muscles, swallowing, throat clearing, coughing and twitches.

I was nine years old when I was so utterly eaten up by compulsion and ritual I began to attack it back as the very thing robbing me of control. My older brother so humourously mocked my inability to control myself. To a lesser degree so did my mother. In doing so they promoted a sense of 'it' not being 'me' and shifted the focus from my feeling the environment was robbing me of control to the sense that my Exposure Anxiety was robbing me of control. It was how they did it more than the doing itself. Done for my benefit, I would probably have taken it as a way of controlling me and been even more resolved to tune them out, to 'win'. Done for their own self-amusement in relieving their own pressure and frustration, amused at each other's characterizations of me, I resolved to burn this bridge and, hence, my own demonstrated lack of control.

I began to retaliate against my own rituals, daring to hold back in spite. I began to dare to mess up the very reassurances I'd just completed, to dare asymmetry, to play hard to get with myself, to always leave myself wanting more. I learned deprivation and began to experiment with the power to modulate my behaviour. My behaviour became my number one project and that had never stopped until this year. Until this year, my achievement was that I stopped being it and started watching it, catching it. At the age of nine, I discovered I could get Exposure Anxiety on my side by pointing out my own loss of control. Exposure Anxiety is like a deaf–blind flea-ridden wild dog in a frenzy. It is so reactive, it will attack or defend itself against anything felt to be the invasion, the robber of control. As the home environment stirred me up with ridicule I used this as fuel. I did not master the Exposure Anxiety. It was as furious as it ever was. Now it was attacking not only the environment and itself, but me. What perhaps seemed like greater turmoil actually showed me a way forward. In the process, of course, I was labelled 'emotionally disturbed' and if a cat with a terrible flea infestation is emotionally disturbed by it, then I surely was that. It took me till the age of twenty-four to find treatment for the under-lying physiological causes when I began to 'de-flea'. It took me until the age of 38 to finally know life without 'fleas'.

The physical responses of Exposure Anxiety

The physical responses of Exposure Anxiety are far more important than the behaviours they cause and these need to be the primary focus of help. The metabolic problems driving Exposure Anxiety cause extreme restless-ness, tension, terror and silent internal screaming. An ensuing magnesium deficiency can cause muscular twitchiness and tremor. The panic state of Exposure Anxiety can cause your throat to constrict so that if you speak you have to push against what feels like someone strangling you from inside. It is essential that the environment understand that however horri-fying this description is, it is usually the only reality the person has known. Good times are the momentary relief from these feelings, often through behavioural reassurances from self, to self. When I hear of able people with Asperger's can be celebrating that they have the condition of 'autism', I feel alone. Exposure Anxiety can be part of the condition of autism and affects so many people, some functionally able, some not; and it is the worst thing I can think of to live with. For me it is not a celebratory part of culture, nor of self, unless the personality itself is compatible with this masochistic defensive adrenaline-driven state. If I were a drug addict, I would not celebrate this as culture or self. To be inescapably addicted to one's own adrenaline at such a personal cost is the same.

In my case, I experience Exposure Anxiety as caused by metabolic problems triggering neurotransmitter imbalance and leading to severe digestive and immune system disorders and the toxicity and functional malnutrition in spite of apparently 'inadequate' diet. Because of this, whilst I am proud of myself with or without the label 'autistic', I support any advances in both conventional and natural medicine which will not suppress the behaviours, but treat the underlying causes.

Severe chronic stress will tax magnesium levels. Treating severe magnesium deficiency is one of the most important factors in reducing Exposure Anxiety. Metabolic problems can cause thyroid problems which are reported to be common in the mothers of children with autism-spectrum conditions and thyroid problems are one of the major underlying causes of Vitamin D deficiency. One of the first indications of this is a calcium deficiency in the mother as the calcium–magnesium imbalance occurs. Vitamin D deficiency will cause extreme deficiency in magnesium.

Magnesium is required to protect the brain and also to absorb B group vitamins necessary to immunity, enzyme production, fatty acid metabolism, nutrient transportation – all with impact on information-processing, overload and the self-protection mechanisms which set in when incoming information is perceived as 'invasion'. Mine, however, was not a case of regressive development. Whilst carrying me, my mother, who had never had any tooth decay, had a succession of them. She had more than ten fillings done before having a blood test that showed I was causing her a calcium deficiency.

The signs of D deficiency were apparent from the time I was a few months old, and yet there was no follow up treatment recommended. Cod liver oil treats D deficiency and would have raised my magnesium levels. Vitamin D is closely linked with vitamin A metabolism and vitamin A is required for zinc metabolism and visual–perceptual development. Such an imbalance leaves the infant open to far greater impact of heavy metal toxicity on the brain and reduced resistance to viruses. Severe chronic anxiety impacts on the gut, immune system, oxidative stress and detoxification mechanisms.

It's important to keep in mind that vitamins and minerals require adequate stomach acid to be metabolized. In states of acute anxiety, levels of secretory lgA in the gut decrease and the stomach generally becomes too alkaline. An alkaline gut promotes harmful bacteria and reduces levels of helpful gut flora. The gut then easily becomes host to Candida infections that not only cause sugar craving but then multiply in the presence of sugar, which results in severe lowering of magnesium levels. Magnesium is needed to use B group vitamins properly and information-processing depends on the adequate supply of B vitamins to the brain. Not only does Candida cause sugar craving which then reduces magnesium, but when Candida has finished with the sugar intake, it uses up whatever is left of vitamin B.

Without adequate stomach acid, the stomach cannot properly break down many foods, particularly those hardest to digest such as dairy products or gluten. Vitamins and minerals as well as fatty acids and amino acids cannot properly be metabolized when there is inadequate stomach acid and enzyme function, including secretin, becomes impaired. This situation is made worse by the misinterpretation of inflammatory and myalgic conditions in people with autism-spectrum conditions. These generally have nothing to do with excess stomach acid but with the auto-immune system in response to a build up of toxins and an overabundance of Candida and harmful gut bacteria all of which are exacerbated by severe chronic stress. When such inflammatory auto-immune responses attack the gut lining (as well as the blood-brain barrier) causing inflammation, the GP may well misdiagnose excess stomach acid. The consequences in someone with an already too alkaline gut are likely to be terrible; they are quite likely to get progressively worse, with the blame possibly put on their 'autism' rather than the treatment.

Treating Exposure Anxiety and the fueling factor of information-processing problems via physiology requires a specialist who has studied the impact of nutrition on health in the field of autism and also understands the relationship between metabolic disorders and neurotransmitter imbalance underlying involuntary behaviours. This is an additional qualification to medicine which takes many years. The GP who has often spent a week studying the effect of nutrition on health in his or her six years of studying medicine is unqualified to counsel parents about the impact of such treatments, and those psychiatrists aware of the effects of neurotransmitter inbalance on involuntary behaviours may have little understanding or respect for the need to balance such treatments with a nutritional approach. Many, instead of admitting their own lack of knowledge in such a specialized area, may actively discourage parents from seeking out trained doctors with these additional qualifications. Only a handful with such balanced qualifications exist in the field, but exist they do.

Knowledgeable practitioners can be found on the DAN list of ARI (Autism Research International) found at *www.donnawilliams.net*. There is also a site for free advice that can be found worldwide at *www.autismmanagement.com*.

Exposure Anxiety and language

The jarring sound of one's voice

It is a well known stereotype that many people with autism do not speak. In fact, the percentage of those who do not make speech sounds at all is very small. Those labelled non-verbal sometimes still sing, hum, chatter under their breath to themselves, whisper at their own reflection, use the occasional verbal string from the TV or have a handful of pragmatic words such as 'car', 'juice', 'home' and many non-verbal children do later develop some communicative ability. A large percentage of people with autism are echolalic and there are two forms of this, immediate and delayed echolalia. In the case of immediate echolalia, the person parrots back (often to themselves) words just heard. In the case of delayed echolalia, words heard previously come up later, often in specific situations which don't always make interpretive sense to others even though the theme might be very fitting with the tone or situational context of the original phrase. Reports of the number of people with autism who are echolalic differ; some say about a third of people with autism are echolalic.

Echolalic children often go on to speak interactively with meaning and purpose, though many remain verbal but not functionally verbal because the nature of how they use language is either not understood by the environment or not used with apparent communicative intent. Functionally non-verbal children with autism, though less easily assessed, are likely to be as intelligent as those who are verbal. Often a child who has publicly demonstrated no verbal or reading skills will still find out how to disassemble a complex object, work a video recorder, find a way to escape a seemingly escape-proof room. In spite of such intelligence, functionally non-verbal children often don't learn from their directly-confrontational environments to sign or indicate in a directly-confrontational way their social–emotional needs other than by pulling someone over to what they want them to get (can't do it for self, as self, by self when before others).

I loved the sound of my own voice but there was no such thing as my first words or, if so, not until I was about nine. At two and a half I didn't respond to language. At this same time I was heard to be chattering to myself in the voices of my grandparents, regurgitating a two-hour long conversation between them in the voices used. I remember being three, four, five and still not responding to people with please, thank you, yes or no. When addressed directly, they got nothing. Yet I sang all the time and I had, by the age of five, a huge repertoire of television advertisements and jingles. By the age of seven this had expanded to copied sentences that fitted certain patterns. I still wouldn't call any teacher by name, nor call my parents Mum or Dad. I could, however, chant with the class, the day of the week, the date and the good morning Miss so and so. If I wanted something, I just took it or I went without. I couldn't ask for the toilet, but I learned to suck the ink from my pen and make a spectacle of myself, which always resulted in being sent to wash my mouth, always with supervision, since I'd been found AWOL too many times.

By the age of nine I began to use my own words, 'foosh' for cat, 'degoitz' for Exposure Anxiety, 'whoodely' for the sound of air moving inside glass goblets as I ran my hand about inside them. I had names for fruit and food I liked and stated these out loud upon seeing them like I was addressing a friend. At school, though, functional verbal communication was near impossible with my teachers and, because my use of language wasn't well understood, I was treated mostly as uncooperative and a behaviour problem until I was about eleven. Those who spent much time with me found the language I had either underused or overused, self-directed and without apparent meaning or purpose, and annoying and disruptive.

Most of what I experienced as me speaking was done through touch and through my eyes. I dialogued all the time with my reflection but rarely spoke a word out loud. My dreams are mostly still like this and when I have dropped things heavy enough to lose a fingernail, I still do not scream nor do I often make sound when I cry. All my language is learned, and that which comes spontaneously, connects spontaneously, is fluent and passionate and mostly non-verbal.

I found it great to hear the sound of singing coming from me even if it was in the voices in which I'd originally heard the song. To hear my jingles, my advertisements, other people's phrases, I loved. To speak my repertoire of my own word-phrases I had no problem. But to hear myself sell out and speak in the language of the external world with intention to connect and with interpretive meaning capable of being understood, this jarred me like a slap in the face. It remained extremely hard to use the language of the external world in a non-stored way and to be simultaneously able to understand myself with meaning. I became so quickly meaning deaf to my own words that the length of time speaking and what topic I was on quickly trailed off into self-entertainment. This was certainly made worse by the fact that, like hearing your voice played on a cassette player, Exposure Anxiety could not bear the self-feedback of my own attempts at interpersonal directly-confrontational social communication. The language would become increasingly obscure, more reliant on characterization as non-me, or peter away to a barely audible mumble addressed at my shoes as I wandered about. Conventional speech therapists have sometimes heightened this excruciating self-consciousness and its crippling effects because they do not understand the mechanics of Exposure Anxiety.

Hearing one's words with meaning

Not only did the ability to process my own speech drop out after a few sentences, but this probably, ironically, made it possible to continue speaking. This was a catch twenty-two. Becoming meaning deaf to yourself means you are working 'deaf' to what you are doing and it rips confidence away completely. Still today, when I do public speaking, the meaning drops out fairly early and I just keep on speaking knowing that I know my topic and could ramble it out in my sleep. I sometimes check with the audience that I'm still making sense but that's all. To stop is to allow Exposure Anxiety to win. And once my own voice sounds like something incomprehensible coming out of my mouth, Exposure Anxiety decreases, for it progressively has no idea what is being disclosed and what there is to 'protect me from saying'. As a public speaker, it is easy to tell myself I am simply speaking out loud to myself and, if people choose to listen, that's their business.

Being complimented is still intensely difficult because Exposure Anxiety rages up within me. Being asked to repeat something is extremely difficult because I often can't remember what I have said, only reiterate the sound forms I just made which happen to be words. As Exposure Anxiety catches up through the repetition, it awakens and that is uncomfortable. After a talk, it surges at me as it begins to process the backlog of what I have said, raging at me emotionally, sticking me emotionally with pins for certain revealing quirky individuality or being too personal, too passionate, too expressive. It prefers whitewashed pure information devoid of self and given in response to a prompt, so it was never mine or me in the first place. During breaks I'm fine if asked frequently asked questions, but spoken to personally and I freeze up, jarred by my own clumsiness which is compounded by the isolation and inability to show easily the person inside.

Exposure Anxiety and the impact on receptive speech

Receptive speech problems are not compounded by Exposure Anxiety alone. Visual–perceptual problems will mean that linking words with visual images may not happen, and it is important to label everything around the house so that words are immediately linked with the experience it goes with. Extreme chronic stress contributes to deficiencies in essential nutrients, especially B group vitamins lost due to leaky gut and will cause severe information-processing delay, so that meaning drops out of speech continually, leaving it as either entertaining patterns of sound or an invasive assault of meaningless noise. Speaking in song and keeping words visual and concrete through mime signing or speaking via objects can be important strategies not only in making language less directly-confrontational and more user friendly, but in helping people 'stay in there longer'. Speaking at a reasonable pace with space breaks and always leaving the listener when they are still wanting more are good strategies both for building receptive language skills and promoting language as less invasive and more user friendly to people with Exposure Anxiety and information-processing problems. Be surreal, be silly with words, play as though for your own benefit, model the impression that words are about having a buzz for one's own sake. When one is relaxed with language, it has a far better chance to begin to come out without trying, if only from self to self.

Speaking in the third person

When someone with Exposure Anxiety refers to him or herself as the externalized 'you', and becomes forced to internalize the expression as 'I', this can take one of several routes. The best possible one is that the person will comply in using 'I', but will reinterpret the 'I' as 'you' internally in order to stop the blocking of all that follows, provoked by being forced into self-consciousness and personal responsibility for the expression. The next best possibility is that the person will shift to a characterization so the 'I' is no longer about him but he can, through the characterization, continue to speak. Although this depersonalization involves an emotional removal from the communication which is unfortunate, it is better than nothing. Another possibility is that the person will drop pronouns altogether and simply begin on the topic, devoid of who it's about or who it's addressed to. When I was twelve and began to speak in a non-stored way, this was all I was capable of doing. When I began to add pronouns it was in the form of 'you' or 'a person' and later 'one'. The person may avoid all pronouns, perhaps even conversation, with the person correcting them. He may, however, continue with others who seem to respect the degree of effort involved in communicating as best as possible in the grip of Exposure Anxiety and who do not stop or seek to correct. Another possibility is that the person may shift one step to the side, no longer using the 'you' which drew attention, nor using the wished for 'I', but now using the third person; his or her own name, 'she' or 'he' or the plural generic of 'they'. Or he may stay with the singular but move to the generic of 'a person' or the formal 'one'.

Psychologists have spent too much time judging the cognition of children on the basis of their apparent inability to 'learn' or 'understand' the 'proper' use of pronouns. Speech therapists and teachers have then been encouraged to force self-consciousness and raise Exposure Anxiety in constant reminder and prompting regarding this 'proper' use. When someone with Exposure Anxiety uses her name instead of 'I', she is feeling herself one step to the side of the interaction. When she refers to herself as 'you', she is looking at the externalized self and reassuring herself of the social–emotional reality that this is not felt as the internal self, thereby allowing Exposure Anxiety to stay off guard. Just because someone is compelled to use the second person 'you', the third person of their name, 'she', 'he', 'they', the depersonalized 'a person' or 'one', does not mean that he or she doesn't know that when you say 'I', you mean yourself, and that other people use 'she', 'he', 'they', 'you' or 'I' in a different way.

A person with Exposure Anxiety may well be compelled not to acknowledge the use of the invasive 'you' when being asked for something because the response denotes an emotional acceptance of directly-confrontational self-in-relation-to-other interpersonal connection. Yet you can ask the same person, 'would Ms Williams please pass the sauce' and you'll likely get your request met.

Why nobody has any names

Forget the politeness. Politeness is a luxury well beyond the daily persistent struggle with pure communication ability when living with Exposure Anxiety. Struggling with the crippling self-protection instincts of Exposure Anxiety in order to communicate is like climbing a steep hill just to say the simplest personal thing, straight out, as yourself in your own voice. Insistence on the condescension and humility of politeness in someone struggling with crippling self-protection instincts can seem as if the environment is rubbing salt into the wound – highly disrespectful and unappreciative on the part of the environment. Getting the T word (thank you), the P word (please) and the M word (Mum) out of me was a major challenge. I was nine. It was by then 1972 and behaviour modification was becoming fashionable. For about two years my mother went to war with me with this kind of stuff and never had we seen such disturbed behaviour surface in response.

Making me say 'please' or 'thank you' at first got avoidance of the topic. Later it got compliance but beneath the compliance a seething rage which broke out as soon as the environment was off guard. People seemed always to find my violent outbursts to be unprovoked. Exposure Anxiety often does not respond immediately. There is simply too much waiting and watching going on. When the heat is off the rage, no longer intimidated, explodes. In my case this meant scowling, punching and slapping myself as a means of paying back the environment (nothing so robs it of control as attacking yourself). It meant holding my breath secretly, vomiting secretly, cutting myself in paying the environment back for such 'invasion' and 'defeat'. It meant eating bad food and drink to pay it back, biting myself to pay it back, refusing to use the toilet to pay it back and mostly giving up public expression, apparent volition and any act of reliance, interest or need.

When I said 'thank you' or 'please' I would only do so to the prompt. I could not dare sell out Exposure Anxiety in simply giving these words 'for free' for to do so would have made me the direct object of my own attack and deprivation. Rather than this being experienced as empowering and caused by the environment, it would have felt like involuntary and uncontrollable punishments. Given the imprisonment I already felt, I could never bear this feeling on top of everything else and I always fought to avoid being the victim of it. I learnt this very young. Extreme adrenaline highs went hand in hand with severe reactive hypoglycemia caused by food intolerance when I was only about three or four and these had me attack myself in states of sensory flooding up to six times a day. By the time I was nine, I had learned what it was to be terrified of 'it'; my body was not my friend and I had best do as I was told, learn to outrun and outfox it or blame the environment. Self-abuse with the intent of hurting or controlling the environment doesn't feel like abuse emotionally. It feels as if your body is merely a palette and the abuse the paints.

Once my mother had 'succeeded' in getting compliance in my saying 'thank you' or 'please' in response to prompt, she went further, requesting she be given a name. At first I went into avoidance but she was the most wilful human being I've ever known and certainly my match, plus she had size and strength. In the grip of Exposure Anxiety I could go without everything, anything. In this state I was the most self-contained, stubborn, proud, defiant child I knew. Still, if I didn't reply to being called by my name, she could use that as the justification to come after me and force me under extreme force to say 'Yes Mum'. Her own challenges made her a terrifying and formidable opponent. When I was nine her control over me became an object of far greater terror than my own Exposure Anxiety and she got her compliance and I got my despair and 'humiliation'. I became progressively robotic. I do not see such 'victory' in attaining compliance as proof that the conventional behaviour modification techniques 'work'.

Exposure Anxiety had never been defeated, ever. I was like a god and I had been forced to my knees and made to speak not just a name, but a title which denoted I was not my own parent, not in my own world, and whatever I felt about her, she was not irrelevant. I was made to use a word that I knew carried a connection between her as my mother and me as her daughter. It meant she was insisting Exposure Anxiety step down from its throne and recognize it was not the parent, she was; it did not have the primary relationship with me, she did. My entire cognition and function-ing was based on those structures. To destroy them had the felt potential to destroy 'self'. It could have been anyone who did this to me – an aunt, a grandparent, a father, a brother. It just happened that, as my mother, she was the only one driven enough, tough enough and bloody minded enough to go to the extremes where she could break a wild horse. But a broken horse, whilst it is more manageable, is not necessarily 'improved'. Later, when my depression had taken me to the point I could not cry or express personal emotion, she did this again. The world can view this as they wish, but she paved the way for so much else. Only by knowing one's greatest defeat does everything less become suddenly so much easier.

I began to call her by name occasionally and by my own volition. It was maybe only a few times a year but I called her by her first name, not by 'Mum' and with it my father got a name too, a made up one, but a name nonetheless. She was given the name of 'the world'; the name she went by. My father, who had relied on an indirectly-confrontational approach, had never been called Dad but had always been given a name in my own language. I called him 'Jackie Paper', from the song 'Puff the Magic Dragon'. I did finally call my father 'Dad' in the two weeks he had left to live. When I first heard the word in my own ears, it jolted me terribly.

This contrast taught me that my mother's force was not the only way. Getting me to use or acknowledge names could have been achieved using reverse psychology or a playful insistence on formal names and titles, on made up names or on something elaborate and surreal. By contrast, using an everyday name would have not felt like such a desired 'joining', espe-cially if it were playfully insisted I not use this. I remember such a response in my adult years at university. A visiting professor insisted on being called by her surname only. I could not. I called her nothing, but I have to admit that, inside, I called her by her first name, familiar and personal, yet in defiance of the expected this became what would have been socially distancing and, therefore, 'safe'.

Until recently many people still got from me their full name: first name and surname. When I reached thirty, instead of finding that an achievement, I saw it as the impact of Exposure Anxiety in forcing me to contort desire to express acknowledgement and connection from the personal into the distant and formal. I retaliated against it, claiming my own life and expression. Sometimes this meant nobody got any name. Sometimes I used only pronouns. Sometimes I used their name but it was wooden and forced in spite, or perhaps to spite Exposure Anxiety within. Later, as I persisted, and especially if I stirred Exposure Anxiety about its great power and high and mighty pride, then it defied me, freeing me up and I could more easily use my friend's name. But should anything have hurt my feelings or provoked too much of a sense of exposure, I shifted, temporarily right back to the formal and one of the first things to go communicatively was the use of names. The love of those people and connection to them, in spite of this, had and always does remain. Sometimes I could acknowledge that in my own world, sometimes not until Exposure Anxiety was off guard. Then I was often on my own, yet in my own world, my connection to others was freed and it was whole.

The pragmatic versus the personal

Words for car parts, food products, commands relating to leaving or going home are more likely to come out than expressions of connection. The pragmatic is not self-exposing and this means that 'juice', 'car', 'video' may be safe realms of communication. I was unable to ask for a drink, a coat, the toilet, but I could use stored phrases (however obscure to others), made-up words, buzz patterns, and I could address objects either about themselves or about other topics going on for me.

Having to operate in an indirectly-confrontational way is very akin in some ways to the experience of a Buddhist lifestyle and can be an adventure rather than a burden. Zen Buddhism takes the focus off other and is about learning how to 'be' as an inspiration to those around you, which is one of the strongest mainstream examples of indirectly-confrontational 'giving' to those around us through 'giving' to ourselves. To understand this pattern of experience, of thinking and being, one does not have to embrace Buddhism as a religion, but it may have something to teach those who live with people with Exposure Anxiety about how to live without provoking self-protection mechanisms.

A world of things without people

When people try actively to join someone through objects, the object is no longer an object, but a bridge. The person with Exposure Anxiety may well, in 'self-protection', burn it. When we truly join socially and emotion-ally with *ourselves* through the object, the person with Exposure Anxiety does not experience this communication as an invasion nor the use of the object as a bridge. This leaves the learning available, untainted, unthreatening to the inner over-protective 'parent' of Exposure Anxiety. The world of things is a safe, controllable realm in which the person can work with and modulate his or her behaviour naturally in relation to the strings being pulled by Exposure Anxiety.

Parents of children with autism-spectrum conditions are put in a very different position at home to other parents. So much that can be taken for granted in other homes cannot in the home of children on the spectrum. Social judgement adds to this alienation. This social isolation turns many parents against their own instincts for what works, and this is often counter to the textbook theories of non-autistic psychologists and so called 'experts'. And the impact of social judgement and 'expert opinion', on already strained family relationships and social isolation can mean that parents end up fighting each other instead of working as a team.

The topic without the person

Speaking on the topic devoid of the person it is about, even devoid of the attachment to self, and devoid of overt conscious acknowledgement of whose attention the communication is intended for, sounds like a very difficult labyrinth to navigate and it is. When I was about twelve, this was how I made the transition from purely stored speech into relatively expres-sive personal communication. I had, around this time, two forms of inter-pretive non-stored communication, beyond those of talking in theme or via TV advertisement. One of these was the use of litanies. These were long lists of the events of the day, as they happened, quite like a news report done from self, to self, but projected outwards in response to a question such as 'How was your day?' The other was that of addressing my shoes or a corner of the window or whatever I could wander my attention onto in order to keep the flow going. A question asking why people reacted how they did and expressing how it made me feel, or asking advice about resolving such feelings, might sound like 'When a person, such a feeling that, inside, so annoying, then wonders why and…'

This, among other forms of communication I used, was called 'waffling' and was generally not listened to, which is just as well or I'd not have progressed to such expressive and personal communication, however impossible it was to understand. Many speech therapists and teachers, rather than taking the heat off by appearing not to be listening in order that communication can flow more easily are instinctively more likely, instead, to focus strongly on the person speaking, even prompting them to clarify whom they are addressing or whom the communication is about. Even if they get the person to respond to the prompting, they may not realize their actions have burned a bridge here and the person with Exposure Anxiety may become progressively more inhibited in initiating interpersonal communication on future occasions.

Getting tied in knots and the impact on trying again

Lack of confidence in the ability to be understood can be very inhibiting and this means parents, carers and professionals want to encourage and praise the person with Exposure Anxiety. Yet, if the very self-consciousness provoked by being the object of focus, attention or sensed 'expectation' is the source of becoming communicatively tied up in knots, then the form of encouragement needs to be extremely indirectly-confrontational in order not to make the problem worse. If someone is addressing the window or their shoes and become tongue tied because of their own Exposure Anxiety, then the environment can help in an indirectly-confrontational way. The environment themselves can respond to their own shoes, to the fingernail they are filing, to the ring they are twiddling, reassurances such as 'There's all the time in the world', 'Yes, it is very difficult when a person…'; and so on, and this makes any sense of 'invasion' far less likely.

Remember that Exposure Anxiety is never so poised as when someone tries something they've never done or succeeded at before. Yet these are the very time the environment feels like making a song and dance and drawing a lot of directly-confrontational attention to the efforts of the person with Exposure Anxiety. Some people with Exposure Anxiety have learned social responses to praise and encouragement. They know that 'a person is supposed to enjoy praise and encouragement'. They watch TV, many of them pick up behavioural patterns of others and know what is considered 'normal' or 'the right response'. Some are driven to emulate these responses. Some are not. I expect that in the context of Exposure Anxiety this might depend on whether the environment was waiting and wishing for such emulation. Mine was not. In fact it was quite the opposite. I remember being told quite often to stop repeating everything and, my older brother was in absolute despair at times that I refused to be a person in my own right in relation to him but was so utterly compelled to use him as something to merge into. Around a third of children with 'autism' are thought to be echolalic and some are echopraxic. Perhaps this is a reflection of the response of the environment in triggering or failing to trigger exposure anxiety around this behavioural response.

Just because a child gives you the stored 'correct' response to your praise and encouragement doesn't mean she has processed her own triggered behavioural response. You may simply have pressed A and got the expected B. That doesn't mean she felt B. If you find she spontaneously initiates the same behaviour without prompt the next time and the time after, then praise is unlikely to have been an inhibitor. If, however, you find that with or without her apparent 'pride' in her achievement, she appears to have 'lost interest' in initiating what triggers the praise and attention, you can be fairly certain the apparent 'pride' in her praised achievement is the equivalent of a stored sentence and can't reliably be taken as being 'from her'. It may be better in future to save the praise or express it in the third person to an object, picking up your favourite toy and telling it how you feel.

Why speaking without self can be as difficult as being 'non-verbal'

Being able to speak but subject to the involuntary avoidance, diversion and retaliation responses of Exposure Anxiety is not the great blessing so many parents of so-called 'non-verbal' people might imagine. There are parents of people who cannot control their own speech or whose speech is difficult to interpret, solely self-directed or pure characterization. For many of these people, they wait, not for language, but for self within language or social–emotional connection through language. For some parents, it is harder to pass their children off as 'normal' when they do speak than when they don't. If a child doesn't speak, it's up to the imagination what the child might have said. If a child does speak but language is taken as 'bizarre' or 'non-functional', the child is taken to be mentally or emotionally disturbed or, in the case of diversion and retaliation responses in verbal communication, badly behaved, spoilt, or lacking in empathy or consideration for others.

There is a vulnerability in being non-verbal but equally a vulnerability in having difficulty with 'functional speech'. Whilst one may be able to speak, that speech may be unreliable either in the expectation that a reply is possible or in the reliability of that reply as an indication of the person's personal reality. In both cases the person may still be unable to ask for very simple things and many people with verbal language can talk on their special topic, but still not ask for their simplest needs to be met. Many 'non-verbal' people have fewer diversions coming out, so the path is clearer in knowing what they think or feel than some 'verbal' people. You may get no verbal answer to your question, but if, instead, you make statements out loud to yourself whilst viewing peripherally your effect, you may find the response in the muscle tone, eyes or reflex responses.

In childhood, beyond ice-cream it was near impossible to find out verbally what I liked or wanted. Even if you got an answer it was fifty–fifty as to whether it was reliable. Other were left to building up a pattern of my responses and 'knowing' rather than 'asking' what I liked. Either I liked the things that were left for me or introduced through playing hard to get till I took these things, or these were actually what I liked. In either case, the 'fly on the wall' can be extremely observant of what colours, sounds, textures, patterns, objects, places or people someone with communication difficulties has 'taken a shine to'. After that, it may not be a matter of how you find a way for them not to receive but how you find a way to inspire them to find, snatch or take.

In my teens and adult years I was often frozen in my personal communication and governed by my own diversion responses and compulsion to reassure myself of disconnection by relying on 'the right answer' (the expected or stored response). This meant I was very easy to manipulate into appearing to agree with the desires and intentions of others. The Exposure Anxiety response, instead of protecting me, found that making such a stand against doing 'as other' was more exposure provoking than letting me be used and abused by strangers. I could no more save myself from them than I could save myself from my so called 'protector', nor could I tell anybody about things for years later nor ask for help in resolving them any more than had I been 'non-verbal'.

Exposure Anxiety and friendship

Friendships in a directly-confrontational world

Friendships in a directly-confrontational world are difficult for people with Exposure Anxiety. On a simple level, being unable to initiate or avoidant can make you look like too much hard work for most people to bother with. Being constantly diverting can be exhausting to others and make you look uninterested or self-interested. Being caught up in retaliation responses can make you so abrasive that you attract people likely to do the same back for different reasons. This is quite aside from problems of verbal communication, inability to hold simultaneous sense of self and other and difficulty handling directly-confrontational interaction.

Problems with verbal communication can be extreme or subtle and I don't think they are any easier either way. As a young child I coped much better making friendships by being virtually functionally non-verbal. I needed only a handful of words to get by and the fact I had a very full repertoire of songs, advertisements and jingles meant I got by.

My first year in school I noticed other children chatted with each other and I couldn't, but because I could speak and I chattered to myself all the time, at this age I simply stood out as 'a character'. The second year was harder and the third year harder again as children had by then all paired off. By the age of eight, life at school was very lonely, hovering on the outside of circles of children, befriending the occasional new kid who hadn't made friends with anyone yet.

Children lost interest fairly quickly. I got lucky when I made 'friends' with a girl a few years older than me. My big repertoire of swear words and the occasional sentence helped me get by quite well when most of our interaction was through doing, adventuring around the streets, going through rubbish skips, exploring building sites, playing in the phone box and riding trams. Losing this friend plunged me into the reality that at school I might as well have smelled of dog shit. I felt like something thrown social scraps. I spent much of my time wandering and trying to amuse myself and not stand out too much, to others or to myself. I got adopted eventually by 'troubled children', those who didn't speak English and other dregs whom nobody else wanted to be around. I feel I was honoured by such colourful company and a richer person for the diversity than had I been part of the mainstream.

Children with Exposure Anxiety, and especially those with receptive visual and auditory perceptual problems, can be incredibly isolated, with or without verbal language. Being meaning deaf and having severe receptive language-processing problems is frightening because you cannot process a reply to anything you initiate. Such children need social situations involving surrealism, humour and doing. When socializing is about doing, the focus is off the self, the inability to hold simultaneous self and other doesn't always matter and the activity is less directly-confrontational.

I was never allowed to do staff room duty because of my behaviour problems (it's not very easy to trust a meaning-deaf, meaning-blind child with the staff room) but ordering books in the library would have been safe. Being given jobs, especially alongside someone else in a similar position, would have been a good way of experiencing social involvement in an 'incidental' way. Having a movie room to go to during lunch times where children can be together without necessarily having directly-confrontational interaction is a positive idea for socializing for those with Exposure Anxiety. Giving children safe building materials (cardboard boxes and tubes are inexpensive, accessible and recyclable) so they can relate through doing on breaks if they are unable to initiate self-in-relation-to-other conversation or sustained activity gives them a joint focus and incidental involvement with each other. I was sent to school with cards and this helped bring children to me. Later it was stamps. Often it was food. I may have been used but for someone with social communication problems it is simply that someone was interested and that I was able to sustain the involvement because it was through objects, and this is what mattered. At other times it was tree climbing and being king of a big log in the school ground, able to keep everyone off until a group of children were lined up trying in turn to get me off the log, which was great.

Encouraging involvement with those who don't speak the same language means non-verbal or functionally non-verbal language is taken as natural. I remember one child who had a catalogue full of all the things she liked (like a scrapbook made out of the Argos catalogue) and this gathered others. As compensations develop and evolve, the person can appear more able even if, in many ways, they are actually not. This can mean that others are attracted to the Exposure Anxiety rather than the person.

Someone with compulsive characterizations can become the entertainment. Someone who compulsively hides within the expected or 'correct' social response can be exploited if there isn't someone on board who really cares, yet holds back enough to allow such a person experience, freedom and life. Some who are compelled into passivity or provoking others into being responsible for all actions might find they attract heroes and helpers, only to last them aside later or keep them in 'learned dependency'. Some who are compelled to never demonstrate the need for help or any personal wants of their own can find themselves being involuntary counsellors and confidants.

Modelling that getting together with others means going out walking, or bringing food for a cook up, joining in making or building something, showing up with a video to watch, playing cards, or bringing over some photos, a video game, or a collection to show are all good ideas. Having 'doing' to focus on gives a focus and structure to social contact and allows someone with Exposure Anxiety to address the topic, the object, the issue and not clam up in feeling they are either the focus of conversation or expected to initiate it. It also means they have a structure that helps them have an excuse to arrive and leave, which are major problems with Exposure Anxiety in daring these very strong moments of self-consciousness and initiation.

Friendships and sense of self and other

One of the hardest things is getting contacts with people who like to be in their own space, and yet who enjoy being around others. When someone with Exposure Anxiety initiates social contact it can seem they aren't 'interacting', more just 'being'. But 'simply being' is a wonderful way of allowing others to be free to simultaneously 'simply be', with each person enjoying the freedom and lack of self-consciousness and expectation that means. So what if you wonder what the person with Exposure Anxiety thinks of you or whether they enjoy your company. They are there aren't they? They are able to let go in your company and be themselves. Why can't that, alone, be enough of an answer? Do you really need the feedback to be in your face and directly-confrontational? You can get that anywhere, from most of the world. Is it really such a tragedy that you can't get it from the person with Exposure Anxiety as well? There is something wonderful in the feeling of self-ownership and freedom to be without self-consciousness that you are able to get from the experience. We don't all have to be 'normal', usual, to be valued, valuable and equal in our social worth.

The teens and twenties are a very difficult time for many people with Exposure Anxiety. It may be hard to find anyone who can appreciate that their way may have to be indirectly-confrontational and about simply 'being' in a self-in-relation-to-self way whilst in the company of someone else.

Friendships and letting go control

Friendships are about letting go of control. Yet Exposure Anxiety is about fearing the loss of control. The only thing that removes this loss of control is the removal of a self-in-relation-to-other dynamic to interaction. Friendship of a self-in-relation-to-self nature where two or more people entertain themselves or are entertained by something external simultaneously, whether that's a film, going walking, swapping cards, trampolining, gardening, swimming…is still valid as friendship.

The main problem is the self-expectation and social expectation placed upon people with Exposure Anxiety to do 'friendship' in the same way as others. What is so wrong with learning which patterns of relating are more problematic than others in order to organize interaction designed to bring the maximum success more often, and not compound a constant sense of social failure and isolation?

Friendships and being 'seen'

Friendships involve being 'seen' and the avoidance, diversion and retaliation responses of Exposure Anxiety are often far from being 'seen'. But there are realms Exposure Anxiety seems to touch less than others in many people. For some people it's art, some it's music, some it's creative movement, gymnastics or acrobatics, running, swimming, trampolining or horse riding. For some it's singing, computers or assisted or independent typing.

It's important to model that friendships can be indirectly-confrontational, revolving around doing, focused on the object/issue and not the person, but it can also be a good idea to engage user-friendly realms of interest least controlled by Exposure Anxiety responses. Remember modelling is not about what the person with Exposure Anxiety is doing, it is about what you, as the environment, are modelling as being worthwhile for your own benefit.

Exposure Anxiety and internal friendships

For all of us, there is the internal and the external world. All that we are in the external world is all that we actually are seen to be doing. Yet our external world may show little communication and involvement whilst our internal world may be full of the 'life in theory'. This is the life we might have lived had we not been cripplingly shy, strangled by obsessive compulsive responses, tongue tied, frozen or caught up in retaliation responses from the very things we seek to connect with, diversions away from our greatest desires, the things which most move us. Many people with autism who have severe Exposure Anxiety have been able to type about their inner realities. Whilst they have acknowledged these dialogues were not heard, these connections not seen on the outside, many such writers have expressed humour, passion, deep empathy, even been in love, when on the outside nothing of the kind was ever seen or thought possible. Alex in the book, *Like Colour to the Blind* was one such character. But I have since met many others, from a girl as young as seven to a man my own age in his thirties, all able to type both with assistance (can't do it as myself, by myself, for myself) and, when they can dare, independently.

It is important to acknowledge that there is a division in society between those who assume that if it existed, surely we'd see it on the surface, and those who know both in themselves and others that this simply isn't true of personal realities. Most of us are not the same on the outside as we are on the inside. Some of us are connected but have trouble showing who is inside. Some of us are utterly disconnected, afraid of going near who is on the inside, finding it a stranger. Some of us have a watered-down version of the inner self that comes out and some of us have an exaggerated version making a bigger impression than who is actually in there. Exposure Anxiety is a master of disownership. Ironically, this is often at the expense of the person being excused of all expectations. Here, the winner is Exposure Anxiety, who now possessively holds the child nobody is looking for. Unchallenged, we no longer see Exposure Anxiety responses in action and the twenty-five-year-old continues to stare into space as his nappy is changed and he is spoon fed. But the same clearly 'helpless' twenty-five-year-old may still have the dexterity to escape a locked room, to do an intricate self-hypnotic finger pattern. There are choices in how we make sense of what we cannot understand according to our own reality. The same twenty-five-year-old may well watch the world like a 'fly on the wall'. He may well play out internally patterns of interaction of the person he might have been had he not been constrained by his own Exposure Anxiety responses – and all you may see is a twenty-five-year-old spoon fed in nappies.

I often had my quiet days or weeks, even months. Their intensity differed. Sometimes I was salvageable, sometimes not. At the age of twelve I had been coping with more than I could handle and I went inside myself for about six months. I wouldn't wash (and remember eventually getting into the bath in my clothes). I slept in my clothes. I ate only to prompt. I stopped speaking except to repeat words back occasionally as if in a dream. I stared blankly into space in a deep state of self-hypnosis. I felt miles away from my own voice and from the same me who at other times had been alive and emotionally expressive, in my own world but showing on the outside. I spent hours sitting on the side of my bed lost in the pattern of the wallpaper. One visitor to the house remembers finding me in the same spot, in the dark, where I'd sat all day. I'd been into this deep still inner space before but never for so long and I know it got everyone motivated to prompt me. Fortunately, I got sent away in that state and the rules changed. Instead of staying in, I turned back out and eventually returned home. But I do know this state of giving up and disowning all connection with the external self.

There are others who find freedom in portraying who they might have been had they been free, convinced the life they are having is not direct expression but performance of who they might have been able to be had they not had Exposure Anxiety. It is the most elaborate and functional display I have ever seen, but I have seen it in those who have been masters of mimicry, memorization of pattern and characterization. It takes one to know one and I'm so glad nobody let me hold them to ransom beyond a few months.

Exposure Anxiety and invisible friends

There has often been the stereotype that people with autism lack imagination. There is, however, a difference between being limited in the capacity to think beyond self or the here and now, and lacking imagination. Nor is inability to socially invite elaboration the same as lacking imagination.

I have seen wonderful art by people with autism, seen displays of humour, non-verbal, typed and spoken, however surreal, self-directed and 'autistic' in nature. I have seen amazing surreal and creative uses of objects used in experiences of 'art', 'music', 'construction' and kinesthetic play in spite of labelling such as 'inappropriate use of objects' by non-autistic psychologists seeking to assess levels of 'abnormality' and 'disability'. I have also worked with children and adults, non-verbal and verbal, who have displayed interaction either with their reflection as another person or playing or dialoguing with someone 'invisible'. This doesn't mean they actually see or hear them.

An imagined stored dialogue of 'what I say' and 'what he says' and then 'what I say back' does not qualify as schizophrenia. When I looked in the mirror, I saw another girl. I could not consciously hold several ideas in my head simultaneously such as that this was glass, and reflection on glass, and that this related to me and to the reflection at the same time and that this meant something in terms of whether or not this was another girl. A toddler with the same level of social–emotional development and information-processing capacity registers as a similar object. When I imagined my reflection was older than me, this was natural. If we have no idea the reflection is self or how similar or different we, ourselves, might be, how could it be otherwise?

Many adults have written about their invisible friends or characterizations, their internal dialogue with parts of themselves. Whilst this may put off those who might otherwise make friends with such a person, dialogue or interaction in one's own world, however externalized, can be one of the only areas of social interaction this person experiences within the confines of Exposure Anxiety. However presentable you wish people to be, the fact this type of dialogue is experienced without social stress, unlike other social contact, means you are putting pressure on very isolated and highly-stressed people without giving them some way of diffusing their need for safe expression.

My suggestion is there's a middle ground. By modelling that you yourself have an imaginary friend who calls you up on your battery-less mobile phone to dialogue, means that when such dummy mobile phones are left lying about discarded, they might just get used in a similar way. It becomes far more socially accepted to see someone dialoging on a mobile phone than simply nattering out loud to themselves in public where this is associated with being 'mad'. If only we were all so healthy and able to unwind and allow each other the same.

Exposure Anxiety and performing friendships

While growing up the topic of not having any friends was often spoken about, which meant I had to set out to contradict it. I was therefore highly motivated to have the appearance of 'friendships'. It didn't matter who someone was, if I sat with them, they were my friend. If we had the same thing to eat, they were my 'friend'. If we wore the same colours this person was my friend. Though between the ages of nine and thirteen was a very rough patch, at thirteen I became intent on performing friendships. It didn't matter whether I liked someone or not. If they could stand me and I could hang about without being bullied, bashed up or made to go away, these were my friends. I was like a fly to shit. My smile might just have well been painted on but I was passing and nobody could now define me as not having friends. Unfortunately, in leaving home at fifteen in a rollercoaster of 'care in the community' style 'relationships', this same rule applied.

Nobody was watching out for me (I wouldn't have let them anyway) but my own experiences still have something to teach those who are looking out for others with Exposure Anxiety. If you are using the mechanisms of Exposure Anxiety against itself in helping someone with Exposure Anxiety, have plan B. If you have modelled that friendship is the goal and the only route to equality and inclusion at any price, be careful what you are modelling. Some people with autism live much more safely with a sense of value in enjoying their own company than being indiscriminately social for the sake of the symbolism. It may make you proud (or at least not ashamed) and get you off the person's case (how freeing) but it can be dangerous.

Exposure Anxiety and friendships: the realistic possibilities

Friendships, real chosen friendships reflective of the person rather than their Exposure Anxiety responses, are possible but it is important where you look for them. There are some people who, because of their own self-image and insecurities, simply don't work well with people with Exposure Anxiety. Sometimes this is because they try too much to 'rescue', 'help' or 'teach' rather than 'be', or because they are too conscious of other people's opinions or their own self-image. Sometimes the other person is simply unable to see beyond the surface to the individual, too purist in ideas of what someone should be, or believing rigidly that the person with Exposure Anxiety isn't trying hard enough to control themselves and 'act normal'. Sometimes the other person might be so full of self-interest and so opportunistic that he or she has more interest in what they might benefit from out of the other person's Exposure Anxiety than interest in the person beyond the condition. Remember that most such people are not overtly bad and many come in the form of people who might appear overly caring and interested.

Some people can see beyond the Exposure Anxiety to the person and who know how to 'be' without vested interest or 'great cause', without martyrdom or charity. Many more opportunities exist today for people extremely challenged by Exposure Anxiety than did before the internet and email, and many people with severe Exposure Anxiety have been able to explore friendships and connections through technology in spite of the obvious possibility of social dangers. Social dangers are everywhere but it is important to remember that the greatest social danger a person with Exposure Anxiety can face is that of being over-protected in ways which exacerbate their own internal imprisonment and rob them of the quality of life they might otherwise explore and expand upon.

Development programmes for being able to stand the experience of self before others

The use of mirrors is important for many people. Not those forced on people through well meaning directly-confrontational attempts to 'break through', but having a full length one in one's room, one in the bathroom, one in the hall and perhaps one in the lounge. This enables the person to get used to self-consciousness before oneself, then, progressively, when running the risk of being observed, then whilst around others. In my house this built a social instinct in me as a child, and also made it more possible to connect, more difficult to tune out to social contact if only indirectly via the mirrors.

Along similar lines, I was left a tape recorder quite early on which I simply became accustomed to as an object. Later I taught myself through trial and error (I would let no person show or teach me) how to operate one and this became part of the foundation of my enjoyment of the sound of my own voice, especially singing. In recent years there have been talk-back toys on the market that could be just as useful, but remember that if you make a point of demonstrating such a toy in a way which feels clearly for the benefit of the person with Exposure Anxiety, you will likely achieve the opposite to your intention – they won't ever explore or use it.

Drama, music and art are important parts of developing a tolerance to a sense of audience to oneself and before others. I was privileged to have grown up with a compulsive comedian with a continuous repertoire of characterizations. This modelled an ability to explore and use such strategies as a forum for my own expression without realizing I was doing so. This lack of awareness is important because most conventional teaching makes the pupil aware he or she has taken on a skill which will only lead to Exposure Anxiety aborting it. But drama, music and art therapies can be about modelling, they can be done as though for the therapist's own benefit and self-directed or directed at the materials or props rather than directed at the person with Exposure Anxiety. A therapist can use someone else's hand to paint a picture in sand apparently for the therapist's own benefit. Keep in mind that to paint a permanent picture via conventional techniques may be far more difficult to deal with than an impermanent, less conventional activity or media in which there is less of a feeling of giving in to the world and its ways. The therapist can use someone else's hands to play notes on a worktop using a spoon, perform to somebody's foot, making the foot speak back in the voice of a put-on character, play a keyboard by foot.

Other techniques include a throwing box into which to dare to throw breakables, jumping from heights into the depths of the diving pool, a shouting room, stomping sessions, rough and tumble play; whatever promotes the safe letting go of control for one's own benefit. Because such activities have no apparent 'use', this in itself reduces self-consciousness, allowing expression to come out which can, incidentally, happen to 'fall out', at which point the audience should not increase self-consciousness. If someone feels jolted by their own sudden self-consciousness in the face of self-expression, the therapist can 'cover' for this with sudden distracting surrealism or characterization. This takes the focus off, allowing the person to continue without having to go into 'disconnection rituals'.

Counselling, isolation and inner world disputes

What are you to do if someone has a falling out with the beaded curtain which has lost part of its symmetry or colour run and is no longer who it was? Or if the computer has gone ahead and blown itself up and refuses to speak to the person who used to be its friend? What are you to do when someone is angry at the reflection for not disclosing the secret of how to get into the mirror? What do you do when an internal character has developed a phobia or obsessional about something and refuses to allow the self to take any action counter to this without 'paying them back' for breaking some internal 'pact' between 'friends'? Where there is no verbal or typed communication, you simply have to guess. It is how you guess.

The 'reaching in', 'invasive' action of asking questions of someone with Exposure Anxiety is the most likely way to trigger avoidance, diversion or retaliation communications. The best way forward is simply to make statements out loud to yourself without focusing directly on the person with Exposure Anxiety. Use your peripheral vision to view their response, the glint in an eye, the swinging of a foot, the stifled smile about to break out in having been 'discovered'. But don't double check whether you are right; you'll be burning your own bridges.

You can use a magic book, wandering around and reading out loud to yourself, a story about something similar happening to someone else. Of course the book can be a note pad with blank pages, it doesn't matter as long as you are wandering about reading it very quietly to yourself. (I say quietly because nothing so inspires a control freak to tune in as a private self-directed low volume.) There are several parts to such a story. The 'mystery' involves the confusion of the environment. The 'theory' involves the hypothesis of what was going on. 'The dilemma' is about feelings. The attempts to deal with the problem via strategy A, B or C is about ideas put into action. The resolution of the dilemma and the realization that arose as a result of the resolution are the toning down of the story. A glimpse at how this dilemma didn't pose a problem the next time lays the foundations for this story carrying over into repetitions of the same circumstance. Of course, if you are too close to home Exposure Anxiety responses may drive the person to make you shut up. It's important not to make this an issue of control over the person with Exposure Anxiety but to make it clear they are invading you whilst you were doing something *for yourself.*

When you haven't been invited, reminding them you'll be with them in a moment should be threat of punishment enough for many people with Exposure Anxiety. However much the diversion or retaliation responses of people with Exposure Anxiety are mistaken for 'seeking attention', the promise of getting 'joining', 'social' attention' on the environment's terms is often the last thing they are seeking.

It doesn't matter if you got your social story wrong, it wasn't about 'them', it wasn't for 'them'. It was just a story you found in a magic book which you were reading for yourself, for your own benefit. If they chose to tune in, that was their choice. Life itself is like this. There are things around us that affect us all the time. You can't cushion people from that, nor, perhaps, would you be doing them a service in trying. Hypersensitive people need sensitive desensitization programmes. The environment doesn't have to be the bull at the gate, however caring or charitable the motivations. It is more strategic to know how to dodge the bull in order to get it to a space in which it can be free, expressive, whole and comfortable.

CHAPTER 5

Environment
Exposure Anxiety at home

Who am I living with?

With stored responses and characterizations it can be hard to know whom
you are living with. The same is true where one parent triggers Exposure
Anxiety and the other is singled out as the person's 'special person' or the
'facilitator' through whom the person expresses themselves. The same is
true where there is no verbal language in relation to others but there is
self-directed chatter at the mirror. The person with Exposure Anxiety is an
enigma and the broader the spectrum of compensations and adaptations,
the more of an enigma such a person is. Imagine for a moment how difficult it is in such a labyrinth for the person himself to know who he is. One
person triggers Exposure Anxiety, another has Exposure Anxiety side with
her, co-opting her involvement. One person triggers freezing and compliance, creating a secondary, even more hidden trap, another person triggers
constant diversion into characterizations. Inside, the person with Exposure
Anxiety may feel whole, well adjusted and connected, but in social contact
may experience himself as disconnected, performing, passive, frozen,
retaliative, avoidance and constantly distracted.

It took me a long time to have any idea which 'me' was me. This was
made harder by the fact that everybody identified 'me' as someone different. At school I was labelled disturbed and usually handled with extremely
contrasting authoritative discipline, being tuned out (constructive) or

excluded from activities (made me want inclusion more strongly, which was a useful thing) or treated like a dangerous substance with a sign saying 'handle with caution'.

Whilst I felt my father saw through my mechanics to the person inside, I felt my mother struggled to know me beyond her focus on the appearance of my behaviour, and she was fixated on the desire for me to learn to 'act normal'. There were times when I felt I had become a science experiment. My behaviour, my Exposure Anxiety and sensory– perceptual issues seemed to become the object of insightful attempts to ease and expand my world, many of which worked. During this time, the cross between my mother's frustration and her efforts made me feel both understood and blamed for my own condition and this was important in my experiencing that someone thought there was a 'me' beyond my involuntary mechanisms, albeit an imagined one, fitting with her idea of who was in there. The impression I got of myself through her was that I was both damaged yet whole though, through not fighting hard enough, I 'chose' to be limited in the consistent expression of this wholeness within the external world. My father both understood my Exposure Anxiety and saw me as a whole child, assuming my humour, my creativity, my girl-ness, my need for play and adventure. I resonated with his assumptions but, most of all, through his absolute surrealism, wild stupidity and daring, he led the way to my being openly expressive and full of character in spite of the restrictions of Exposure Anxiety.

Exposure Anxiety and why it's not rejection

In some families, both parents have a shared plan, and however much their approaches are uniquely their own, each is compatible with the other. There are some families, however, where the approaches are not in sync and a 'good cop', 'bad cop' dynamic develops. On one side of the family you may have the 'facilitator' (sometimes possessively co-opted by Exposure Anxiety on the basis of 'can't do it for myself', 'by myself' or 'as myself' mechanics). On the other side you may have the perceived 'enemy' (perceived as the one 'waiting', 'wanting', 'watching', 'hoping', ever ready to pounce and expand upon the first hint of expression or acknowledgement and, therefore the most likely recipient of involuntary avoidance, diversion and retaliation responses). However much the 'enemy' is loved (and the defensive response of Exposure Anxiety does not internally necessarily exclude the possibility of love, nor compliance with 'the enemy'), it is this role that is most experienced by the parent as 'rejection'. This is especially so if the other parent takes the role of 'special person', or the 'facilitator'.

Exposure Anxiety responses can look like distance, lack of interest or rejection, but they are not. The person may be so hounded by their Exposure Anxiety, so beaten to the starting line by it, that the person themselves is rarely seen externally. But many people with severe Exposure Anxiety have still expressed verbally or through typing that they are distressed that others may not know they are like or loved.

Exposure Anxiety and proof of 'getting through'

If you are looking for proof with someone with Exposure Anxiety, you might be shooting yourself in the foot. Proof is about jolting conscious awareness. Proof is about a feeling of being watched, monitored, 'invaded'. The most likely response to a need for proof is avoidance, diversion, retaliation responses or empty compliance, essentially handing a copy of 'you-ness' back to you. If you want proof with someone with Exposure Anxiety, learn to 'be' as though for your own benefit. Stop 'trying' all the time, and the person with Exposure Anxiety might continue with his or her self-dialogue a little more 'out loud' because 'the heat is off'.

If you have a question, remember questions trigger a sense of self-consciousness, being exposed and 'on the spot'. With Exposure Anxiety this often makes the answer unreliable and either an attempt to get rid of the questioner or a case of giving what has been stored as the 'right' answer, rather than their own. Making a statement out loud to yourself whilst not focusing visually on the person your statement is set to trigger should trigger body movements, the glint in an eye, the hint of a smile or a twitch. Just watch your body language doesn't look focused on them and eagerly set to pounce. You can later learn to read these as you build up a vocabulary of the language of behaviour. It's OK to have only half the answers to a mystery. Chill out and you will often get far more that is real and from self than your eagerness may get by force.

The tragedy of 'positive' reinforcement

Carers want to feel they are making a difference. They are told that positive reinforcement will help make that difference. But with Exposure Anxiety, the more you expect, want or promote something, the more the self-protection response says, 'Don't do that again, that triggers the external world into invasive attempts to connect'. You know when praise works because it really does work. You know when it doesn't when your job as carer becomes harder and harder. So what can you do if your ability to praise or give attention makes you feel more and more impotent to help?

Well, positive reinforcement doesn't have to be directly-confrontational. It doesn't have to jolt conscious awareness of one's own actions, expression or achievement. Remember, many non-autistic people play down their abilities tremendously just to avoid being the focus of attention, even some who, at other times, command attention strictly on their terms and when they want it. If someone loves coloured lights, tinkling sounds, making showers of confetti out of the toilet paper, loves being swung, you have your positive reinforcement. You don't have to say why you've suddenly launched into this 'reward mode', the person with Exposure Anxiety will have mapped that they had just done X, Y, or Z and it was immediately followed by having a buzz. If, on the other hand, you actually say, 'Good for you Max, you did Z, wow, that deserves a big spin', then sure Max feels good about getting the swing, but simultaneously Exposure Anxiety is also triggered, raging and competing against Max's enjoyment of his reward. To Exposure Anxiety it is as though his very enjoyment is like salt on the wound named 'defeat in being conquered by an invader'. Sure, he gets the reward, but when the buzz has settled, his rage may demand he disintegrates the feeling of connection. He may well follow the reward by kicking you, destroying something to distance you or in hurtful payback to himself.

I always suggest that if praise is verbal with someone with Exposure Anxiety that it not be given in the immediate context of the action or expression you seek to reinforce. If it is, you may find the drive to initiate such an action next time will be met with internal anticipation of the impending 'invasion' you know as praise. I also suggest it be given about the topic rather than focused on the person, such as 'Wow, it's great when the shoes get themselves done up' or told in a quick made up story in 'the invisible book'.

Just because someone smiles, this doesn't mean they are enjoying the praise. It can be that they know they are meant to enjoy it, that this is the 'correct' response. It can be that they've learned the smile means you leave them be much earlier than if they give no response. It might be they really do enjoy it, but that it also triggers Exposure Anxiety, each competing with the other in a tide and undercurrent shifting relationship. You know when it is really a felt smile when the person enjoys and initiates the praised activity of their own accord next time, interested in its expansion for hope of further being praised and feeling good about him or herself. There are others who get self-satisfaction in doing something only when there is no observation and no praise. They may even bring something for your attention, yet destroy it later if praised. You can always write your feelings about what you liked about the experience, focusing on the object/issue not the person and leaving the note for 'discovery' somewhere out of common view before others.

Exposure Anxiety and its pressure values

Exposure Anxiety has a number of pressure valves. One of these pressure valves is the insistence on small doses of communication or interaction. We all have our threshold of tolerance, beyond which the survival response dominates and takes over whether we like it or not. Another is self-hypnosis, which is essentially, the ability to tune out conscious awareness that one is or just has connected with the environment.

The first of these is often labelled attention problems. The information-processing problems common to autism-spectrum conditions are all triggers in themselves of the self-protection response of Exposure Anxiety in a state of overload or threatened impending overload. But there are times when the need for small doses can look like ADD when it is really Exposure Anxiety. Similarly, there are lots of instances where 'self-stimulatory behaviour' (how stuffy and negative these terms can be) can be due to other things. Sensory–perceptual fluctuations, fragmentation due to being extremely mono, muscular sensations relating to deficiencies in the supply of nutrients to the brain or due to chemical high such as the cocaine-like effect of Salicylate intolerance or the LSD-like effect of an inability to properly digest dairy or gluten are all examples of this. But 'stimming' can also be solely part of the pressure valve aspect of Exposure Anxiety.

So many times after having dared something which triggered heightened self-consciousness, I was compelled quickly into either 'disassembly behaviours' (such as shredding or tearing things into tiny pieces') or 'self-hypnotic' behaviours such as throwing myself backwards repeatedly, jumping on the bed, spinning, rocking or tapping. These were not the chemical highs of buzzing on colour, light refraction, echo or acoustic resonance which caused me drug-like highs. Nor were they the movement compulsions associated by allergy- and toxicity-related muscular tension and twitching. The problem is, in the care fields, all 'stimming' is put into one basket marked 'stomp on it'. My view is, know what you are working with. If you are looking at something that can be turned into an interest or skill, do so. If you are looking at something which is chemically based and causing the person discomfort or exclusion, then find out what's out of balance and get it rebalanced. In many cases such problems come down to treatable neurotransmitter imbalances, digestive, immune or auto-immune system problems or toxicity issues which can be set straight without bombing the person's humanity with excessive or ill-fitting courses of psychiatric drugs. If the stimming is part of the pressure-valve mechanism, taking it away may cause big retaliative repercussions as if to say, 'Can't you see I need to do this so I don't have to attack you or myself?' If this is the case, you can take the hint that your approach, however well motivated, may have been too patronizing, too directly-confrontational, too 'caring', too 'helpful', too persistent, too 'other directed', too 'encouraging' and, essentially, experienced as too 'invasive' for that person's Exposure Anxiety to tolerate without adjustment.

The last three pressure valves are that of can't do it for myself, can't do it as myself, can't do it by myself. 'Would you like a biscuit?' may be the only way to get a biscuit. Getting it for yourself may be blocked by Exposure Anxiety but your wanting one may trigger competition: 'I didn't do it for myself, I did it because they had one and I wasn't going to be left out. I'm just following my shoes. I didn't use the toilet, it's just where the pee goes. I felt sorry for the jumper so I put it on. It wasn't me, it was the dog. I was only singing. It was just part of a jingle. I didn't say anything, my fingers just typed. Make me.' If you take away these means with 'Oh, good for you, look what you did', 'You can do that for yourself', 'No, say 'I want a biscuit'', the person is left with all that is left for defence – avoidance, diversion, retaliation.

With all the pressure valves sealed up, if you stomp on avoidance, persisting on a response, if you hassle and hassle beyond diversion, then you'll get retaliation. In a family the self-abuse of someone retaliating against their own drive to reach out is very painful to live with. In my family, getting suddenly very busy, nobody jumping in to help, everyone acting like my attempts were absolutely an everyday thing, made this easier. There was no praise. Thank God, there was no praise. Visitors didn't know this but they soon learned after my displays of sudden self-abuse or object throwing. Equally hard is when these retaliation responses are aimed at others. Sometimes this is at the person most trusted and relied upon, as though the person is attacking themselves by proxy, their externalized self. This is never so true as with the person in the role of 'facilitator'.

Exposure Anxiety and the divided family

Exposure Anxiety doesn't just happen in divided families, it can, itself, divide them. In any family, members of the family can play complementary roles or those which clash with one another.

A parent can put him or herself in the position of 'saviour', but unless the person with Exposure Anxiety makes them 'their special person', they remain at arm's length. The role of the 'facilitator' is not one that the carer gives himself or herself, it is one that the person with Exposure Anxiety assigns to the person they use as the stand-in self. In that sense there is often a possessive, controlling relationship of subtle, often non-verbal hinting given by the person with Exposure Anxiety. The facilitator is trapped by his or her 'caring'. This can feed the learned dependency of the person with Exposure Anxiety. Worse, the possessiveness of the person with Exposure Anxiety and the draining nature of the emotional blackmail that can go on silently between the facilitator and the person with Exposure Anxiety, can split the family into a 'good cop', 'bad cop' dynamic. Here one is treated as 'the invader', the other being subtly emotionally blackmailed into accepting responsibility for the person who uses them to communicate with the world. The facilitator, in learning to play hard to get, by getting a life, by tough love, small doses, being aloof, puts the person with Exposure Anxiety into a position where they have to chase what is slipping from their grasp. Someone with Exposure Anxiety will often be compelled to use extreme self-convinced helplessness to black-mail the person back into the co-dependent relationship, sometimes bat-tering themselves to make their point. Exposure Anxiety is like an addic-tion. The more the facilitator gives in to the emotional blackmail and the controlling possessive nature of the relationship, the more the power of that possession grows. With this feeling of power, the phobia of the potential loss of power should the facilitator assert a life of his or her own or connections with others also increases.

We all have the potential for this but the person with Exposure Anxiety can, in the wrong situation, take this to the max. I had often established 'a special person' but this is always short lived and in my proud and haughty state of hair-trigger desertion, most couldn't pass my tests or trust so I con-nected at arm's length; but I knew the dynamic and the potential for the dynamic. It takes a certain kind of martyr to sacrifice their selfhood and life to the role of facilitator.

In reacting against the harmful autism theories of 'blame the mother' prevalent in the sixties, the focus is now so much on the child, the profes-sionals often seem to forget that whilst certain environmental factors have not been the cause, they can certainly exacerbate Exposure Anxiety and develop it in extremely counter-productive ways. The extreme chronic stress of Exposure Anxiety is one of the most controllable exacerbating effects on information-processing problems, yet there is little advice what to do environmentally to reduce it and much advice being given that increases it.

Punishing someone who has already been punished

In the home, all children are naughty, all of them, even those with autism. A child with severe Exposure Anxiety, especially with severe information overload, is so caught up just coping, there isn't time for much naughtiness and some naughtiness is a wonderful sign of a colourful child, of child-hood itself and of individuality. But, contrary to the stereotypes, people with Exposure Anxiety can often sense when something is not wanted. In fact the more it is not wanted the more that doing it makes Exposure

Anxiety feel good about creating distance, controlling the desire of others to connect. Just because a child is switched off to general information-processng doesn't mean it isn't highly switched on in the grip of a defensive and reactive adrenaline-driven state.

Distancing behaviours can be intensely amusing or satisfying for some children with Exposure Anxiety. This repertoire might include wiping snot on someone you like, putting them off with masturbation or through exposing yourself. It might include making someone squirm by pursuing them to smell them or grab their hair. It might include filling one's room with excrement so it becomes disgusting to others to be in there or doing a pattern that makes others leave the room or unable to enjoy themselves in the same room.

So, naughtiness, naughtiness affects us all. The difference is, does the person with Exposure Anxiety have a choice? The compulsion to distance others can swing violently with the desire to connect, making it very hard to then punish someone for the compulsion to distance. But why should such distancing behaviour be reinforced as acceptable when others are robbed of the power to do the same or enjoy the use of the same room? My view is that people have a right to enjoy themselves to some degree but enjoyment derived of a compulsive power trip because of the adrenaline-addiction state of Exposure Anxiety is not really about freedom nor choice, nor interest. Tic-like and compulsive behaviours are driven and about a lack of choice. Without choice, I cannot, however driven (and boy was I driven), call this 'interest'. For me interest is about choice and freedom and that's what I have outside of the power issues caused by Exposure Anxiety. Not all people with Exposure Anxiety, however, identify against the dynamics of the condition. Perhaps that is the fine line between the autist and the psychopath.

If the only enjoyment we know is the power trip of Exposure Anxiety distancing, triumphant retaliation, the secrecy of avoidance, the humour of diversion, then this is still all we know of enjoyment and without any of it, however undesirable to the environment, we lose our love of life. But, however much Exposure Anxiety-driven behaviours have the power to amuse or cause a rush, my view is they are only acceptable to a degree and as long as they don't deprive or harm others.

I used to annoy the hell out of my older brother when I was in the same room. He could not watch the television because I wouldn't stop playing with the controls, messing up the picture and sound for my own buzz and the enjoyment of feeling his resentment rise and knowing I had driven him out of the room. When I wasn't doing this I was throwing myself repeatedly back into my chair getting more and more active as I felt his annoyance and my excitement build. I played with words and sound patterns and jingles over and over, drowning out his ability to have his own headspace or enjoy the TV. I had wanted company so I had gone in there but once in there was blocked by Exposure Anxiety both from initiating shared activities or from sitting still and quiet (which increased self-consciousness) whilst he enjoyed the room. He ridiculed me. I felt victorious. I had got to him. He shouted for my mother. I was immensely powerful and adrenaline rushed like a drug. He shouted so often our pet cockatoo started mimicking so the whole neighborhood heard. Later, when my little brother started behaving in a way similar to me, I repeated his shouting to have my brother 'eliminated' from my room. Of course, in both cases, this fed both my brother's jubilance and my own, making it huge a reward to wind each other up in these terrible non-verbal vendettas. But what they taught me was this. There are times when the Exposure Anxiety behaviour is a statement of 'you've been too in my face'. It may be saying, 'you have been too persistent', 'too focused on me'. It may be saying, 'give me space', 'back off', 'what happened to your own life'. These kind of messages may be worth listening to because they can lead to better results and a feeling of being respected and thereby instilling a capacity, likewise, to respect as best as an adrenaline addict can.

But there are times when Exposure Anxiety is driving the person simply to be a powermonger in situations where the other person is powerless to affect them on their own terms. If you want to punish a child for the power trip of such Exposure Anxiety-driven behaviour, don't say 'don't'. This is the fastest way to reward them. With an adrenaline high. Telling someone 'this was unwanted', 'bad', 'will make them unpopular', you hurt the child within, but Exposure Anxiety is writhing with victory.

My brother should have been provided with his own TV in his own space where I was excluded (he eventually got this and lived outside in a converted garage – he has now forgiven me). Left alone in the lounge room, the Exposure Anxiety would have no longer been triggered and I'd have been left there, alone with myself. Had I chosen aloneness, I'd have not been in there. The imposed aloneness I'd have been left with was the consequence for my inability to calm myself, my inability to leave every few minutes to release the pressure on Exposure Anxiety and allow my behaviour when in the room to be more manageable.

Where someone puts snot all over you, making them put more is the quickest way to create a sense of expectation and connection, triggering the Exposure Anxiety to reject its own distancing behaviour as one which invited 'invasion'. I have chased a child with the arm it sought to bite. I have expressed artistic appreciation for spittle patterns.

Of course, with masturbation and exposing oneself, this issue is more difficult. Sending the person out won't work, you just reward them by 'having got to you'. But observing their choice and saying that as it puts you off, you are taking the TV/music/dinner with you to another room means they are left without the victory. There has been no put down, no opposition, simply the environment making choices for itself and them being left behind because they chose not to fight their compulsion or find ways of heading off the need to distance such as self-calming or being present only in small doses. Moving the TV, music, games into the kitchen because so and so chooses to use that room to expose himself or mastur-bate means you may have to congregate in the kitchen a while, but the person with Exposure Anxiety will eventually give up the room. They may migrate into the kitchen, and announcing that people have come in here to enjoy themselves without the distraction of 'anyone's' masturbation or exposing themselves may mean the person sulks a while. But eventually you can probably gradually move back the 'feel of the lounge room' piece by piece, as though testing out whether you are all ready to go back to using 'that room'. The most likely response on the part of the person with Exposure Anxiety may be to act as if nothing ever happened. Annoying as such measures may be, they may be more effective than the conventional behaviour modification ideas of punishment and reward. These take account of the motivations and anti-motivations of the person but, in my experience, never take into consideration simultaneous motivations and anti-motivations of the Exposure Anxiety.

Heading off such behaviours by sending the person out of the room to fetch things every few minutes is a good plan because it gives them a break so that Exposure Anxiety comes down. Remember, even if you are watching TV, doing something else, the person with Exposure Anxiety can still wind themselves up simply knowing they wanted to say something, initiate involvement and so forth, but couldn't. So you may not see the trigger of the Exposure Anxiety heightening.

Exposure Anxiety and self-help skills

Exposure Anxiety peaks in situations of greatest expectation and desire of others. What this means is that those activities which are not wanted or desired are those most likely to be easily expressed without being blocked by Exposure Anxiety, whether the person wishes to be taken over by such compulsion or not.

People with OCD or Tourette don't always enjoy their obsessive or ticcy behaviour, and nor do people with Exposure Anxiety always side with what is coming out. Often the self-directed payback behaviour for some people is so extreme that they become terrified of challenging their Exposure Anxiety which holds them to ransom like an internal terrorist. When a person with Exposure Anxiety has performed a behaviour that was deeply unwanted, then stands blank and disowning of it, it may well be that once the Exposure Anxiety has diffused through the behaviour, you are now facing the person themselves, who in experiential terms, 'didn't do it'. When someone with OCD or Tourette is gripped by obsessive or ticcy behaviour, these are generally not experienced as 'them', but as 'a possession' kind of feeling. People with Exposure Anxiety, having lived with the condition since infancy, can have a much harder time knowing self from the condition. Some of the most severely affected, however, such as facilitated autistic writers, have typed about being imprisoned by this 'non self'.

Families want to get on with life and the greatest pressure of sensed desire on the part of others revolve especially around eating, speaking, looking, dressing, playing, learning, exploration, affection, consideration for others and toiletting. I know I dressed myself from about the age of five because I remember going to school with clothes over my pyjama bottoms. Before that I didn't really care if I spent the day in what I'd slept in and I know it was usual for me to be in a nightdress in the afternoon. I remember at the age of seven or eight putting my underpants on my head as a hat and putting on my jumper as trousers so I know I played with clothing. Nobody at home ever stopped or controlled or ridiculed what I wore and I often wore cotton summer clothes in hail and rain and sweltered in jumpers I'd worn with nothing under in the summer. Although I might have played on dependency with a chosen 'special person', there was no way I was letting anyone else have any part in dressing me. I suspect, had such a person suggested they'd be in soon to help me, I'd either have been out the window or dressed by the time they got there.

It took a long time to get me to brush my teeth. I remember learning this around the age of about seven and mastering it by nine when my younger brother got wonderful toothbrushes which sparkled, had bells inside the handle, and buzzed, as well as a toothpaste dispenser which meant toothpaste got used but went everywhere. Again, there was no direct pressure or expectation in spite of huge numbers of fillings. I brushed my teeth because my brother made me feel I was missing out on the buzz he was having in using his brushes.

I found it very hard to understand most toys and perceived each piece as the toy itself. I can remember two incidents where my mother modelled play and once she'd abandoned the activity, it often took days or weeks, but I did follow many of these leads in exploring play. Most of my own play was about merging with the feel of an object or experience, so involved doing the same thing over and over again to a drug-like high. But I did flick through books at school (again lots of modelling, absolutely no expectation) and memorized a few of them word for word, though meaning was impossible. I developed a great sensory relationship with books. I felt a personal interaction with the surface of their pages and covers, with their smells and with favourite 'visit pictures'. I think of these as 'visit pictures' because 'climbing into' the feel of a picture was like having a visit. I felt a personal interaction with the indexes and the ordering of the books by colour, size or numerical or alphabetical order.

Eating both was and was not a problem. I had no Exposure Anxiety about helping myself, particularly when out of view or left alone in the house, and would take food easily when it was completely on my terms. Eating meals at the table was problematic and I fell off my chair from swinging and rocking it more times than I can count and generally got through meals by playing with the food (modelled by my father). Almost completely I 'lost track' of the cutlery (I expect Exposure Anxiety helped in upping the avoidance of what was desired or expected). I was often made to take my food away. I remember phases at the table but I don't remember it as a general thing. By the age of nine I was given my plateful of food and sent out to the lounge room. I seemed capable of eating anything edible as long as I didn't focus on eating. I almost never finished a meal whilst warm and I'd pick at the bits of it sometimes over a very long period. My older brother was a good model in that he provided no expectation I eat my food, but I often remembered what the food was because he was eating his and any competition for mine triggered me possessively to scoff my food. I remember a time when there was special food just for my older brother, especially fruit. I was told to leave it alone. I attacked the fruit bowl. What wasn't known was that as someone highly salicylate intolerant, fruit (though pears and mango are safe) affected me like someone on cocaine and I became much more unmanageable after a fruit binge.

My mother had agoraphobia and needed help with shopping. She didn't ask. She would, instead, put the money and note in my hand and send me out saying what the money was for and I'd go down the street. Her tone was always one of absolute assumption, as though I was a tool, a version of herself by proxy. If I returned without what she'd sent me for (which was about a fifty–fifty chance), she sent me back out.

With the help of the shop keepers using the shopping notes, I learned to shop. Nobody was there to watch me and, in the supermarket in particular, I helped myself to things I liked before leaving in my own time. Eventually, because nobody stopped me, I didn't do this. When there was washing to be done my mother didn't ask, she just indicated 'arms out', borrowed my outstretched arms and filled them up with washing and heading me for the washing machine. Again, there was the absolute assumption that I would work it out. Even though she knew I had great difficulty understanding, she knew I would do most anything to avoid being 'invaded' and controlled. This meant that provoking her to come after me again later and interrupt me being in 'my world' was less rewarding than dumping the washing at the machine.

From the age of about eleven I straightened my own bed because I didn't like the mess. My mother had modelled the making of her bed out loud to herself and I knew how to make it tucked in tightly at the sides. After what felt like a year of having the same sheets, I changed my own sheets, finding clean ones on the shelf and putting mine in the washing machine (I'd tried this two years before as well when peeing the bed made it uncomfortable.) I did the dishes because of the bubbles and the clinking sounds of cutlery in water. It was not a way of getting praise, it was a way of getting rid of attention and losing myself in the pattern.

I never made myself a lunch (there were no school dinners) and had always had lunch money and knew how to say 'five of chips', 'five of potato cakes' to the person taking orders. But when my little brother started school, I was about eleven or twelve and I was told to spread his sandwich for him. I had by this time learned how to make a sauce sandwich (my brother and mother modelling for themselves and leaving me wanting), but the co-ordination of the whole thing for a lunch took until I had done this for my brother. Then, I managed to compete and do it also for myself (why do I do this just for him when I get nothing). Then I took my own sandwiches, however badly made. Unfortunately, what wasn't known was that my metabolic problems meant I was also gluten and dairy intolerant and I may as well have packed drugs for school lunch.

Battles about consideration for others were a waste of time on me. My 'sorry', in the hands of Exposure Anxiety, meant nothing. I didn't even know if I was or wasn't sorry. In the grip of Exposure Anxiety fifty per cent of my actions and expressions were involuntary. Things just were, they just happened. I knew in my body it wasn't choice but I had very little concept of what choice was. I never thought, and then did. I was always left observing whatever had 'popped out'. The most common instruction to my brothers in relation to my behaviour was 'leave her alone', 'take it in the other room' or to me to 'get to your room' (which only had me compelled to escape and be 'vindicated'). I am, nevertheless, a person of great compassion and empathy for others and it's hard to understand how I developed that. I was never expected to care for animals (in fact my mother's difficulties modelled the opposite), but finding lost and abandoned animals in my neighborhood certainly instilled a great caring in me for things which couldn't help themselves, perhaps similar to my inner self which was defenceless against the dominance of both Exposure Anxiety and the problems in my family. I identified with children being bullied, perhaps because I felt bullied inside and the strong approach of my equally adrena-line-addicted mother and the struggles of my brother in coping with me, certainly had me feeling sorry for myself as much as I felt artificially strong. I had a great empathy for my younger brother (though he harassed me through my territorial relationship to my room and belongings associ-ated with 'mine') who had similar struggles and was greatly dominated by anxiety, phobia and compulsion. I had great resonance with those who either didn't speak much or didn't speak English, perhaps because I had struggled to navigate language with meaning in ways that eventually had me understood and seen as something more than 'disturbed'. I had great empathy for those made victim by violence because of the domestic violence in my own home and for those who were homeless and poor because of my own experiences with this.

The greatest battle in my home when I was growing up was the toilet. As a child I wasn't toilet trained till I was three and a half. Even then I held on for days. At school it was impossible to ask for the toilet so I often simply tried to walk out and later tried to be sent out through sucking my pen till my mouth was full of ink. At the first house, I was afraid of the entrapment of the outside toilet but it was also not within the house so there was less feeling of being observed, known to care, the defeat of 'com-pliance'. I also loved the abalone shell ashtray in there which so diverted my attention onto the mother of pearl in the shell.

At the age of seven, however, we moved to the next house and here I developed a problem using the toilet. I was OK at first, though I often went in the bath. Later I developed fascination with going in the bath in my clothes, then taking my clothes off. My retaliation response against letting go also meant I was having great problems with constipation around this time and this was making me vomit and created expectation by my mother that I use the toilet regularly. At first I complied, going in, coming out, saying 'yes'. But I wasn't going. I absolutely was frozen from going when someone waited, ready to ask. My body simply wouldn't listen. It wouldn't connect. Eventually, I went, instead, secretly in the garden, refusing to accept 'defeat' and when I peed in the house, it was in the bath or basin not, as desired, in the toilet. By the age of twelve, I'd developed such a phobia about the toilet, revolving around the expectation to use it and that it was 'theirs' and 'their way', that I began peeing in my room, making patches everywhere and covering each new one with a rug. This coincided with my pet Tom-cat developing a habit of going in my vinyl bean bag – so the cat had provided the modelling and, later, the cover. The cat was blamed for the smell and banned from the house. Eventually, my mother lifted one of the rugs to find it moldy and wet and there was war.

She was stony and silent, put my brothers and me in the car and went straight to the GP. She announced to my brothers calmly we were all here because 'Donna has been pissing in her room'. She then, after the disbelief, snickers, and beginnings of taunting, ordered them to shut up and say nothing about it. I was left sitting on my own. They emerged back from the GP's office and the car was driven to the hardware store. I was frozen and terrified, with no idea of the consequences but utterly exposed. My mother came back out of the store and threw a potty into my lap in the back seat saying 'There you go. You'll piss in that in future.' On the return to the house, never had I been so eager to erase my behaviour, disprove my need for such measures, and disarm her of this strategy by making its necessity redundant. I still went in the bath and the basin but also now in the toilet. The bathroom was mirrored, wall to wall so I was now much happier being in there in the company of myself. There was a musical toilet roll holder so you could play music on the toilet. Don't worry, twenty-five years on, I'm over it, I'm toilet trained and house friendly. But those were the dynamics.

At the age of fifteen, I was taken out of my fourth failed secondary school in three years and as I sat at the table my mother announced to my father that I could either be a machinist or a cleaner. It was also joked that I could be a stripper as I could dance. Much as this may shock some people it is a valid profession and could have been a relatively sensible idea with strong social support if I'd been drawn to it. People have to remember that my family were uneducated, felt intimidated by professionals, had no label and no support services and I was born in the sixties when autism was barely known about. I also had no maths skills, could barely read with meaning and had impaired social communication and difficult social behaviours. A job was picked for me and within a week I was in a factory to be trained as a machinist (job lasted three days). I went on to have thirty jobs in the following three years, from stock rooms to ticketing, from department stores to pastry shops, from housecleaning to working in a meat-works. I lasted anywhere from days to months but until I was eighteen, my friendly demeanor and cheeky face got me all the kinds of child labour opportunities that predominantly non-English-speaking employers had to offer on my working class side of town.

I ran away from home at fifteen and a half with someone I'd met a week before. I had money from my job, called a taxi (I had practised with phone books for years), put all my things in and arrived, to this person's shock, at the other end. I refused to go back but ended up homeless after a few months. My behaviour in believing myself capable of independence was impossible, and after having me back for eight weeks, my mother had two choices, make me a ward of the state or put me in a flat and hope for the best. She did the latter. I didn't know how to manage time, when to eat, how to create a routine. I burned everything, including myself. I locked myself out and lost my keys every week. I had all my utilities turned off from not knowing what bills were or how to pay them. I paid my rent on the doorstep when I'd forgotten to go up the hill and pay it. I had no idea how to eat, shop or cook properly. I spoke to any stranger who stopped me. But I refused to ask for help or contact my family, and when my mother came to see me and sent my younger brother to my door to get me, I refused to have contact. I held out for three years with the exception of a sewerage flood which resulted in ankle high sewerage throughout my flat. Only I know what I was like and that had she or anyone tried to stop me, I'd not have been in a flat but on the other side of the country or living on the streets. What I learned in that state of independence taught me great compassion for others and made me a member of the community in which I had to work on myself to be accepted as equal. It was bad but the only other choice with no services or professional help was to imprison me. I'm still standing. I'm also whole and I'm happy.

Exposure Anxiety, social events, restaurants and holidays

Social events, restaurants and holidays, these are hard things for many families of children with Exposure Anxiety. The more the surroundings are unfamiliar, often the more the Exposure Anxiety peaks. Some children work better with structure as long as it is self-owning without pressure to interact or express themselves personally. Some children desperately need at least the first half-hour to be unobserved and 'fly on the wall' before they can accept being controlled by the environment in unfamiliar surroundings or structures. After the initial reassurance of freedom and lack of expectation or 'invasion', the chance to be in the clear structure provided is often reassuring, as long as it's presented in a way that doesn't provoke Exposure Anxiety. Focusing on the object/issue rather than the person is important and modelling that you are enjoying things for your own benefit is also one way of showing the peace flag to Exposure Anxiety in new situations.

I was not taken to social events, nor restaurants. I stayed with my parents in motels and played in the grounds (gravel pits, fishponds, exploring plants and stones, walking 'boundaries', swings). I went to two holiday farms with them and was later sent off with my older brother (not to his pleasure) and my cousin (which was great). I was sent to stay with two different cousins quite often (one great, one a very difficult experience). One lived in high rise flats and it was a controlling environment that caused mostly aversion responses. The other lived in a house where we were free to be outside and in the streets and I explored schoolyards, trees, building sites, shop counters (had a thing about getting behind shop counters), car washes, petrol stations.

Parents and siblings need respite from children with severe Exposure Anxiety and it shakes up the Exposure Anxiety responses. One thing is certain, holding the family to ransom doesn't diminish the complications of Exposure Anxiety. So, however much it continues to be a factor out in respite, it is worth it to the family to get some head space, some personal space, to miss the person with Exposure Anxiety and be relieved when they come back. Of course parents worry. But controlling someone with Exposure Anxiety in a directly-confrontational way may bring out the worst. Worrying and caring and trying too hard may bring only learned dependency and more reactiveness as well as creating divisions in the family as others seek balanced give and take relationships with each other but find that the problems of the person with Exposure Anxiety dominate.

It is important to know that the Exposure Anxiety response is not all that the person is. Usually, there is someone very different who would be there if you reduced the Exposure Anxiety and parents often see glimpses of this person. I am nothing like I was before dietary intervention and treatment for toxicity, nutrient and immune system issues.

Explaining Exposure Anxiety to others

Parents need the community to understand Exposure Anxiety in their children. They are under enormous pressure to over protect their child and are often praised for their martyrdom which may do nothing to aid the independence of their child and may actually promote learned dependency. Being able to jump to the prompt is not independence. It is not the expression of the personality. It is not the self. In the end, we have ourselves. There is no prompt. To know self-satisfaction, we have to know individuality. If all we've known is the satisfaction of jumping to the prompt, this is knowing 'one's place', 'one's role', but it is not the glorious adventure of discovering and developing self.

It is important that others understand that Exposure Anxiety means a child needs tough love, humour, freedom, personal space, unclinging warmth and a parent who can model the enjoyment of life. It is important that others understand that making the child the focus, that being overly helpful, that waiting and watching and being ever ready to praise can actually rob a child with Exposure Anxiety of his or her full potential to develop.

It is important to get the community to understand what an indirectly-confrontational approach is, why it is used with Exposure Anxiety, how it works and how to be of use. Its useful to build a communication network which provides freedom to express potential but with a safety net to keep the person safe from social dangers.

It is important to explain to others that people with Exposure Anxiety may be more capable than they appear, and that in spite of severe information-processing delay, they still have the capacity to rely strictly on pattern even without having interpretation in the moment of the experience. You may want to explain that, because of this, tough love may appear uncaring to others but that love is also about empowerment. It's important people understand that when any person is in a foreign land unable to understand the ways or communicate, even without the ability to use their interpretation capacity successfully, they have many skills of mapping pattern they can still rely on. They can still function relatively meaning deaf and relatively meaning blind, though, of course, it can be extremely daunting and may make them cling excessively to 'a guide'. Many such foreigners live in foreign countries, neither using the language nor understanding the customs and they do so sometimes for decades. They also have the disadvantage that they have often not always lived like this, it is not second nature to them. Those who have someone they use constantly as the go between and translator are far less likely to seize these skills for themselves. There may be no motivation to do so and life may be easier, staying how they've always been, albeit out of sync with the new foreign country.

It is important to explain that people with Exposure Anxiety may be interested, caring and considerate, though their behaviour may show the opposite. You may need to explain that seeking to directly control the person can make them even more out of control of their behaviour. You may need to explain that, whilst they may think you need to focus more strongly on your child by modelling, triggering and manoeuvering in a directive but indirectly-confrontational way you take the heat off, self-consciousness decreases, self-protection responses decrease, and your child can better dare the vulnerability of showing more of the interest, caring and consideration he or she has inside.

You can explain that people in a highly defensive mode will generally over protect themselves from the invasiveness of attempts to help, yet often have the potential to find intricate novel ways of getting what they want. Because of this, being aloof and playing hard to get whilst modelling all kinds of skills that could be later used by the person with Exposure Anxiety, you empower your child. You also retain a strong sense of self and family life that provides a secure structure full of information.

You may wish to point out that it is equally likely that rather than causing the child's 'autism', parents observed as aloof or distant may have been working instinctively on the Exposure Anxiety in their child. It is equally possible that rather than having caused their child's Exposure Anxiety, parents are vulnerable to being misjudged by a society which does not understand the mechanisms of interaction when living with someone in this trapped and often upside-down state. Co-dependency is not love, empowerment does not involve offering dependency and independence usually flows from want rather than compliance and want is found in having one's own space and the necessity to activate it. You might remind them that different approaches work for people with different kinds of difficulties and each might be valid. An indirectly-confrontational approach can still be considerate, warm, humourous and rich with understanding and caring.

Exposure Anxiety at school

Exposure Anxiety can manifest itself in a completely different way at home than it does at school. If at home an indirectly-confrontational approach is used, you may find someone with reasonable self-help skills who is capable of entertaining themselves, even exploring things. If then at school, there is intensive on to one with focus across the table directly on the individual and a reliance on compliance, you may hear of the same child waiting always for the prompt and rarely thinking for him or herself, seeming lost and totally reliant on others. On the other hand you may hear of a relatively self-managed child who is utterly out of control, caught up in constant diversion or retaliation responses, seeking to escape or interrupt the surroundings constantly.

Where at home there is constant focus on the child, ever ready to jump in and help at the first sign of distress or threat of self-abuse, you may find the same child at school if they provide intensive one to one attention. Conversely, you may find you barely recognize the same child if this child is left to flounder in a group of thirty mainstream children with a support assistant who holds back, refusing to take over. You might find someone who desperately seizes the structure and seeks to follow the lead of the flock or someone who covers under the table eventually coming out in 'snatches' before trusting they are not the focus of attention and progressively joining in without prompt.

This echoes the experience of many undiagnosed people with 'autism' in the sixties and earlier (diagnosed in their twenties and thirties around the 1980s and 1990s) who were not in special schools but left to sink or swim in mainstream, without funded support. Some of these people were non-verbal til mid, even late childhood and some with marked problems with 'functional language', often got the label 'disturbed'. This was before mainstream awareness of the label of 'autism' when the label and its stereotypes were much narrower than today.

Today there are unfortunate assumptions of incapability where the adaptations of the person with autism are rarely acknowledged or allowed to evolve and ideas of 'normality' rather than 'individuality' dominate. I have known functionally non-verbal children with no apparent self-help skills who appear utterly meaning deaf and meaning blind with no sense of pain or cold. Some of these same, seemingly 'incapable' children, however, can still organize themselves in complex tasks of their own volition. Some have driven themselves to operate a video or dismantle a crate containing the object of their obsession, or dismantle plugs or light switches, delicately manoeuvre a climb to a great height, find ways of escaping and ways of manoeuvering the environment into taking over. We must distinguish between the brain-affected state of information-processing delay, and mental retardation. We must equally distinguish between social–emotional retardation which holds back the acknowledgement and display of ability and the cognitive capacity for ability.

Where professionals cannot reconcile such apparent ability with such inability, they simply put the huge potential of sensory mapping down to 'autistic behaviours' rather than looking at what it tells us of the dynamics that stifle the same capability elsewhere.

Who is this person?

In school, the child is in danger of being confused with his or her behaviour. Teachers or assistants unable to see through the cracks may only respond to the condition and never see the potential. Their 'professionalism' is partly responsible here because they may feel impotent if the most fruitful way to help is to model without helping, to allow people frustration out of which is born motivation, to not take the bait when invited or emotionally blackmailed into taking over. They are equally under pressure to control their clients, to 'reach them', to come up with 'proof' of achievement. Teachers in particular are under impossible pressure that limits their ability to alter their approach. Policy, funding restricted to certain approaches and programmes, the national curriculum and a position dependent on 'proof' and 'results', restrict the individuality of the teacher in the classroom. The luxury of seeing the person beyond the behaviour gives way to 'controlling the disruption'. But assuming capability, refusing to be baited or played, constructively letting people live with the consequences of their defence responses, these things can still fit in.

In mainstream classrooms, the problem for a child with Exposure Anxiety will often revolve around the areas of greatest external control and expectation. The expectation to stay in the room or sit in a chair will often mean the child can think of nothing but escape. Leaving the door open (if the corridor is quiet) can make some children more likely to stay than be compelled to go. Sitting on the floor could be an option and there's no reason why work can't equally be done on the floor if that makes someone feel 'less controlled'. Given the choice, sitting in the chair stands out less, creating less of a sense of exposure, and is more likely to then be chosen. Keep in mind that what often looks like attention seeking is often about controlling the environment or setting oneself apart, distancing. The same child, given the choice to be 'different' may prefer to disappear into not needing special arrangements.

Sitting next to the child can, similarly, make them more thrown into avoidance, diversion and retaliation responses. Sitting on your own at another table but still able to help if really needed might give the child more ability to control his or her behaviour and do some things for him or herself. The constant asking or counting of time doesn't have to be responded to literally. It may mean 'I'm not keeping up. I really feel self-conscious.' The answer then is to non-disruptively model giving yourself a rhythm and suggesting 'I like this, when I feel like I'm not keeping up, it feels really calming.' It might mean, 'I'm bored because I don't understand' (the answer then is, 'sometimes it all just sounds like blah blah. I think this is what they are saying,' – and demonstrate to yourself in a visual and concrete way). It might mean, 'I feel lonely and I want to talk but don't know how to make you talk to me'. The answer would be, to oneself, 'Oh it is hard to sit so long, I get restless and I'd much rather talk or do something else, but I'm just going to listen/work for a few more minutes first.' Respond to the real content, not just the words. You may be surprised at the response. It's OK to get it wrong. Dare to be imperfect, to make a mistake.

Exposure Anxiety and 'proof'

Leaving available the materials for an activity may still trigger 'expectation' and the defence against it. When expected to paint with the brush, I painted with the wooden end. When expected to look at a book the right way up, I glanced at it upside down whilst walking past (for many dyslexic people, they grasp the word equally well upside down. Instead of leaving conventional materials such as paper and pen, you can occasionally be surreal, leaving cardboard or wallpaper and sand and modelling the use of the sprinkling of sand as a writing or drawing or maths tool. You can take pupils outside where they can write answers in the sand with their feet, or use something like puddles of water to dip feet and make mathematical representations using the footprints as number groupings. You can 'travel' throughout the playground, introducing 'country' by 'country' in the different areas as a way of playfully demonstrating geography. You can draw a huge body on the ground, filling it with representations of the organs and going on a tour of digestion as part of biology.

Life is a balance of the conventional and the surreal and this shake up is part of emotional development in feeling ourselves either pressured or held back by our own reluctance in the face of the new. When all that is provided is the conventional, we create emotional imbalance. By being occasionally surreal and expansive in your use of materials to address a topic, you model it as fun for one's own sake. This makes it less possible to predictably pinpoint the focus of what you are rebelling ('protecting yourself') against. Even if the person with Exposure Anxiety will usually hold back totally from what is novel and new, you will be providing a very important lesson. The person with Exposure Anxiety who resents their inability to enjoy themselves in something novel and new becomes progressively more self-challenging because of the feeling of frustration and 'being kept out' by their own mechanisms. Unlike conventional activities, those which appear novel and fun but in which the person was unable to dare to participate, stay with the person longer than the more conventional lesson where they may have complied to the prompt but felt no personal motivation. Teachers think so much about getting results, that they forget that subtle shifts in identification and motivation, expressed or unexpressed at the time of an activity, are still part of development and results. Not everything is seen, on the spot, especially with Exposure Anxiety and especially when combined with information-processing delay.

Some people with Exposure Anxiety love structure and cope wonderfully in it. Others feel expectation is clearly defined in conventionally-structured activities and have a clear focus of what they are compelled to oppose. If doing the same as others provokes a feeling of 'defeat' and 'connecting' and triggers Exposure Anxiety avoidance, diversion or retaliation responses, providing the person with something totally different with which to do their work can work. It is the most likely way to have them want to 'disappear' from being singled out and grab someone else's pen and paper (for to take one of their own would be choice, self-expression and defeat). But if you then jump on them for taking someone else's paper and pen, you'll have pushed them too far. What you can do, however, is to recognize a great and novel idea and suggest everyone swaps pens and paper (not expecting the person with Exposure Anxiety to do so) and this makes everyone now equal and you haven't rewarded the snatching of other people's things. Expecting 'manners' when someone has done their best within the confines of their Exposure Anxiety will only establish a subtle but entrenched war. You can't remove the underlying causes of the self-protection responses and you can't wish the Exposure Anxiety away, even if it doesn't fit with words like 'appropriate' or 'manners'. What you can do is work with the Exposure Anxiety to the benefit of the child and the classroom.

Multiple choice questions work to trigger responses. The person with Exposure Anxiety may attribute the answers not to themselves but to being provoked into correcting the paper. Multiple choice questions can be purely pictorial and can be worked into communication boards. Facilitated pointing or typing can be used to feel for the person's response in relation to your own movement towards potential responses on a picture or word grid. It should never be assumed that someone who hasn't appeared to learn to read or cannot read fluently with meaning hasn't mapped the association of individual words with experiences or concepts, especially preconsciously. Keep in mind that whilst the conscious mind may have great limitations in reading or understanding what is read, multiple choice questions don't have to rely on conscious accessing.

Putting the wrong piece in a puzzle, the wrong word in a sentence, a word in upside down, something written twice or misspelled, a piece left out and walking off as though you haven't noticed is one of the ways to trigger someone into 'correcting'. But shower them with praise, stick their achievement in their face, and you may soon find they suddenly lost this skill. Here, it is the teacher who has failed not the pupil. The teacher failed to 'speak the language of indirectness'. The desire for correctness or per-fection is sometimes an extreme motivational force in people who are tightly controlled by Exposure Anxiety. The reluctance of teachers to deliberately be 'wrong' means this mechanism is under-utilized in classes.

Teaching language with people with Exposure Anxiety

The more you are waiting, wanting, needing someone to use language, the more that language becomes the focus of a sense of 'impending invasion' and 'entrapment' and the more this aspect of functioning becomes the focus of Exposure Anxiety responses. For some people this may mean they'll only use pragmatic language but avoid personal communication. For others it may mean that speaking to oneself is acceptable but respond-ing directly, interactively with the environment provokes alarm bells inside, making them feel anxious and out of control. For some it may mean they can use yes or no but can't give away any level of self-exposure through language beyond this. For some it may mean they can respond but only in someone else's voice or in obscure language or only when prompted but not of their own free volition and initiation.

To stimulate language as self-expression you have to work to diminish self-consciousness about language. To take the heat off, language has to be not the focus of the activity or feedback but purely incidental to the partic-ipation in something else that is the focus. Activities which are completely non-verbal are more likely to provide the sense of stifling silence and the exposure of environmental silence, causing Exposure Anxiety to jump in the opposite direction – the compulsion to fill the void as a way of losing self-consciousness. This may be with sounds made to oneself, with humming, with tapping, with singing or sudden stored lines. But if you attempt to engage the person directly through these communications, Exposure Anxiety can quickly shift and the protection again gets focused on the issue of language and the person clams up. Keeping to oneself and getting on with things may be one of the best ways to provoke someone into wanting to provoke you. If you fail to respond to physical or behav-ioural attempts to provoke you, the next step may well be to bait you with sound, especially if it is known that's what you are always waiting for. Responding as though sound or language are purely incidental to your focus, you can provoke the person to come after you further using this tool of sound or language as her provocation. Don't expect a miracle in a day, but following through such a programmeme, you may progressively turn around the links between Exposure Anxiety-related self-protection mechanisms and their focus upon language.

Labelling everything with the names and descriptions for everything touched, handled or encountered is one way of building up vocabulary as you read things in a whisper to yourself as you use them. Like gestural signing, this links the words directly to their related experiences. By demonstrating the privacy of this self-entertainment, it compels the person with Exposure Anxiety to tune in far more acutely. This way, the person with Exposure Anxiety sees language not as something between him and other people but about people and experiences in the world, built up in user-friendly self-dialogue with the objects/ feelings/places themselves.

Teaching the curriculum with people with Exposure Anxiety

When I was in school, it was virtually impossible to understand what the teacher was saying or doing. I mapped huge amounts of information and found I'd processed them eventually outside of the context in which they occurred, albeit generally preconsciously. Nevertheless, one can only stand so much of this sensory flooding before the discomfort and loss of control of information overload follows. There is also the sense of starvation of life and experience.

In a classroom dependent on interpretation, where knowledge about the world is conveyed through the interpretive media of written or verbal blah blah blah, I had little processing capacity to keep up with this interpretive representational experience of the world. Outside of school, I did exactly what I liked. I played with the patterns of traffic like a mathematician. I went onto people's property to explore their plants and ornaments, the structure of their glass porches. I explored the inside of printing works, textile factories, soft drink manufacturers, packing warehouses, paper manufacturers, car washes, corner shops, rubbish collections, building sites, cemeteries, tram networks, other schools, elevators, high rise flats and escalators.

I had the most remarkably privileged childhood for someone with autism. I had nobody with me and I was free to have a hands-on experience of what existed in the world, where people went, what they did. I couldn't ask questions (except a stored one of 'What are you doing?' – which usually got me found and chased out) but here there was no language, writing, drawings to have to interpret. I was encountering immediate sensory reality. Being in complete control of the initiation of these experiences, they didn't trigger Exposure Anxiety and I was free to explore, to look, to wander, to collect momentos.

My ability to use discovery learning also led to my doing so at my father's work place where he eventually co-opted me into searching secondhand cars for 'treasure', washing the seats, washing the windows, cleaning the cars. I extended this into his office and he co-opted my behaviour into tidying and ordering things (which also meant I'd take certain things, tear them up and dump them in the incinerator – though not always the ones he wanted in there).

A good key worker could do background preparation for a discovery learning programme, preparing targeted environments and getting co-operation from the community. The person with autism could be introduced to the community via a business card that explained on the back how Exposure Anxiety works. The environment could be prepared and also know that attempts to share or join with the person will likely cause abandonment of the activity, whereas getting on with their own thing will allow the person to be free of their involuntary self-protection responses and explore.

There were some places I went which were a physical danger, others a social danger. But there are many places where exploration with someone else being a self-owning shadow-presence, are relatively friendly. The advantage for me was that by the time most people had asked each other who I was and what I was doing there, I was done with the experience and was already leaving. The degree of trust I have of myself in spite of severe feedback problems, and the degree of belief in my equality with others in spite of Exposure Anxiety, I largely put down to my opportunity to experience discovery learning.

At home as well, this was generally how new items were introduced. They were generally not given, they were left, not wrapped, just placed about in positions as though they'd always been there. It was generally understood by the language of my behaviour that to give too directly and wait and watch for a response was to impose a sense of the gift being full of 'you' not about 'me'. The degree of Exposure Anxiety this would raise would taint the gift for a long time afterwards. This made it difficult or impossible to 'befriend' gifts or new items and peacefully tolerate their use or contact with them as part of my own world (and anything like this triggered anxiety so didn't stay in proximity to me). Whilst seen by many people to be 'rude' or cold, I have learned in adult discussions since that this way of giving comes very naturally to some people because of their own well-disguised Exposure Anxiety.

If the curriculum is something taken over to the person and stuck into their space, it can be like throwing down the gauntlet. If, however, the subject is an experience that people are able to go to and explore this is a very different relationship to information. If I was teaching maths, I could use collections that represented numbers and bring these numbers and the mathematical operations to life through moving through them laid out on the floor. I could jump my way through multiplication or post away the numbers in subtraction, I could spin collections involved in addition, play rhythms with multiplication and shred collections involved in fractions. I could feel the mathematics. I could live it. I could make it an experience of body which got around mind and which, learned through kinesthetics, might last longer than learning in a mind subject to fluctuations and information-processing problems. If I was exploring literacy, I could move with the moving words, feel the texture of words, bring words to life with mime signing. I could, especially, make words that were not about meaning but pure sound pattern and silliness designed to break the link between words, self-consciousness and information-processing whilst incidentally make written language into play. I could teach typing with a huge drawn keyboard on the floor and dance out my sentences with my feet. I could learn to write in sauce on a block of wood to avoid the Exposure Anxiety connection between self-expression and the expected symbols of pen and paper. I could be teaching the curriculum with less self-consciousness, through doing, through body, without the emphasis on proof of knowing and accept that doing is a kind of knowing, a knowing in body. The most important thing is that learning is accepted and that the teacher feels the time spent is constructive.

Exposure Anxiety and transitions

When someone initiates an exit, it's within their own control. When others initiate a transition, the person is not in control. Not only do they become subject to a flood of information in the transition but transitions are almost always directly-confrontational, self-in-relation-to-other and conscious-ness jolting – all bad dynamics for keeping Exposure Anxiety low. But there are ways of making transitions indirectly-confrontational.

1. TAKE THE FOCUS OFF THE TRANSITION

This might mean following the command of a magic hypnotic pencil in front of you. It might mean being a pack of quietly-treading gentle tigers, sneaking their way to Room 32 to pounce into the chairs in there. It might mean being a tram conductor singing passengers into line before the tram moves down the tracks to meet the bus outside.

2. TAKE THE FOCUS OFF THE PERSON

Remove yourself by going into character, essentially removing the sense of 'invasive control' from any potential control issue. Or allow the child with Exposure Anxiety to make the transition as something other than him or herself or to attribute the responsibility for his or her actions to the volition of an object or force other than the teacher. Or tap, sing or create rhythms on the way for the teacher's own sake to reduce self-consciousness.

I have had children with Exposure Anxiety seize control in a 'go on make me' refusal to get off the floor. If they can work down there, I provide them their materials in this place of choice and some quickly find sitting in a chair much more appealing in defying being 'met'. Similarly, I have simply got onto the floor and engaged a child (verbal or not) directly in social chit chat to myself aimed at them, which usually provokes a quick exit in avoiding what suddenly gets taken as an unintended invitation to be social. I have had 'come and get me' children giggling in a corner. By getting on with my activity and playing hard to get, they are forced to come after me to egg me on. I do not try to include them, but tell them I'm busy and I'll be with them in a moment, which seems to diffuse the teasing invitation in which I have now created neutral territory out of a winner–loser position of chase–chaser.

Where a child is unsafe or volatile I have 'removed' and 'navigated' them without direct confrontation towards the area they have to go using 'whirlywind'. Whirlywind is not me, it is a blustery, arms flailing wind which rushes and spins and directs itself at all kinds of things including children in the way. A whirlywind can move in wild changing directions, navigating an avoidant, potentially retaliative child humourously down a corridor, away from a gate, herding the child out of danger or back into the safety of the home class without even using language (in fact whirlywind blurts and blusters). Because, in being a characterization, there is no self-in-relation-to-other, and action can be taken without provoking easy personal retaliation.

Making transitions is also about familiarity. Instead of introducing the child to a new surrounding in the hope it will become familiar, you can borrow or copy key elements of the new environment and leave them lying about in the familiar environment of the home or old class for 'discovery'. If a child has never encountered blackboards, chalk, desks, plastic chairs, recess bells, these can appear one by one in familiar areas of the home as if 'for a visit'. Act as though they are either for your own use or 'invisible', as if you are surprised by their existence now they've been pointed out to you. Then, having become familiar, they 'disappear' again. This means that when the child then encounters these things again somewhere else, they become the seized familiarity among the dreaded invasion of the unknown and unfamiliar. This can be done with all kinds of transitions, a pillow case from an intended respite placement, the smell of an essential oil used (or to be used) in a new surrounding, a curtain fabric or piece of carpet which will be encountered elsewhere. The, 'Oh we have something like that' feeling instils a sense of being in control.

Asking for the toilet and eating with others

I had to ask. I had to show I had need. I joined with. For someone with Exposure Anxiety these are not felt as achievements but as defeats, as though the authority of others, one's own vulnerability, conquered the individual. This makes indicating need for the toilet and eating with others particularly hard tasks for some children with Exposure Anxiety, particularly at school.

By using reverse psychology, you might counter this. By providing a seat away from others in the lunch hall, possibly behind a brief semi partition, the child with Exposure Anxiety may feel 'you understood' and be grateful for the personal space and privacy in something so challengingly personal and admitting of need as eating. It may also be that this will be taken as an exposing act of demonstrating 'knowing them too predictably' and this may cause a retaliative response of defiantly joining the group. By giving in to this too wholly, too gladly, you'll trigger a catch twenty-two and the child may go into a rage. But if you act like you are 'tolerant' of the child's choice but won't expect it of them next time, nor the time after, you'll more likely find the child will stay and you'll have diffused Exposure Anxiety as a dinner table issue for now.

Asking someone (verbal or not, high functioning or not) with Exposure Anxiety to take another child to the toilet is one way to have them then seize this opportunity for themselves, especially if not expected or asked if they need the toilet too. You can address the pee/poo instead of the person, wondering out loud to yourself (through song if necessary) if there's one that might need to go for a swim in the toilet bowl. You can humanize excrement by making the toilet bowl like a bubble bath it wants to go into, leaving the child out as 'incidental' to the need of the excrement. If someone chooses to smear to put you off and distance you, you can always comment on the activity as might an art critic or TV chef, comment on a work of art or attempt at presentation. There is nothing that discourages the reward of distance so quickly as someone attempting to engage the person socially via their own distancing media, be that spit, excrement, swearing, mess making, damaging something. If the word 'no' is a reward in terms of a 'throw down the gauntlet' adrenaline rush, you might as well consider the surreal alternatives if they have a chance of working.

I was asked recently about 'responsibility for one's own actions'. In the self-owning, self-in-relation-to-self social–emotional reality of chronic Exposure Anxiety, the self-in-relation-to-other foundations for building 'responsibility for one's own actions' is poorly developed or missing. Yet teaching it is also teaching Exposure Anxiety what you want and expect, and that can be self-defeating. An indirectly-confrontational approach is designed to build this via another route. Without the underlying groundwork, preaching 'responsibility for one's own actions' may be like colour to the blind. It may be just words, a verbal bashing stick saying 'you are not like me and my way is superior because it's common and on that basis I will control you'. People can still become well adjusted, warm, inspiring, empathic people, even without a sense of self-in-relation-to-other if their Exposure Anxiety continually undermines their motivation towards developing that important skill.

Exposure Anxiety and self–other abuse

Self–other abuse can be used by the person with Exposure Anxiety to control others in school. This can be taken as dialogue that the approach being used is felt as too invasive, too controlling, too tightly dictatorial or prescriptive or that there is something being sensed other than what's portrayed on the surface. It can be taken as dialogue that interaction has been in too big a dose or that the child's own volition has been sensed to be invalid. It can be take as an indication that reduced lighting or turning off a fan might reduce the overload triggering heightened Exposure Anxiety retaliative responses, or simply that someone had foods they can't chemically manage. But self-directed or other-directed abuse can also be addressed by saying directly and decisively, 'Hold those teeth a moment, I'll be right back', returning with gardener's gloves, leather jacket or whatever you need to protect yourself or them. You can say, 'Hold that foot. You can kick me in just a moment', returning with the cricketer's pads on your legs. 'Hold that hand. I'll bring my hair right back', returning with a wig on.

You can also put this on them to protect them from their own 'choice' to choose abuse over self-calming. Exposure Anxiety drives to abuse are like a drug. I found them incredibly hard to tackle, made so much worse by nutrient deficiencies and toxicity issues. But however involuntary the abuse, there are still two other choices. Controlling oneself is generally not one of them. Running in circles or jumping is one of them because when you run, you exercise out the adrenaline and it can be progressively slowed back down and stilled to a walk. Another is self-calming such as rocking, tapping and humming, but in an extremely self-abusive state, this may not be extreme enough to compete with the adrenaline rush, and running and jumping may be needed to avoid self-calming being intermittently broken by bouts of abuse. You can appear to give the person choice about their abuse. Give them 'Yes but...', be that the wig, the cricketer's pads, the pillow stuck to the wall for the head-banger or whether it's the 'soft biting' with the arm pushed at the individual rather than pulled away. Exposure

Anxiety driven self-abuse will often pull back away when expected to continue by others.

Triggering versus accessing

In the classroom, the emphasis on accessing is one of the most constant provocations of self-consciousness and Exposure Anxiety and traps the person in an image akin to an apparent self-fulfilling prophecy of inability. Relying instead on triggering-based activities rather than accessing-based ones, and with activities directed at the object/issue rather than the person, you minimize this complication.

Drama, dance, music, writing

Mind and consciousness are like a gradual sunrise that takes time to come up. In the meantime, we are not stagnant, waiting for life to happen. We map everything, letting information-processing take care of itself. We map rhythm and pattern, pitch and volume, the form and flow of movements around us, of objects, places, people. This is the music of life and we feel it with our bodies, long before we identify mind with self; this is the realm of sensing, and we all began there. Some of us stay here longer than others.

Music has a particularly special place in the foundations we all came from. Whether we hear it in the footsteps with which an individual crosses the floor, the visual rhythm with which someone holds and puts down a glass or the flow and shifts of how someone sits in their own body, music, is everywhere and it is our first language. It has the most important of all places in the lives of those who find the realm of mind a place of rusty cogs and heavy effort – the stuff of overload, shutdown, information-processing delay and the sensory chaos that ensues. Such is the stuff of developmental conditions such as those in the autism spectrum, those I have lived with all my life. Music has the convincing power to restore order in chaos, to reassure that, in spite of an absence of sensory cohesion, something whole and wonderful, flowing and consistent still exists outside of us in the world we might otherwise easily give up on as being non-user-friendly. It is a place where those who struggle to keep up with the rate of information, left meaning deaf, meaning blind at the time of incoming information, still can meet with others in a form of communication and a state of involvement I call 'Simply Being'. More than this, music has the power, when haywire chemistry tells you that emotion and connection with others signals the threat of death, there is at least one social realm that remains safe, indirectly-confrontational and accepting of the right to 'lose oneself' as an act of self-calming in order to stay.

Music was an exceptionally important part of my life, not just in the unprocessed patterns around me (I couldn't understand three sentences in a row until I was nine) but in the form of classical music, sixties rock and roll, blues and TV jingles and theme songs. The emotional journeys of classical music gave me an experience of emotion no degree of severe exposure anxiety could later erase. I heard people through it. It helped me stand the music of their voices in spite of the chaos. It gave me a basis for sequencing. Rock and roll gave me humour and stored lines, blues gave me a comedian's timing. TV jingles and theme songs formed the main content of my personal language – a language of 'feel', 'theme' and 'topic', and although it may have been part of my being seen crazy and disturbed (it was the sixties and seventies and autism wasn't well understood) it was the bridge to the language I have today.

Music therapy is about building a safe space, a meeting place, somewhere to feel equal, a foundation of experience in which to remember in our bodies a spectrum of emotion and connection among others equally 'being' in their own space. Music therapy can be modulated and defies the confines and rigidity of social convention. Through song, we can address topics where directly-confrontational language dare not go (or would not be tolerated with meaning on-line). Used with people with severe exposure anxiety, it can be used as the Pied Piper, the musician giving small doses, as though purely for his or her own sake, playing hard to get and always leaving the activity with the person wanting more. It can be modulated to show that those in the directly-confrontational self-in-relation-to-other world can also be indirectly-confrontational in a self-owning way, demonstrating that life is not so black and white but has a whole spectrum in between.

Drama, dance, music and typing can all be used in an indirectly-confrontational way to stimulate communication as 'incidental'. Many cannot cope with these topics in classes where the focus is on the individual. But where exploration of tools in drama, movement, music and typing are freeform, the individual can find his or her own way to use costume, puppets, music and movement, rhythm and instruments, a keyboard and what to type patterns with. In such a class, the teacher, as fellow student, becomes a self-owning, self-in-relation-to- self model of exploration and inspiration of ideas rather than 'instructor', 'carer', 'teacher'. For me, 'instructor', 'carer', 'teacher' are from a self-in-relation-to-other, directly-confrontational, accessing-based structure and developmental reality. This may well equal 'being invaded', 'being controlled', 'being made too self-conscious', from the social–emotional developmental reality of someone who is primarily indirectly-confrontational, self-in-relation-to-self and who works on a level of triggering of preconscious unknown knowing rather than conscious accessing. So the two structures, which are meant to meet, clash. What's more, only one is considered 'normality', 'respectful' and 'correct', which can be an insult to someone who has a different developmental reality. You can't build a bridge with insults and it takes humility to inspire humility.

Story telling and hypnotherapy for people with Exposure Anxiety

Counselling can be done by a therapist in a self-directed way with those requiring an indirectly-confrontational approach. It can be made visual and concrete, focused on the object/issue rather than the person. It can involve the use of triggering rather than expectation on the client to use consciousness-jolting accessing. But even using an indirectly-confrontational approach there are three obstacles to relying on psychology to address developmental problems in people with Exposure Anxiety.

The first of these is certainly that physiological causes may need to be addressed. The second is that many people with Exposure Anxiety have auditory-processing delay. This means that some may struggle to get a full percentage of even literal meaning from interventions based on words. Others may get fluent literal meaning but have little or limited ability to process auditory information beyond the literal to the significant at the time things are being said. auditory-processing processing delay have the same problem understanding or keeping up with themselves. They may speak with meaning but have no or little idea what they have said. They may speak with apparent awareness of the significant and yet know what they said, what it literally meant, but have little idea of why they might have said what they said. The further complication of this, however, is that therapy involving verbal language is a grind: hard work and a quick cause of information overload.

Finally, there are essentially two minds in the person with Exposure Anxiety: the defensive/self-protective mind, and the non-defensive mind. The counsellor is working to help the self, not the defence arsenal. Yet some people with Exposure Anxiety can remarkably map out what is expected of them and use this mapping to divert the therapist, or passively comply, or to build up an arsenal of how to play the therapist defensively. This isn't necessarily a conscious process and most mapping of pattern is something sensed or felt – kinesthetic rather than reliant on informa-tion-processing such as interpretation. The point is, if the defensive self uses such an arsenal to further 'protect' the self against the invasive attempts by the therapist to influence or connect, then the therapy is futile.

It is here that storytelling and hypnotherapy can have greater benefits. The abstract, even surreal nature of storytelling and hypnotherapy can mean the defensive mind cannot map what is expected and use it to retain divisions between self and other or between the therapist and the self. Sto-rytelling and hypnotherapy can be so slippery, there is no foothold for Exposure Anxiety. Furthermore, even if someone has quite marked auditory-processing delay, still very meaning deaf in the moment of the telling, the process is still likely to work. This is because even though someone appears not to understand visually or auditorily in the moment doesn't mean they haven't mapped the pattern of everything and this grad-ually becomes worked through on a preconscious level. The person may be completely unaware of what he or she has understood, but the emo-tional–social impact of what was understood still causes an internal shift at some level. I have heard this reported by the families of many functionally non-verbal people who appeared to react to events several days or weeks after they took place, at which time there seemed no apparent understand-ing. It is the nature of the brain eventually to work through its backlog, however limited in resources. Furthermore, storytelling can be done with mime signing, and playing out via representational objects or pictures and so requires less processing time in linking words to meaning. Hypnotherapy can be the language of emotion rather than mind and involves journeying through dynamics, patterns, shifting feel of situations and so may rely less on the drudge of information-processing of every day blah blah.

The definition of a reward

For someone with chronic Exposure Anxiety, the definition of a 'reward' or 'punishment' might be quite different. For most children, inclusion is a reward, exclusion a punishment. For the child with Exposure Anxiety, inclusion may be an expectation, an imposition, an entrapment. Exclusion may be equated with personal space, freedom and a lack of external control or expectation. Playing hard to get, keeping things small doses, always leaving the person wanting more may promote involvement with someone with Exposure Anxiety. The opposite, attempting to join verbally and socially via the medium of the unwanted behaviour very often leads to this bridge being burned.

Approval and praise are conventionally taken to be rewards. Disapproval or ignoring the child are conventionally taken to be attempts to inhibit the same behaviours from recurring. Yet for the child with Exposure Anxiety, approval and praise may equate with an intolerable degree of connection sensed as uninvited 'invasion'. Disapproval may be equated with having the power to distance others. Being ignored can mean losing inhibition, but it can also mean being disempowered when a child is insistent on provoking a response, in which case, I'd use the 'yes, but' strategy. The 'yes but' strategy means you encourage the unwanted behaviour whilst manoeuvering it. 'Gentle kicking' whilst pushing towards the kicker is an example of this. So is, 'No problem, I'll just get a cup of tea and be right back' is another example of acknowledgement but distance, not playing the game but refusing to enter into an escalating stance of confrontation, counter confrontation.

Getting stars might be OK because the focus is on the work, not on the person. Getting a pragmatic reward or a right to 'buzz' can seem a good trade but is hard to then interrupt, take away or limit with someone who is limited in her simultaneous sense of self and other.

Food rewards are a problem. Most children with severe chronic Exposure Anxiety will have metabolic problems which require special diets. Furthermore, chronic stress exacerbates gut and immune system problems and many children crave and are actually chemically addicted to the foods which they cannot matabolize or have allergies to and which cause drug like highs with obvious effects on behaviour about thirty minutes later. Eighty per cent of children on the spectrum are unable to properly digest dairy or gluten according to Paul Shattock. Sixty per cent are unable properly to metabolize salicylates, which are high in citrus, grapes, berries, cola, cocoa, chocolate, caffeine and artificial colourings, flavourings and sweeteners, according to studies by Rosemary Waring. Phenylketonuria is thought also to be a common cause of autism and is known to provoke chronic anxiety and involuntary behaviours. It is treatable through a specific low protein diet but many subclinic cases are not picked up on and are left untreated. Many people on the spectrum have been found to have low stomach acid and an alkaline gut, often meaning high toxicity-related Candida levels (which use up vitamin B supply) and low magnesium levels, all exacerbated by sugar intake. The ability to use food as a reward is thought limited so as not to set the child up for an increase in the very behaviours and difficulties which will sabotage what they've just achieved and been rewarded for – hardly a pattern you'd want to reinforce. This leaves a limited range of acceptable rewards, such as sliced pears and mango, rice crackers, plain crisps or corn chips (where a child is not allergic to potato or corn). The only other alternative for dietarily-managed children is to use 'safe' food rewards supplied by home.

School dinners, sugar and the impact of diet

I've been a consultant to schools where I've seen spaced-out or hyperactive children, very pale and thin, with allergic 'shiners' under their eyes, indicative of treatable food allergy and food intolerance. I've seen these same children in the lunch hall with lasagne full of gluten and casein (milk products), covered with tomato puree (high in Salicylates) or sandwiches full of gluten and spread with margarine full of milk products and followed with sugary deserts full of dairy products. Dairy and gluten are the hardest foods to digest and lead to opiate-like responses, akin to LSD. Salicylate intolerance causes a cocaine-like high, making it very hard for children to hold back or slow down, increasing sensory fragmentation. I've seen children turn even paler twenty minutes after lunch, with major outbursts. I've seen two children with tremor and cold fingers and nose together with sudden onset panic attacks indicative of reactive hypoglycemia common to food allergy and toxicity issues. Yet day after day I'll see such children with lunchboxes stuffed with sugary snacks which exacerbate the hypoglycemic see-saw, crisps full of additive given to children on the spectrum. Children need fun and food they like. Interesting, exciting and safe school lunches are possible for children with special dietary needs, but getting awareness of such things by GPs, school pediatricians, parents and those who control school dinners and distribute them, is actually a bigger challenge than learning about special diets themselves.

Exposure Anxiety and the playground

Nowhere is a child more expected to initiate or flexibly accept the initiations of others than in the playground. This makes it a difficult place for children with Exposure Anxiety. Avoidance responses can mean a child looks happier being alone, uninterested in the activities of others. Most children won't interrupt if they think they will be pushed away or 'ignored' and they need to see the other person is interested in them to feel confident to take the risk to be social. This means children with involuntary avoidance responses are often left alone.

Children caught up in involuntary diversion responses seem to be unable to play 'properly'. They appear not to care about 'the rules', not to 'follow the game', not to 'pay attention'. Sometimes they become the clown of the group, often the source of amusement, entertainment, but also a tolerated source of frustration. Children who respond with retaliation responses are often considered frightening and unpredictable. They quickly get a reputation that is a bit like an invisible 'keep your distance' sign. They may attract those who want to be seen to be wild or tough and this can mean they might be set up as 'the troublemaker' which is not actually what they are. Being given any social role, however, is sometimes better than having none to the lonely self dominated by Exposure Anxiety responses.

An assistant facilitating activity in the playground for a child with chronic Exposure Anxiety responses might think about how to organize activities that don't trigger these responses so often or so extremely. The avoidant child can easily be incorporated into very self-owning activities.

Looking at things through coloured cellophane, throwing leaves about, rolling down hills together, trampolining, swinging, jumping on beds, skating – all are activities less likely to leave this kind of child isolated.

The diversive child needs to be expected to constantly shift in order to defiantly stick at any one thing. An obstacle course, a box of costumes, musical instruments or cardboard boxes out of which to build structures, are ideas which can allow constant shift whilst staying involved in the whole. Being in charge of a Camcorder during an event means the emphasis in involvement is not on the child but on the filming. In charge of mowing, sweeping up, being the one to collect everything up, all give an emphasis outside of the child and a sense of progression in an activity that provides continual shift and movement. Diversion thrives in stillness. Keep things moving.

The retaliative child needs flexible activities which are likely to leave the child behind so that he or she chooses to keep up but can participate with his or her own separate 'flavour'. A treasure hunt or a 'find it' game of 'hot/cold' can put the focus outside the child and inspire everyone to go for the goal for their own sake, compelling the retaliation child to 'get there first'. Tug of war, limbo competitions, tightrope walking, whatever activity intrinsically hints of 'You can't', is most likely to inspire, 'Oh yes I can'.

Exposure Anxiety and bullying

Avoidance infuriates bullies, robbing them of a sense of significance and power and compelling them to want to 'get a response'. Of course the more directly-confrontational the bully is, the more the determination to avoid grows. It is only if the bully tried to join in with the person in avoidance that their Exposure Anxiety would escalate to diversion and the self-protective retaliation response that would keep them safe. But the bully isn't trying to join such a person. People caught up in involuntary avoidance responses are also singled out by abusers because they appear not to notice or show they care about what has been done to them. There is a challenging enigmatic nature to the aloof child which can be misused by an abuser as 'teasing' them into contact with such a child or used to try to justify their behaviour by trying to 'help'. The avoidant child also appears to be so private and secretive that the behaviour of the abuser is more likely to go unseen by others.

It is extremely important not to suffocate the freedom of exploration and movement of the avoidant child as this is their best avenue to expression and learning. At the same time it's important to model and inspire the use of pointed or typed communication in those who can't speak up, even if this is via a communication book of 'word-pictures' in word grids on different topics on each page. Many thought unable to read or write have still demonstrated an ability eventually to step into assisted typing and it is this 'voice' which may help protect them. The avoidant child may need a 'fly on the wall' shadow, not there to take over, but to help protect against bullying.

Diversion responses can make someone look as if they are having fun, as if they don't mind. They can also be infuriating, especially to parents. Children with constant diversion responses can be subject to excessive attempts to control them or 'teach them' through physical restraint, sometimes abuse. They can be made complicit in their own abuse as a result of their giggling or squealing taken to be signs of enjoyment. Their ability to escape can challenge some people to want to win by entrapping them. Bullying someone caught up in diversion responses may centre around their inability to control themselves with an emphasis on 'how mad' or 'disturbed' such a child is.

Writing can be very hard for children challenged by diversion responses. They may rush themselves, constantly compelled to break off from the activity. Typing can become much faster and the result of the word on the page clearer to read. The diversive child can say far more far more quickly through typing, sometimes, than through writing, and this can be a source of disclosure, dialogue and protection as can a book full of communication word grids used in pointed communication. Physically, the ability to spin makes it hard for an abuser or bully to hold a grip, so modelling this playful escape mode of becoming 'whirlywind' can be a useful tool for a child who may be unable to initiate real self-help in running away, biting or screaming. Remember that everything you teach a child regarding running away, biting or screaming might be needed one day. Another reason to teach 'small slow running, gentle biting, quiet screaming'. You can always teach them to modulate the intensity should they need to.

Retaliation responses usually come out when someone is trying to join with the person with Exposure Anxiety. But being attacked is not an act of connection, but of distancing. The person who appears so retaliative may actually freeze under such a confrontation, going instead into avoidance. The retaliative child is liable to be egged on into dangerous situations through challenge and it's important to model the retaliative response of retaliating against the retaliation itself, the ability to give up on reacting and walk or run off defiantly instead. There is no point reasoning about a more well-adjusted response and explaining such a response to a child dominated by retaliation responses means you may actually disempower them by compelling them to reject your teaching. The response has to make sense to Exposure Anxiety defensiveness. The retaliation child doesn't usually become a bully, but may well involuntarily attack the people he most seeks contact with, making him feel like a danger to others and mistrustful of himself.

Teenage years: complications for the young adult with Exposure Anxiety

The teenage years are very trying for people with Exposure Anxiety. Avoidance, diversion and retaliation responses might have passed as a child, but as a teenager hormone levels become erratic, and on top of this there is the challenge that others are all competing for the assertion of their own maturity, which makes the person with Exposure Anxiety a likely scapegoat. Expectations of more personal and focused responses become increased in secondary school and the expectation to respond in a self-in-relation-to-other fashion now becomes intense. The fact that the person has got this far without these skills means there is the added fear of discovery of this deficit so there are added attempts to hide this. This means the self-protective responses now not only centre around protection against self-consciousness, against connection, against defeat, but now also against discovery. This makes the person intensely vulnerable and under pressure like never before. As others race ahead in their social skills, able to cope on all these levels, this creates something akin to being naked under floodlights, one's difficulties highlighted by the relative lack of these in others. In my view, removal to a special needs school needn't be necessary but removal to a unit sensitive to how to deliver learning whilst accommodating a social–emotional developmental delay may be needed. This could deliver the same intellectual level of information but the style of delivery might involve a continuation of an emphasis on triggering rather than accessing, modelling rather than teaching, exploring and through this understanding, rather than expecting proof of understanding before the right to explore. It might involve the teacher's participation in lessons as though for his or her own benefit rather than that of the pupil, and keeping things visual and concrete, perhaps even mime signing to cut down on required processing time. It might involve focusing on the object/issue and not on the student and learning through doing, rather than through mind with the consciousness-jolting this involves and its relationship to triggering Exposure Anxiety. It might involve making learning incidental to the doing, modelling learning through sensing and mapping of pattern, in which understanding becomes incidental, rather than relying primarily on interpretation over 'getting the pattern'.

Those who remain in the mainstream structure might need to tape lessons as they may have been so gripped by Exposure Anxiety as to be unable to fully process or properly participate in them at the time. These can then be played on going to sleep, allowing them to sink in without using conscious awareness or triggering Exposure Anxiety responses through 'trying'. Such students might need to go twice to the same class or lecture if available, the first time getting some of the content and involvement, the second time, familiar with it and less 'on guard', able to begin to think and respond to the lesson. Such a student might need access to the materials in their own time and space to utilize the advantage of teaching themselves broadly on the topic. Students with visual–perceptual problems may be helped by low lighting, avoiding fluorescent lighting or through the use of tinted lenses. Addressing food intolerance and food allergies as well as nutrient deficiencies may be able to help struggling students on the autism spectrum at this age, even if earlier dietary interventions have never been tried. Medications which help balance neurotransmitter levels may also help those with challenging, involuntary behaviours to manage a greater degree of self-control.

At this age there are huge expectations to 'act normal' and compare notes on experiences, whether you are socially–emotionally at this level of development and have the cohesion to process your experiences or not. This increases the fear of 'discovery' as a pressure on top of all the others caused by Exposure Anxiety. It is therefore important that people have alternative social networks, such as rambling groups, chess clubs, computer games networks, singing groups, martial arts, film clubs. These might be whatever they can be involved in socially through 'doing', so they remain confident, active and involved, with a sense of social success and inclusion rather than failure. With people with Exposure Anxiety the key to this may be in choosing activities which are very self-owning in which contact is not directly with the person. The isolation of being the only person with severe chronic Exposure Anxiety can be overwhelming in secondary and post secondary school levels. It's important to find a way to feel useful if you can't become personally involved, such as helping out in student services, sorting equipment, working voluntarily in the canteen. It's also important to have at least one person you can just let go with and be yourself. Even if this is your pet dog, your hamster, someone you look after or even sitting with your favourite tree, you need to feel there is some space in the world, however alone, where you are able to be fully yourself without comparison to others or disappointment in yourself.

One of the hardest things about being a teenager or young adult is that people want personal interaction and conversation. The person caught up in chronic Exposure Anxiety avoidance, diversion and retaliation responses can have major struggles with being personal. Some will defensively bombard others with personal information to disempower them from asking for such information. I call this jumping out the cupboard before they open the door. This 'distancing behaviour' using the personal can achieve just that, distance, even though the person with Exposure Anxiety may have wanted to connect, in spite of being compelled by that very desire to distance. Some will hold others off at arm's length, keeping everything tightly controlled, formal and pragmatic. They may be so self-protectively blocked from using the personal they themselves cannot, in the course of interaction, find it. It may still, however, resurface, once the heat is off and the person is on their own or left behind by others. This creates a terrible isolating catch 22.

Some will so compulsively divert they are considered to be unable to take anything seriously. They may use compulsive characterizations to deliver important personal communication but the delivery distracts from the content and the personal message is not taken personally because the person didn't give it directly 'as herself'. In *Nobody Nowhere* I wrote about Julian asking me, 'When do you ever get off the stage?' and this really sums it up. He was trying to be personal and connect and all he could get near to was a compulsive performer caught up in involuntary diversion responses. Some will be so caught up in freezing and avoidance responses they appear to have nothing to say, to be uninterested and uninteresting. Inside, they may have much to say and a deep desire to connect; or they may be cut off from that, unaware of having anything to say, or of any desire to connect. Yet they display a degree of frustration and despair that tells the story of what is beyond conscious awareness.

It is important to have a medium via which the young adult can defy what is coming out on the surface. Many find that whilst behaviour and verbal language become corrupted in the hands of Exposure Anxiety, writing, and particularly typed communication, somehow gets out with less contortion or restriction. This is not so for all and some require a 'safe person' with them to feel OK about disclosure between them and the keyboard. Typing worked, in my personal case, because of the movement and because, unlike verbal language or behaviour, it was directed not at a person but at an object. The movement was so impersonal, the simple tapping of fingers, unexpressively, uniformly onto keys that make little feedback noise, nothing to jolt recognition. Somehow, Exposure Anxiety seemed unable to 'see' my fingers. It monitored everything, every body movement expressive of self, every utterance, every thought involving desire and connection, but it couldn't see my fingers. Also, the ability to talk, not to someone else, but to the keyboard means no matter how much someone else wanted to hear from me, I felt physically convinced that my dialogue was not with them but with myself, about them as a topic.

Providing the opportunity to disclose one's real self through typed communication is not just important for 'non-verbal' people and people without good 'functional verbal language', but also for teenagers and young adults whose personal language is challenged by Exposure Anxiety. Through typing they may be able to form relationships, discuss issues,

reply to questions, make arrangements, disclose feelings but, most important, disclose the difference between the inner self and the one coming
over because of Exposure Anxiety. This helps outsiders to make real connections, in spite of the surface behaviour and communication. Also,
having specific non-verbal time and instructing others on how to 'simply
be' can allow the teenager or young adult to enjoy himself as himself with
far less contortion and save verbal communication for the keyboard.
'Simply being' involves those activities that allow a sense of being in one's
own world whilst in company. Playing with light, pattern, sound,
movement, enjoying nature, involved in construction or sculpture, even
skating, walking, trampolining, swimming, horse riding, computer
games, videos and chess – these can all be 'simply be' activities.

Exposure Anxiety and work

Exposure Anxiety can sometimes get off guard when the self feels securely
hidden behind a sense of purpose. This means that sometimes, there are
people with Exposure Anxiety feel less exposed on a personal level at work
than they do at home. Some jobs and activities provoke Exposure Anxiety
more than others. I have had production-line jobs where I felt my own will
was given over to the machine or the process and I felt quite calm and at
peace in myself as part of such a process, however seemingly
unchallenging this may have seemed to an outsider. I had thirty jobs in
three years between the age of fifteen and eighteen and if there's one thing
about Exposure Anxiety, it can dig its heels in and refuse to budge or it can
be ever ready to avoid, divert, retaliate or run. Exposure Anxiety can make
you stay when you really should adapt or move on. It can make you
sabotage or run at the very point you are becoming valued, noticed or
known. So it's not just the job, it's the control dynamics and social climate
of the job, which both need to be taken account of.

I worked best where I could 'lose myself' in the work, not notice I was
even noticing. Audio typing, copy typing, production line work in a
printers collating, quality control on a production line in a meat works,
ticketing rows of garments in a clothing factory, counting in stock rooms,
filling stock orders to go out, sorting and tidying department store shelves,
cleaning; these were very lulling jobs. It was such a relief to have a single

aspect of life where Exposure Anxiety got off my back and out of my gut, where I could just stand and 'be' among others.

Serving customers or answering the phone to people was problematic. I could address the issue or the topic, but the expectation to build rapport or connect personally meant constant struggles with Exposure Anxiety attempting to take over. One shop I worked in, I snapped at people in sudden shocking stored lines of 'What do you want' in strong distancing tones. Another, I went into stored phrases on the telephone, appearing snappy, self-entertaining and obnoxious and often slamming the phone down on people. I was constantly told off for ignoring people which was my way of controlling myself or protecting them from my own diversion and retaliation responses should I push myself too far when in avoidance mode. Walking out on jobs was very common. Sitting at the bus stop unable to force myself on the bus to work and watching them pass until I was late for work, then terrified of this and forced to never show up again was also common. Serving customers could be fine if it was a production line, one-size-fits all response required in which I was able to focus on the product and the supply without the interpersonal niceties. The handing over and receiving of money was also an issue to someone with extreme self-protectiveness against a sense of self-in-relation-to-other. The saying of please or thank you was so very hard. I learned to ignore their money till it was put on the counter and then I'd take it from the counter. I learned to put their money on the counter. I learned to clear plates without asking. I learned to say 'Q' for 'thank you' and 'some… if that's OK', instead of 'please'. This was extremely hard for the environment to accept as my best efforts, let alone the desired response. I think, however, a simple card of introduction explaining this would solve some of that. It could say, for example:

> Hi, in case my ways are a bit confusing I thought it right to let you know, I'm not being rude, I have Exposure Anxiety. This involuntary self-protection response means I find it difficult to easily or consistently connect in a personal way. I will try my best to be of help and service. Thank you for understanding my somewhat 'different ways'. We are all different.

There are some people with Exposure Anxiety who do not feel at all exposed in making 'chit chat' and in fact feel safe hiding behind it. I had one job where I sold newspaper space door to door and although I felt gripped with dread to initiate conversation, I was able to focus on these people's shop businesses and on how I might bring this to life in an advertisement and shape the conversation around that. I didn't experience dialogue as interpersonal and the freedom to be in a job that allowed me to explore shops and be free to walk down the street, was much less Exposure Anxiety-provoking than working in a room full of other people. Dialogue, when someone came into my space and I was unprepared, triggered Exposure Anxiety, but dialogue where I had invaded their space on my terms with my focus, did not. Unlike being cornered on my own territory, having invaded theirs, it was me who was free to leave. They had to stay with their shop, vulnerable and exposed to all who came in. Jobs involving doing, the moving of things, planting, ritualistically assisting people across the road, are all focused on 'doing' and involve the freedom to move as part of the work.

The social climate, however, was always the weakest point for me. I'd have loved to work without any breaks. When I could I took my breaks whilst walking. When working in the city, I took my breaks in the bedding department of the local department store, enjoying the private feeling of being in what felt like a 'home space' with a bed and a sense of containment and cosyness. I have no formal religion, but I escaped into a small church to be in a dim, candle-lit, quiet, non-interactive space. I went walking in the local park, spending time with trees. Though I hardly read, I spent time in the library either of the establishment or the local library. I'm not a train spotter, but I sat at bus stops and tram stops and watched passing public transport. I spent my breaks tidying my work space or that of others if they let me. I walked around the streets photographing graffiti. I disappeared to the toilets. I hovered on stairwells. I wandered about the factory floor. I'd have spent time with pets if there were any. I'd have watered the plants if there were any. Where I was expected to stay or to want to stay in a staff room or to go out with others, I felt gripped with dread. Though I had the deepest desire to be like others, to find it as easy as them, this took great effort and focus and the slightest letting up of control over my communication and behaviour meant Exposure Anxiety would run it instead.

I think it's important in taking a job that the person with Exposure Anxiety has a plan for breaks. What is nearby? Is there a TV, are there magazines, is there a park? What will you do if that plan is blocked for some reason? Can you take a video game, a deck of cards, comics, a Walkman? Is there a language you'd like to learn on your breaks via tapes? Is there some reading up you'd like to do or a part-time open education course you could focus on? Can you take your own lunch and drinks? Is there a small space you can have to yourself? Sometimes just having these 'escape routes' is enough to be able, instead, to choose small tolerable hit-and-run doses of social interaction with others on breaks. If these alternatives, this private space, this freedom, makes the difference between being able to stay in a job or constantly manoeuvering yourself out of one after another after another, then it may be worth it. A card of explanation to fellow employees can help avoid the gossip, alienation and back stabbing that can come from being too mysterious, too enigmatic, too different. Be up front and you have nothing to hide. The mystery is over. My own card would probably read something like:

> Hi, glad to meet you all. I live with Exposure Anxiety. This is an involuntary self-protection response that makes it hard for me to easily commit and stick with social involvement, a bit like social claustrophobia. If I seem aloof or uninterested, it's just that it's hard to relax with this condition so I give myself other things to do and lots of space. I might pop in with the group from time to time but wanted you people to know I've lived with this problem all my life and it's nothing caused by any of you. Thanks for understanding this 'differentness' and I look forward to gradually getting to know you all in what will probably be small doses. Thanks for bearing with me.

Staff members not wanting to leave the person with Exposure Anxiety out of activities but sick of asking and getting no response or feeling snubbed, can start an invitation board out in the hall, with a write up of what's happening this lunchtime or where everyone's going with the addition 'feel free to just drop by. All welcome, maybe see you there.'

I found it so hard that when I was invited directly I was quickly triggered to avoid, divert from or reject such an invitation. General public invitations were easier, less reeking of the heavy weight of commitment and the entrapment that entailed. Notifications on walls were more likely to have me drop by than direct invitations. Remember that if the person with Exposure Anxiety always 'disappears' at lunchtime, you can always have a note system, stating you wonder where they go to, you don't want to be missing out. It might be more interesting than what you do. If you ask if you can come along you'll quite likely get the involuntary self-protective response of apparent indifference that is really off putting to many people. But if you don't ask and just announce your decision to come along, not to be with them, but because you are interested in the activity, you'll likely find an easier response. Remember, this may be someone who finds a sense of self-in-relation-to-other to be very difficult to manage or cope with. Being self-owning, there for the activity and not the company, might really take the heat off and allow the person with Exposure Anxiety to find you do not provoke this inescapable internal discomfort which follows them through most of their social life. Under these social rules, it may be possible to later include others by the same pattern. But keep in mind that many people with Exposure Anxiety will pull away from the activity if they sense that interaction has become a self-in-relation- to-other activity rather than a self-in-relation-to-self one that happens to be done in larger numbers.

Being told what to do can be a big problem with Exposure Anxiety. If the person with Exposure Anxiety has put this responsibility on you to tell them what to do or prompt them, then you telling them often means they can 'disappear', doing 'as you'. But if they have not initiated this from you, your attempts as boss to ask them to do something or do it your way can very easily be taken as an invasion and trigger avoidance, diversion or retaliation responses. Certainly, it is likely to trigger protectiveness against the sense of self-in-relation-to-other that is necessary to adapting to your needs as employer. The only way they may be able to appease and calm their own Exposure Anxiety-driven sense of 'invasion' at such an attempt may be to continue on their own track. This may mean doing their own way, to prove to themselves you two have not 'connected', they have not been 'invaded', they have not conceded 'defeat'. But you are the boss. What do you do?

To start with, model, don't teach. Observe the way being used by the person with Exposure Anxiety and then take over, as though for your own benefit rather than theirs. You could say (out loud to yourself) something like 'That's really interesting how you do the task that way, I prefer the faster/neater/shortcut/clearer way like this'. You would say this not to them but out loud to yourself directed at the work, not the person and then just walk off. Here you may have a better chance of instruction being not compliantly listened to but taken on board because it gets around the defensiveness. It may take a bit of repeat modelling such as 'Wow, you're still doing it that old way, budge over a minute because I'd just like to do a bit of this the faster/neater/ shortcut/clearer way. Thanks for that.' This doesn't attack the person's way of doing the work but demonstrates their way is the old way, the slower/less orderly/long winded way. They are left with a nagging awareness that someone else had 'beaten them' in productivity, had a way that worked better than their way. They will feel a lacking which will drive them to try to stop you finding any need to take over again, beating you to it. Instead of having to continually re-define their sense of self in relation to the boss by insisting on staying the same as they always were, the focus shifts to keeping the boss away by making the boss's expertise redundant.

Giving instructions in a visual and concrete way, perhaps on a white board, with symbols for concepts so the interpretation sticks, is a way of telling the board rather than the person. The person can then take the instruction from the board without feeling they are selling out by 'connecting' in a self-in-relation-to-other way. The board becomes the neutral territory from which the instruction is not given, but taken. Similarly, the boss can have a query-board in the hall or, more privately, a 'suggestions box'. The board can either be a white board or a board for post-it questions or statements. Using the board means the person with Exposure Anxiety doesn't have to approach the boss and can still say 'I can't' without confronting the self-in-relation-to-other obstacle. Remember the person with Exposure Anxiety may be more likely to make statements than ask questions. Statements are just dialogue out loud to oneself but even the thought of asking a question may provoke a sense of self-in-relation-to-other which may trigger avoidance or diversion from the question or the asking of it. The boss may be more likely to get statements like 'The computer doesn't work right' rather than 'How can I get the computer to process…?'

Social dangers in the workplace and the person with Exposure Anxiety is an issue. Keep in mind the social danger may be from the boss him or herself. Modelling a dialogue via notes between employees can be the problem or the solution, but at any rate, social dangers thrive where there is secrecy and privacy. People with Exposure Anxiety are often the person, because of this, to be singled out as the ones who won't disclose, who won't speak up. Social dangers are also possible outside of the workplace where people with Exposure Anxiety seek to escape the social involvement of breaks. Contacting those in charge of overseeing such places and letting them know who to contact if there is trouble can be a good plan whilst allowing the person with Exposure Anxiety space and privacy. Keep in mind that the more you try to control or hem in someone with Exposure Anxiety, the more they may run. Giving space and lack of expectation is often the best way to enable them to more easily protect themselves by coming back to involvement in the group where they cannot be so easily made a victim of their own secrecy and privacy.

Counselling strategies with people with Exposure Anxiety can mean speaking out loud to yourself and using social stories which focus on the issue/topic rather than the person. Keeping things visual and concrete, using your social stories whilst sketching diagrams or representative cartoons can help some people tune in because the emphasis is off them and there is no sense of being directly invaded by someone's 'blah blah'. It's often a good idea to tell two parallel stories, one which represents how things are happening and the other to demonstrate how they might otherwise have happened. This allows the person with Exposure Anxiety an aerial shot of the contrast and a position of openly choosing with which to identify without being compelled out of self-protectiveness to reject the one expected of or desired for them. Remember to frame your social stories so they make social–emotional sense and work constructively for the person with Exposure Anxiety. In other words, such stories shouldn't purely reflect the social–emotional reality from the perspective of someone without Exposure Anxiety.

In my view, Bach Flower Remedies can be important in helping people get work, stay in it and make choices. In particular, Cherry Plum for fear of losing control and doing what you dread and Rockwater for self-denial, stricture, and rigidity and being a purist, might help some people to ease up about influence. Alternately, Walnut can help people to protect themselves from being overly influenced by others or too oversensitive about change. Red Chestnut can help people who worry compulsively and are compelled to take over. Rescue remedy can help in panic attacks or facing extreme stress, including that of initiating interviews, which I think can be more scary than having teeth pulled.

Exposure Anxiety and independent living

Independent living involves being responsible for oneself and, occasionally, getting outside help. Being responsible for oneself in front of other people is different from being able to survive when completely unobserved and left to your own devices. Many parents assume that the child's ability is based on what they see and have never left their child to fend alone in a survival situation. Yet there are some so called 'low- functioning' children who have becomes lost, either in the city or the outback, who have survived quite remarkably until they were found again or caught.

One of the greatest problems with people having the chance to be independent is the 'prove the capability in order to get the opportunity' mentality. I'm thirty-eight. Had anyone waited and watched and tried to teach me to learn how to keep track of time, run a bath without flooding it, leave somewhere without locking myself out or understand how to organize paying a bill, cooking to a recipe, asking for help or not speaking to strangers, then, until recently they'd still have been waiting. When one is hungry, one eventually grabs food. When one gets locked out, one is forced to draw attention or break back in. When something floods one is forced to draw attention or take control. When utilities get cut off, one is forced to adapt to the loss or draw attention to get the situation sorted out. Exposure Anxiety means that asking for help doesn't come naturally and that the person may go to extreme lengths to 'provoke' help indirectly or to hide the fact it is needed. This can make the person look far less capable than she actually is.

It is possible to create a fairly user-friendly apartment for someone who can't ask or organize due to the inability to liaise with others or show in a self-in-relation-to-other way that something has bothered her. Utility bills can all be put on direct debit to take care of themselves. Food that requires little or no cooking or preparation can be delivered. Washing can be collected, delivered and put away without the tenant having to 'care' or take responsibility or liaise. Technology can also compensate for a lot of practical responsibility. The biggest need for help may well be in helping parents to cope with sticking by tough love in order to allow their child to discover for herself her own drive to use self-help skills. Because of the degree of internal opposition, the motivational factors have to be more extreme to combat this opposition to exploring or progressively, through trial and error, using the skills needed. It is the school of hard knocks and it is a very tough to ask parents to give space when every instinct is to watch, help or assist without having been asked to.

Modelling doing for other and taking for self may be an option for some people. Cooking not for self but for the invisible person or teddy at the table may be a way that the self can then choose not to leave that food unappreciated and uneaten. Getting a blanket not for self, but for the dog, then competitively choosing not to go without may be a way of getting something for self. Getting a glass of water not for self but for the plants and then testing whether it's OK to drink may be another. Modelling the getting on of shoes, not for self but for the poor hurt feet, may be a way of getting a preconscious message through about how to utilize self-help skills when blocked from taking direct conscious action on one's own behalf.

This modelling may provide the database for someone with Exposure Anxiety developing tricks for doing for 'self'. But as most life skills education is directly confrontation, those with severe Exposure Anxiety usually are the last ones to 'discover' or subconsciously pick up the self-help skills necessary and so are also the last ones to be put in situations of independent living. So it may need to start with heavily modelling how such skills might be achieved had the modeller him or herself been living with extreme Exposure Anxiety. Presently, there is no such training, no literature on how to implement such a programme and no real understanding on the part of non-autistic professionals as to the basic mechanics of living with Exposure Anxiety from the inside. Those who live with Exposure Anxiety can hardly dare expose it. But without someone doing so, it would never be understood.

It is not only self-help skills which shout 'I exist', 'I care', 'I can', and someone modelling such daring for their own sake can only be an inspiration, but many skills beyond this are needed. Answering the door, telling people to go, leaving the house, shopping problems, saying 'thank you', asking 'please', saying 'no', asking for help, all of these may be difficult with Exposure Anxiety. Keeping in mind the 'in front of the public rules' of 'can't do it for myself', 'can't do it by myself', 'can't do it as myself', you will know your options. Having a helper may work but will promote learned helplessness which is why it's so attractive as a cop out for Exposure Anxiety. Can't do it for myself can be constructively utilized in doing for the dog, for the plants, for the jumper, for the feet. You can even warm up the house just for the poor cold house! If you can't use your skills in an Exposure Anxiety-provoking situation unless it is not as yourself, you can still do as someone or something else. Again, this comes down to modelling, always as though for one's own benefit, from the time the child with Exposure Anxiety is quite young. It's OK to go shopping as 'the mad shopper'. It's OK to ask someone to leave as an undercover police person. It's OK if you can't dare to leave the house, to suddenly go on a mission to save a tin of beans from the supermarket. It's OK to say 'please' with the voice of a high society socialite, to say thank you as though you are someone being awarded an honour. It's OK to say 'no' as a schoolmaster, to answer the door as though you are in a TV advertisement. The worst that will happen is that the child will be thought of as funny, colourful or mad and that may be a lot better than being helpless and without any apparent survival skills. A 'no' or a request to leave doesn't even have to be verbal, it can be expressed through gestural signing. What you model as communication doesn't have to rely on verbal ability. The person with Exposure Anxiety may not even take up your characterizations at all for these are about you and to take them up may be felt to be an open sign you sought to 'join them' in a self-in-relation-to-other interaction. But they may, however, take up the deeper level; that if blocked from doing as self, it is always possible somehow to utilize some other role to do things in that role without selling out.

Being unable to do as oneself, for oneself or by oneself may limit flexibility or even close out the development of many or most 'friendships'. This depends on the area and some communities tolerate, even incorporate developmentally-challenged people better than others. In my teens and early twenties, living in apartments in communities where most lacked a higher education, in areas challenged by high crime and unemployment, I was just one of many wild and colourful characters and that probably meant I was engaged by more people than I might otherwise have been. I met as many 'good' and simple people as I did opportunists. But someone living independently will possibly be as socially isolated as in a house they might be in a block of apartments, and possibly no safer one way or the other. Those who, for their own safety, live in assisted independence, still need their personal space. If this is someone with Exposure Anxiety, the same rules of motivation may apply.

Exposure Anxiety and adult relationships

Exposure Anxiety can make relationships extraordinarily difficult. On the one hand the person with Exposure Anxiety may be frozen out of initiation, especially if the other person is in pursuit in any way. On the other, although many people with Exposure Anxiety feel safe in the passivity of compliance, they then often feel hemmed in and controlled, compelled to sabotage or escape from the situation or take their frustration out privately on themselves. This means it's important to help people manoeuvre their Exposure Anxiety responses in relation to their partner. The person with Exposure Anxiety may need to know it's OK to initiate through a letter or note, or to initiate activities where the focus is always on something external or about doing. Some people meet others through walking the dog or befriending the other person's dog. You can model that it's OK to ask others to be a little less enthusiastic, a little less in your face, to ask others to play a little hard to get to help counter the apparent 'shyness' of Exposure Anxiety. You can model that it's OK for a partner to push the person with Exposure Anxiety away instead of promoting the much asked for controlling co-dependency in which the person with Exposure Anxiety plays a progressively frustrating passive role. Only in pushing the person with Exposure Anxiety away a little do they stop focusing on how hemmed in or robbed of control they are in their self-made passive role.

Meeting people can be a problem if you can't cope with compliments, pick-up lines, small talk, sustained eye contact. But though the media and youth society portray that the way to meet people is through the 'in your face' scenarios of the pub or the club, this is where you are likely to meet a certain kind of person. Compliments to total strangers, pick-up lines, small talk, sustained eye contact with unfamiliar people, these are actually not reality or real contact in my view, they are part of a mode of behaving, a role. If you are not part of that scene or feel invaded or expected to invade others or out of control in this scene, this doesn't mean you have no hope of building social contacts. A lot of contact in pubs and clubs is superficial. People in a high state of excitability or anxiety are subject to sensory flooding which can make pubs and clubs one of the most difficult of all environments to relax in. In such a survival state it is common to switch off from information-processing and rely only on mapping pattern; on sensing. Someone highly sensing may well be very confused by the dissonance between what they sense and what's portrayed on the surface and this makes the job of trusting and relaxing even harder in a superficial atmosphere. On the other hand, some people with Exposure Anxiety, ironically, feel less exposed when around people who are so superficial, posturing or melodramatic that they can't actually 'see' the person with Exposure Anxiety. Although such superficial connections might, for some people, be easier, they can leave a hollow feeling which ends up compounding feelings of inner isolation.

Developing a relationship with someone who can't easily relax with compliments, nor stand the sense of self-in-relation-to-other necessary to the spontaneous thinking about or giving of compliments, means someone with Exposure Anxiety often ends up in very particular kinds of relationships. Such people can be seen as playing hard to get, attracting those who like to pursue or refuse to accept apparent 'defeat' in being closed out, or are intrigued by the mystery or enigma of someone so intangible, unable to pin down. The person with Exposure Anxiety may be an involuntary compulsive clown who attracts someone who loves to be entertained or play the more 'straight', 'serious', 'organized' or 'practical' partner. The person with Exposure Anxiety may be so seemingly rejecting, he or she may attract someone who compulsively seeks to please or cajole and such a relationship can easily build a kind of sado-masochistic dynamic. The person with Exposure Anxiety may appear so apparently incapable or indecisive that he or she attracts the dominating or overly 'caring' partner, too eager to play 'teacher', 'social worker' or 'martyr'. But someone with Exposure Anxiety can get lucky and attract someone who has been attracted to the person beyond and in spite of his or her condition and simultaneously accept that he or she may have to manoeuvre the partner's Exposure Anxiety to have a flexible, fluid, ongoing and mutually rewarding relationship. That's probably a rare find, but, in my view, a possible one.

The partner of someone with Exposure Anxiety may have to accept that compliments aren't absolutely essential to the connection with a partner and must certainly not to take the lack of them personally, nor see the inability of the partner to accept compliments as any kind of personal insult. Demonstrating an interest, initiating a conversation, suggesting new things to do, places to go, all of these may be blocked by an instinctual aversion to a sense of self-in-relation-to-other. The partner may have to use an indirectly-confrontational approach to trigger suggestions rather than relying on pressure, expectation or direct requests which trigger the very self-consciousness which then may block the reply. In short, the partner of someone with Exposure Anxiety may have to have a tough skin, be self-owning, be good at self-entertainment and be always ready to cheerfully get on with his or her own life for its own sake.

It is important that people with severe Exposure Anxiety know which traits in others are likely to shut them down and which are likely to help them open up. When seeking friendships and relationships, people with severe Exposure Anxiety are left without hope because every time they get an opportunity to connect, the directly-confrontational self-in-relation-to-other nature of the approach freezes them or kills them off inside. It is important to model the social possibilities which involve indirectly-confrontational activities and in which communication is not central but incidental, such as walking groups, chess clubs, playing cards, watching a video, playing computer games, doing art together, being in a play, working on a construction, singing in a choir, or playing in a band.

It's important to model making statements in order to provoke discussion rather than asking questions. Questions are very difficult for people with Exposure Anxiety to answer or initiate, as they are clearly self-in-relation-to-other in nature. Statements, on the other hand are self-directed and therefore self-in-relation-to-self. Model that speaking out loud to oneself for the benefit of the interest of others is a valid form of communication, that it's OK to address your watch, your shoes, the clock on the wall, if that's what it takes to keep talking out loud on the topic raised in someone's statement. Model that looking briefly at the other person in the room can be seen as treating them as equal to everything else in the room and isn't necessarily an indication of intent that the dialogue is aimed at this other person rather than out loud to oneself. Model that it's OK to leave little post-it notes addressed to nobody in particular on the fridge door. Model that it's OK to communicate via typing on a computer keyboard, saying what you'd say to yourself. Model that it's OK to use 'Hi' instead of 'Dear so and so' and to sign off letters purely with your name or even just 'Bye' if that's what it takes to not clam up in self-directed verbal expression through typing. Model that it's OK to be surreal, to use characterizations, to speak through objects as a way of having both freedom and the expression of love.

When it comes to touch, initiating intimate touch is one of the hardest things for many people with Exposure Anxiety. Model that it's OK to ask for physical contact through writing if the person cannot dare initiation. Model that it's OK to just come up and lean on the person if that's the only non-controlling, non-invasive initiation of touch that can be coped with. Model the enjoyment of forms of indirectly-confrontational touch such as reflexology, massage, hair brushing. If someone can't cope with accepting touch when it is not self-initiated, it is possible to leave a note, not invasively directed at the person but expressed as though written to yourself, stating 'here is the hug I could have given'.

Adults seeking to develop sexual touching need to know that pushing oneself through the motions isn't anything to do with experiencing intimacy. Doing it isn't experiencing it. I have been there, got the T-shirt and I know. An adult with severe Exposure Anxiety can find it extremely hard to get past performance to experience. This is especially because the more the other person seeks to please, to care, to help, or sees the process required as a means to an end and not an end in itself, the more the person pressures themselves just to push themselves through the act. This cuts the person with Exposure Anxiety off inside from the experience.

As a person with Exposure Anxiety, especially combined with information-processing delay, be careful of offers to 'help' or 'teach' you. After writing *Nobody Nowhere* I had someone move into my house who seemed uninterested in sex and patient to 'help me build up tolerance to touch'. This person was also deeply afraid of emotion but, unlike me, had cut it out of his life and lived totally in character with the outside world. Seeing his real self made me feel quite trusted and he dared me into marriage which I went through of my own stubborn volition, just to see what the experience of being married to someone was like. It is not just those who care who can learn how to dare a person with Exposure Anxiety into pushing themselves into situations they are not motivated towards of their own volition. Whilst this mechanical sensuality was better than the blatant 'taking' on the part of others that I'd experienced before, I knew I could take this or leave this. Something was missing. I'm very glad this person did not wish to stay with me and that I went on to have the chance to find out what that missing connection was. The fact, however, that I had gone along with these 'lessons', had direct implications the day after the second wedding anniversary for what this person could or could not ask for under law as part of a divorce settlement. It was a very costly lesson indeed.

A partner has to be chosen by the person with Exposure Anxiety and that is probably the hardest part. For how does someone with Exposure Anxiety know they have chosen when they often cannot openly choose, nor even acknowledge their choice. Most people with Exposure Anxiety seem simply to 'find themselves' in a situation and assume, therefore, they chose it.

To 'accept' is not the same as to 'choose'. Assuming you gave yourself enough time and space to know this was what *you* wanted, and assuming you did not merely 'accept' but 'sought' to secure the connection, perhaps you can feel safer that you had chosen. It is essential that the person with Exposure Anxiety feels equal with a partner.

The person with Exposure Anxiety can make a plan to not consider sex, only proximity. Make a plan to not consider sex, only sensuality. Make a plan to not consider sex, only exploration. Where sex is intentional, it will freeze most people with severe Exposure Anxiety. Where it is incidental, even held back from, and where the atmosphere is sensual, emotionally safe and indirectly-confrontational, it has a chance.

Understanding partners can leave their clothes on, accept not looking at each other or even touching each other, simply lying, experiencing their own space whilst listening to music or enjoying coloured light. From here, they could choose to close their eyes and smell each other's hair, use their faces or feet rather than hands to feel the texture and form of each other as if they were each sculptures rather than people. There could be insistence on simply exploring each other's hands or feet rather than focusing on holding or anything invasive. There could be an insistence on laying in each other's laps, with and, perhaps later without clothes, and sharing hair brushing whilst watching coloured moving light, listening to music or watching TV. The important thing is that the person with Exposure Anxiety has *chosen* this involvement, not merely 'accepted' the offer. This means the person had a choice. It means they had time and space away from the influence of what was being offered and that the person with Exposure Anxiety wanted the involvement enough to chose of her own accord.

The choice of who to explore this with is an important one, and many people, even those with some very nice traits, are also pretentious, directly-confrontational, impatient or full of their own expectations, assumptions or vested interests, and may be too much so to be flexible. Finding someone who can work well in this way with an adult with Exposure Anxiety is like finding a needle in a haystack

Sex for most people is a major aspect of self-in-relation-to-other. Someone who has spent his whole life avoiding developing safe familiarity with the sense of self-in-relation-to-other may never say 'I love you'. He or she may directly never use 'us' or 'we', may find it difficult to refer to him or herself with a term that so denotes an acceptance of self-in-relation-to-other as husband or wife.

The development of attraction doesn't have to involve sense of self-in-relation-to-other. Someone can become attracted to someone else on the basis of what they so like or love about themselves that they experience as externalized in the other person. Auto sexuality doesn't have to involve thought or feeling about anyone other than oneself. Nor does attraction. But this is often seen as 'selfishness' by those who are very self-in-relation-to-other. The social rules relating to sex and attraction may not easily make sense to someone with Exposure Anxiety and their own attempts to explore sexuality may be seen as insensitive to their partner. This doesn't always have to be so.

Someone who is self-in-relation-to-other, attracted to someone else who is self-in-relation-to-other, will usually find relative understanding and acceptance of each other's approach in relation to sex. Someone who is self-in-relation-to-self, attracted to someone who is self-in-relation-to-other, might find 'something missing' or a 'clash' of approaches. The couple may be unable to dialogue about it, each generally assuming his or her own reality as 'normal' and the only one it is possible to perceive or experience. The self-in-relation-to-self person who gets together with another like him or herself, however, may find that two hedonistic self-indulgers work quite well together. If they are lucky they may create such a sense of self-ownership in the actions of each that Exposure Anxiety doesn't so easily jump to protect from a sense of 'invasion'.

Most important, auto sexuality can have a place within a relationship if someone is developmentally blocked beyond this – and there is also far more to intimacy than sexuality. Sensuality and intimacy can happen in an utterly self-owning way, done for one's own benefit or focused not on the person, but the foot; not on the person, but the hair. Intimacy can also be about 'one's own world' and not everyone feels most fulfilled when they 'have' what they are attracted to. Some people actually enjoy far more the safety and privacy of experiencing their felt connection in the secrecy and privacy of their own world.

Again, between like-minded equals, nobody has to lose. It is also important to remember that intimacy and sensuality is about more than consciousness-jolting touch or words, it is about atmosphere and having a shared focus. Some people have a great intimacy and sensuality in cooking and eating. For some it is about watching an open fire, sitting with candlelight and music, being out walking together at night. For some people it is connection via email or the shared silence and concentration of a good game of chess. Like any relationship, it is a matter of finding not just personal compatibility but a compatibility of one another's systems. Without this it can, with even the best of intentions, be extremely hard for partners to give each other the patience and empathy needed to build a relationship without overwhelming self-sabotaging control issues. People need to reach a level of relaxing in which being comfortable in their emotions and body becomes possible and from this sensuality, even progressively self-initiated sexuality may evolve and this can't happen in an atmosphere of 'self-sacrifice'. Without this time and space for the empowerment of self-motivated self-initiation, going through the motions of sex may simply be an isolating pragmatic exercise.

In particular, I feel that sexuality is something people with Exposure Anxiety can feel great defeat or isolation about. Pushing oneself beyond the will's own limits of tolerance can mean cutting off from connection with the physical self, emotional self-abandonment, and dissociation from one's self-expression. Yet most people in this situation attempt to deal with such an instinctive emotional cut off through counselling or psychology, as though this gut reaction is an issue of mind. Exposure Anxiety responses were usually there before mind or concepts even took a foothold. Many have tried to use mind over matter but this generally can't counter involuntary dissociation. This was true for me. First I tried simply to mirror the expectations of others, as though the inner connections would follow. After many years I managed the assertiveness and self-expression before others of insisting on my own isolation, finally protecting myself from the sexual expectations of others as well as no longer internalizing this pressure upon myself.

After six wonderful years of feeling in control of the body I barely considered mine, I was manoeuvered into a position of trust under the guise of a friendship. This developed into a programme to 'help' me explore physical contact without dissociation that I felt proud to manage, albeit with a clinical detachment akin, perhaps, to a doctor observing an autopsy. It was only at the end of this three-year relationship that I met someone I took the next step with, realizing emotional drive, not mental commitment, was what really drove people not merely to challenge themselves towards, but desire intimate physical connection. This coincided with taking Glutamine, an amino acid which increased information-processing to the point I discovered the heaven of shared 'social' in which I knew what it was to be 'with'. I had understood sexuality as a role, then as an understandable action involving my body. Now I was suddenly deeply confused because sexuality was not being pushed or expected by me, it was pushing me. It had its own momentum in which I was merely following and, strangely, compelled by the loss of control. I phoned this friend and announced I wanted to sleep with him. He knew I didn't have the social skills to understand his response and I explained that if he showed up without blankets I'd know this was OK. I did do exactly that, I slept with him, enjoying the sensuality, experiencing, in my own world, 'sexuality', but slept. I did not have sex. What was important was not to act upon this feeling, but to developmentally spend time getting used to having the desire and knowing it as mine, feeling in control of it and letting it show me what to do about it. It took me five more years (on Glutamine and with the help of hypnotherapy) to get things together emotionally, socially and physically, rolled up into one ongoing relationship and when I did, I asked him to marry me. Fortunately, he said 'yes'.

Whilst nutritional supplements and special diets helped me reduce anxiety and keep up with processing enough to lower my extreme Exposure Anxiety responses, it took hypnotherapy to make it possible to embrace sexuality with any depth of tolerance. This was not the kind of regression-based hypnotherapy involving going back into the past and attempting to 'recover painful memories' blocking me from development. I have a savant-like memory and can acutely remember almost anything really in too much detail and clarity, so recall was never my problem. The hypnotherapy which helped me was that of guided imagery which wove 'dreams' and helped build bridges and resolve developmental blocks to sexuality by addressing these abstractly through storytelling in a way which went beneath conscious awareness. My conscious mind, and there-fore Exposure Anxiety, was unable to fathom the implications of the pat-terning inherent in the hypnotherapy sessions. I simply found that my way of responding on a social–emotional level was changing, challenging my mind to readjust in making sense of these changes. I was thirty-five when I went through this. It took another three years of the three-way relation-ship between Chris, me and my Exposure Anxiety, to finally know the relief and freedom of a relationship uninterrupted by our unwelcome guest and its involuntary avoidance, diversion and retaliation responses. I married a resourceful, adaptable, patient and fabulous man.

CHAPTER 6

Ways Forward

I lived within, taking for granted the confines of Exposure Anxiety as though it was self. Later I swung between a battle to join the world and a battle to keep it out, differentiating self from my invisible prison warder, then siding with it to spite the world at the first disappointment or stress. Only in my mid-twenties did I, by accident, stumble on special diets that decreased anxiety and disarmed Exposure Anxiety to set emotional development as myself free. I have spent the last decade learning why it is not me and why it imprisons me more than it protects me.

There are strategies for working better with Exposure Anxiety, even turning around the way someone has come to fiercely defend and identify self with their Exposure Anxiety responses. But the most important strategy for combating Exposure Anxiety is eradicating its underlying cause. Its underlying cause is the inability to keep up with incoming information. There are ways to address overload to disarm the drive behind Exposure Anxiety. To improve the ability to keep up with incoming information, three simultaneous approaches are needed:

1. Address neurotransmitter imbalances underlying the tendency toward a state of adrenaline addiction.

2. Treat leaky gut as a means of improving the fuel supply to the brain for improved information-processing.

3. Reduce environmental overload as a means of artificially cutting down the rate of incoming information in people unable to properly filter incoming information.

Leaky gut syndrome

By the time Exposure Anxiety is recognised, the impact of severe chronic stress on gut and immune function is already in place, consolidating a developmental downward spiral. It is therefore important to address this catch 22 from both sides. Metabolic disorders are known to affect around eighty per cent of people with autism-spectrum conditions. These can include the inability to digest dairy or gluten products or foods high in phenol, salicylate or phenylalanine. They can include multiple or specific food allergies affecting the brain, as well as low stomach acid, impaired pancreas and liver function and malabsorption problems broadly referred to as 'leaky gut'. Immune deficiencies are known to affect around twenty per cent of people with autism. These can mean a high toxic overload on a body already suffering from malabsorption and a susceptibility to repeated or chronic infections, further impairing the body's ability to use its nutrients to keep up with incoming information and manage acute chronic anxiety. These biochemical issues may be relatively manageable in most children through dietary and naturopathic intervention (specialists can be found on the DAN list of Autism Research International). The treatment is often costly and funding, even through private health insurance, isn't always available. But altering diet can, with experimentation and creativity, be done very affordably and this can reduce the burden on digestion, compensating for malabsorption, helping the body to detoxify and the immune system to defend itself. Olive oil, oily fish, lemon juice, tahini, linseed, fructose, millet, rice, buckwheat, 'nut milk', and garlic are all reasonably attainable and affordable aspects of 'food pharmacy' for those able to metabolize these, and cutting out refined sugar, msg, aspartame, colourings, flavourings and preservatives costs nothing. These can be one small part of minimizing the problems of leaky gut and immune problems at home and there are often creative ways of disguising these things to bring them in gradually into even very restricted diets.

Many people develop malabsorption and problems metabolizing vitamins and minerals due to a lack of stomach acid, the signs of which are often mistaken for excess stomach acid and wrongly prescribed contra-indicated antacids. Chronic stress helps turn the gut alkaline and an alkaline gut provides a home to fungal infections such as Candida and means many harmful bacteria multiply without being killed off by stomach acid. An alkaline gut means there is not enough acidity to properly metabolize the fatty acids and enzymes necessary to break down foods in the diet adequately, properly metabolize the vitamins and minerals necessary for information processing in the brain, or keep up with toxicity issues in the body. There is a simple home test which is thought to indicate whether there is a lack of stomach acid. Eat beetroot or take four ounces of beetroot juice on an empty stomach. If the next urine is red, it indicates that there is probably not enough stomach acid to break down the red pigment.

Betaine Hydrochloride with Pepsin (HCL) is a stomach acid supplement which is believed to restore stomach acid, helping to improve digestion, metabolize nutrients to do their job both in information-processing and in reducing chronic anxiety – both provoked by information overload but also compounded by things like B vitamin and magnesium deficiencies, but lemon juice is also a good way to increase stomach acid if it is too low. Pure cod liver oil, which is available in capsules, is thought to help reduce gut alkalinity and has helped improve information-processing and reduce anxiety in some people. Omega 3 fatty acids and Evening Primrose oil have helped some people in the same way. Glutamine is used to counter high anxiety and depression states and is understood to re-line the digestive tract, improving digestion, raise T cell count, improving immunity, and help people to detoxify as well as improving the integrity of the blood-brain barrier. Epsom Salts baths (don't drink it) is also believed, through absorption through the skin, to help reline the digestive tract and assist in detoxification in people with salicylate intolerance and glucosamine sulphate is known to help in related ways. Mega multivitamin– mineral supplements in easy-to- metabolize form may help speed up information-processing and combat some of the effects of anxiety in those who, because of digestive system problems or severe chronic stress, are not properly metabolizing nutrients in spite of an adequate diet. Probiotics such as acidophilus and anti-fungals such as garlic may help a disturbed gut lining to restore the natural balance in people who have developed digestive system problems, particularly where there has been repeated use of steroid or antibiotic use. Extremely important with Exposure Anxiety is the way such dietary additions or changes are brought in, and that people persistently protecting themselves from sensed 'invasion' and loss of control, find the way these things appear in the household to be non-invasive and not directly 'about them'. Changes are likely to cause a period of withdrawal symptoms. If changes are made in a way which only serves to exacerbate chronic stress it can be like trying to put out a fire using kerosene.

Treatment of leaky gut restores the ability of the brain to keep up with incoming information. The process of this treatment includes detoxifying the liver, pancreas and brain tissue from the impact of long-term flooding of undigested proteins due to leaky gut. It also involves improving the digestive system so people are better able to get the vitamins, minerals, amino acids, fatty acids and so forth from their food to their brain where it is used to keep up with the rate of incoming information. Severe chronic stress also leads to suppressed immunity, which in turn leads to an increased tendency toward inflammatory myalgic conditions and allergies. Some specialists are looking at treatment of immune system problems such as deficiency in secretory lgA leading to leaky gut in some people.

Deficiency in secretory lgA underly chronic ear, nose, throat and lung infections and impair enzyme production. Acute chronic stress lowers secretory lgA so its treatment must not only seek to raise lgA through supplementation but also address the severe chronic stress which contributes to generating such a deficiency. I have been using dietary intervention and supplementation for fourteen years, treating leaky gut for six years and treating immune deficiency for the last year. I combined these approaches with the implementation of an indirectly-confrontational approach by my home and social environment, techniques to environmentally reduce information overload (including the use of BPI tinted lenses), cranio-sacral therapy (which assists in the flow of celebral-spinal fluid to the brain), patterning exercises for left–right hemisphere integration in the brain and hypnotherapy (which uses storytelling to alter emotional responses). I used a very multifaceted approach. I also used Glutamine, which is a non-dependent amino acid that re-lines the digestive tract and raises white cell counts responsible for immunity. It is also used in the treatment of depression, alcoholism, diabetes, schizophrenia, immune deficiency, cancer recovery, and now in the field of autism. Glutamine is available from GNC (General Nutrition Centres) nation-wide but dosages are not properly known or regulated at present. Every up has its down side and long-term excess doses of Glutamine may cause glutamate excess if the brain has raised levels of Quinolic Acid. Quinolinic Acid is a damaging neurotoxin which excites glutamate receptors in the brain. The Dove Clinic in Winchester, UK, offers a urine analysis test for levels of Quinolinic Acid and those interested in exploring this can find the contact at *www.doveclinic.com*. The work of Dr R Blaylock, author of a book called *Excitotoxins*, may also be of interest to those looking to further understand this area.

Quinolinic Acid builds up in the brain when undigested proteins or gut bacteria cross the blood-brain barrier in inflammatory, myalgic conditions, and in cases of hypoxia (depletion of oxygen supply to the brain). Hypoxia can occur in cases of high oxidative stress where the blood becomes so coagulated it cannot properly transport oxygen and nutrients to the brain. Hypoxia also results from episodes of severe hypoglycemia – so common in children with gut, immune and toxicity issues, all exacerbated, if not sometimes caused, by the severe chronic stress of Exposure Anxiety. Quinolinic Acid build up in the brain has two other interesting connections. One is that it uses up seratonin and tryptophan, contributing to the loop of neurotransmitter imbalance affecting impulse control and adrenaline addiction implicated in the development of severe Exposure Anxiety responses. Quinolinic Acid is also cited as associated with epilepsy and the relationship between the loss of control experienced by those with epilepsy and Exposure Anxiety may be an area enlightened by further research in the field of neurobiology.

If undigested proteins contribute to toxicity issues affecting anxiety, some of the work by Dr Danczac in Manchester may be of interest and can be researched through *www.autismmanagement.com*.

I also live on a caffeine-free, sugar-free diet to raise magnesium levels, which reduces anxiety, and also because sugar increases the problems of leaky gut by feeding a fungal opportunist called Candida. Candida lives off the body's vitamin B supply, starving the brain of its ability to use this vitamin for information-processing. Sugar, also, thereby, decreases the effectiveness of treatment for leaky gut including the use of Glutamine. I'm also dairy-free because I can't digest milk and have a milk allergy which has LSD-like effects. I am also gluten-free as gut problems mean I can't digest this either. I also have to be careful of Salycilate-containing foods or I'm so ADD that I get both manic and phobic and compulsive, not to mention being unable to start or stop activities. I continue to tackle immune system problems as I've only had lgA for a year and now, after a lifetime without it, my body still can't recognize a virus it already had last week (I've had measles about six times). I have also only recently had a normal white cell count after having always indicated a deficiency. I had virtually no IgA (an immunoglobulin responsible for signaling intercellular immune response). This apparently occurs in around eight per cent of those with autism, with twenty per cent having low IgA. The condition is often treatable to a degree, and since being on immune boosters I have had a follow-up blood test showing normal IgA. So I am one of those who may need ongoing help for an immune deficiency and its impact on digestion, toxicity, neurotransmitter balance, neurotoxicity and the supply of nutrients to the brain, including those essential in coping with anxiety and managing one's own reactions and behaviour. With the balancing effect of Risperidone 0.5mgs having recently eradicated my Exposure Anxiety it will be interesting to see what impact that loss of chronic stress will have on my systems' self repair and maintenance. The imbalance of neurotransmitters can also be caused by subclinical phenylketonuria, so it is worth checking if this is the case.

Caffeine and anxiety

Caffeine peps people up. It raises adrenaline levels which makes people more reactive. That's not a problem for most people. But if you are already either hyper, or highly reactive or highly stressed because of information overload, caffeine only makes the problem worse. Yet chocolate, which is high in caffeine, not to mention milk and sugar, is given as compliance rewards to people with severe Exposure Anxiety. Sure, they crave it, but it often means their defensive reactiveness issues just get more extreme, not to mention the effects on madly fluctuating blood-sugar levels in people whose digestive system problems may well have lead to pancreas toxicity and hypoglycemic attacks. Tea is also high in caffeine, as are cola drinks.

All of these are widely given to people with severe Exposure Anxiety in residential care homes, with the tragic effect that their behaviour of is then often 'treated' with tranquilizers and other behaviour-suppressant drugs – many with severe long-term side effects. Interestingly, caffeine, together with Aspartame, MSG and soy are all reported by Dr R Blaylock in his book, *Excitotoxins* as being neurotoxins, essentially affecting neurotransmitter balance in the brain with implications for balance and organ function throughout the body. Caffeine and anxiety…caffeine withdrawal and irritability… May be worth thinking about.

What do we do with those adaptations?

If we tackle the information-processing problems, the Exposure Anxiety doesn't just go away. It gets less because it's no longer 'driven', but someone who has spent years living on adrenaline, lives like an addict. My experience is that even if I hate the anxiety, my body seeks another rush, however uncomfortable that makes me.

If the environment continues to display the same kind of *perceived* desire to 'invade' via words, eye contact, 'discussion', 'demonstration', 'teaching', the learned response is still to respond in accordance with the rules of Exposure Anxiety – aversion, diversion, retaliation and can't do it for, as or by myself. Also, if the person has had severe self-abuse because of Exposure Anxiety responses, the person concedes to this control, siding with Exposure Anxiety, and identifying with it. Similarly, if the person has always been identified *by* their Exposure Anxiety responses, they have no other sense of self, no other framework of reacting. It's important to begin to respond to the person beyond the apparent Exposure Anxiety. Don't take the aversion, diversion, retaliation as the person's 'self'. Step into the aversion, co-opt the diversion, accept but tone down the retaliation. You are taming a wild horse that is out of the control of its owner. So the second stage of countering Exposure Anxiety is that of building want, countering anti- motivations, undermining identification with the condition.

Building want, countering anti-motivations, undermining identification with Exposure Anxiety

How to get people with Exposure Anxiety to do for themselves, by themselves or as themselves presents a dilemma for many carers, let alone the person with Exposure Anxiety. Those who've been able to achieve 'compliance' often later dump or 'lose' these skills they have taken on. If you gain expression or skills that are not connected to self, they represent feels like a façade, a cardboard reality, a parody. It can work for survival if you are really pushed, but it is not really the kind of stuff you can use as a basis for an enjoyable existence because it's disconnected from any internal emotional intrinsic reward. Such apparent 'success' may feel intensely alienating and isolating. This is the 'high-functioning' person alone in a crowd and as buried as they ever were in spite of appearances. So compliance is only half the bridge; without the other half, it just hangs there.

A matter of expressive volume

When you are with people who suffer from Exposure Anxiety, turning down the 'volume' of your own 'directness' decreases the sense of 'audience' that triggers and raises Exposure Anxiety, and can help them turn up the 'volume' of theirs. Think about it. Being aware that someone is waiting, watching, needing and eager for your contact is extremely inhibiting to many non-autistic people. Some hate attention and compliments when they have not actively sought or initiated them and play down their abilities when the spotlight is put on them, even at the cost of denying or appearing to have 'lost' the ability that is causing the attention ('I'm really out of practice', 'No, really, I can't even remember how to do it', etc). Yet within the behaviour-modification movement there is a blind assumption, often amounting to something like a religious conviction, that desiring attention is 'how we all work'. This idea that we all do best when praised and noticed, with persistent reinforcement, is actually not a reality for all people, autistic or not.

Similarly, the compliance model, that assumes we learn best when forced through an action, is fiercely defended by the behaviour modification movement. Yet how many non-autistic people lost all desire to learn a musical instrument because they were forced into learning out of compliance? How hard is it to remember for one's own sake that which someone else keeps drumming and drumming into you as important? Often, internal avoidance of what we were coerced, cajoled or forced into out of compliance becomes the last thing we can remember how to do. Emotion is the drive behind recalling and using what we have learned. What we were driven to out of our own volition stays with us and is un-erasable, however much we wish it away. The only difference here is that the non-autistic person's self-protective mechanisms aren't so excessively high as to inhibit demonstration of ability at any cost.

Desire to please others, to be praised, to get attention, may work for those in whom Exposure Anxiety does not turn this experience into a torture. Some non-autistic people love to please others, to be praised, to get attention – and some have grown because of this and become balanced people, and some have become dependent on the feelings and views of others and are not so balanced. Some don't mind attention or praise so long as they've initiated the request for it, and otherwise may feel invaded, robbed of control. Some are inhibited by attention and praise and will pull away from whatever skills put them in the limelight, relying instead on those which they can do more privately or without calling such attention to themselves. The same is true for people with autism.

In the absence of external help, there is a range of behavioural strategies that help people with severe Exposure Anxiety. These techniques generally involve an indirectly-confrontational approach and can help extend someone into daring self-discovery and rejecting what their chemistry constantly tries to teach them by its onslaught on emotion.

Nobody can dictate which approach is right, because every person is different. Some people with Exposure Anxiety prefer not to experience selfhood and find the prompted expectation to comply helps them not to feel so self-aware or exposed. Others are fiercely defensive of their own world, their self-containment, their personal space.

Parents often have an instinctive 'feeling' about how their child responds even if they can't understand it. They know whether they get most initiation and expression when they happen to be busy with their own thing, when they are sleeping, when they are noticing someone else. The only problem is they've never been taught to use this awareness as a strategy to achieve involvement and communication in an indirectly-con-

frontational way. Conventional directly-confrontational behaviour modification techniques are easier for parents to understand, but may not match
what they instinctively know about how their child works. Yet many, in
desperation, comply with this approach in the absence of help with alternative approaches, which might work better.

The Option Technique works almost in antithesis to conventional
behaviour modification techniques. Yet I see it as almost equally problematic. It was developed by the non-autistic parents of a boy with autism in
the seventies. These were very loving, socially-oriented people who
probably didn't experience severe Exposure Anxiety themselves and the
approach was developed with the best of intentions and happened, in their
case, to work for their child. The Option Approach involves, while being
very non-intrusive toward the child, mirroring the child's movements,
interests, sounds in order to 'break into the child's own world' and bring
the child 'into theirs'. The problem with it is that, although it may make the
non-autistic world appear very user-friendly and comprehensible, it
forgets one very essential element. Whilst this approach certainly makes
sense from the perspective of information-processing problems, it doesn't
make good sense from the perspective of Exposure Anxiety. Whilst some
children have benefited from the Option Approach, I have seen others who
have not progressed or who have progressed in ways which haven't helped
them cope with the expectations of a self-in-relation-to-other non-autistic
world.

One of the things missing from the Option Approach is that, whilst the
activity of the child is mimicked, this doesn't take account of how voluntary that activity was in the first place. Some children diagnosed with
autism don't have very high Exposure Anxiety and their main problem is
information-processing problems or impulse control. They may very much
intend their own actions. If they pick up a drum, go to the mirror, start
humming, they may intend to do these things. Exposure Anxiety doesn't
work like this. Particularly when there is a sense of audience and of the
impending 'invasion' of sensed 'other', the activities which come through
in the grip of Exposure Anxiety are not voluntary, they are compulsions
and most often self-defensive ones involving avoidance, diversion or retaliation responses. When the environment assumes that these are expression
and mirrors them back, trying to join someone through what they didn't

intend in the first place, the most likely result is a confused social dialogue. Here, unwittingly, Exposure Anxiety responses are being taken and reinforced as expressions of 'self'. As the environment continues to confuse and treat equally Exposure Anxiety involuntary avoidance, diversion, retaliation responses/communications and those responses which were actually intended as being equal demonstrations of intent, it can compound the very thing it seeks to break down.

The person with Exposure Anxiety can develop a heightened alienation and a sense that the environment doesn't understand. The person may developed a heightened despair that the environment can't distinguish their activity as a person from that coming from their cage itself; what is being reflected back at them may well be their own trappedness – hardly a polite, enjoyable social message. Second, the fact that far from playing hard to get, the ever-readiness of the environment to co-opt all expression, not for their own sake, but for that of the child, is the very thing which triggers Exposure Anxiety into taking over. Whilst the original intention may have been to be as self-owning and aloof as the child itself was, the problem is that many people with autism can sense a fraud at a thousand paces. Whatever behaviour you put on, however much you perform as though your involvement is for your own benefit, the person with autism may sense, like a snake, the subtle inconsistencies in your body and movement. This may, unwittingly, demonstrate you are trying to trick them and are actually in the activity for their benefit, not your own. Yet what the person with Exposure Anxiety may be showing you again and again is, don't focus on me, be self-owning, do as though for your own benefit.

Not all children diagnosed 'autistic' have severe Exposure Anxiety and not all are so limited in their capacity to use interpretation that they remain reliant on the system of sensing. Some children diagnosed 'autistic' rely more strongly on mind and interpretation and certainly some children later diagnosed with Asperger Syndrome function this way. In these children, the complication of sensing the dissonance between what's being projected and what's contradicting it would be less of an issue.

Another aspect of the Option Approach is that it involves keeping the person in the special Option room, essentially a mirrored room where a rota of volunteers continues to keep company with the child for hours on end, waiting for the child's expression or activity to emerge. For some people with Exposure Anxiety, this could be sensed as imprisonment and extreme loss of privacy. Most of what people initiate is done in privacy or when they think they are not being noticed and when they feel free to escape and recover from the emotional shock of their own dared self-expression. I loved mirrors and was compelled towards them, often in spite of severe Exposure Anxiety when others were in such a room. Nevertheless, I was *always* free to leave. It was this freedom to leave which was one of the most motivating factors in testing myself into initiating coming back time and again. Yet what I see in approaches to 'autism' is almost always using a kind of control or imprisonment, however pleasant we paint it. Imprisonment of any kind compels us not to stay but to obsess on hiding, avoiding, escaping or complying in order to win reprieve.

Being able to use an indirectly-confrontational approach is like a dance that involves poise, grace, a sense of privacy and self-containment, creativity, and humour. It involves addressing yourselves and your own emotional needs and how these compel you to pursue too strongly, need too much. It may involve learning to drop your fierce goal of teaching and learn, instead, how to play, be surreal, to buzz, and to do so as though for your own benefit. It involves thinking about what you are enjoying modelling and incorporating important life lessons into your self-directed play/modelling. It may involve singing to the bubbles in the sink. It may involve jumping to number patterns as you cross a floor covered in categories of objects. It may involve spinning with the word 'spin', running with the word 'run', tapping plastic as you coo to yourself the word 'plastic'. But most of all it involves being possessive about this modelling. For someone with Exposure Anxiety, nothing is so awakening than watching someone else obliviously in their own world as though they, for a change, instead of you, are the ones under glass. Turning this approach into an education is an art. The Pied Piper didn't use compliance. He was just playing his flute merrily and enjoying his playing as he made his way through the town. And the rats and the children followed and nobody could stop them from following this hypnotic, self-possessed display. Maybe there's a lesson in that.

It may be parents will need counselling to reach the social–emotional space and cognitive direction required using and developing an indirectly-confrontational approach well. This is especially so when many will have been indoctrinated by a compliance-based system of education, upbringing and discipline. In spite of their own awareness that much of what they have learned may have nothing to do with this approach, may even be the opposite, they are still, nevertheless indoctrinated. Counselling may not help them change this pattern. Counselling addresses the mind, but the mind may be clear about what's what and the behaviour still doesn't follow. A lot of our patterning is in body memory and emotion. Hypnotherapy and assertiveness training may help some parents to find the kind of space where the use of an indirectly-confrontational approach flows more naturally. There may even be hypnotherapists and those involved in assertiveness training who may be able to visit parents in their own homes if their commitments make it difficult to get out.

I have found Bach Flower Remedies helpful for some parents in turning around their own behavioural patterns. Star of Bethlehem can be used for dealing with grief and how it may compel a parent to try too hard, be too impatient, too directly-confrontational. Others such as Wild Rose can help instil a sense of joy and adventure and Rockwater can help people to be less rigid and purist in their ways. Chicory and Walnut can help break old patterns and help people get a sense of their own boundaries back. Oak may help parents accept their own limitations and reduce emotional pressure on their child. Red Chestnut, Cherry Plum and Mimulus can help people let go a bit, especially if there are issues such as constant worry, fear and fearing loss of control. Rescue Remedy is used to help calm generally and cope with a sense of panic. These are available through health food stores where wider literature is available on them.

Parents of people with Exposure Anxiety may be very stressed and frustrated people. They may have very high adrenaline levels themselves which make them over eager and pushy, too quick to worry, too quick to fear and overprotect, too quick to control and overdirect. Some, like my own parents, may have neurotransmitter imbalances, toxicity issues, digestive system problems, immune system or allergy problem related to those of their children, and parents should consider getting help for themselves too.

If your stress-driven emotional states are interfering with your ability to help someone with Exposure Anxiety, take a look at how you deal with stress. If you are exhausting your own adrenal system through chronic stress, depleting your vitamin–mineral levels and increasing toxicity with things like cigarettes, lowering your magnesium levels (your anti stress mineral) with high sugar diet, if you are hyped up on MSG, aspartame and caffeine (including in tea), these are things you may be able to control. You don't have to become a saint. You have choices and you make them because of things you want from yourself and in your life.

Aversion, diversion, retaliation responses as language

Avoidance, diversion and retaliation responses are natural. When someone's adrenaline levels, however, are artificially high, these avoidance, diversion and retaliation responses can go so overboard that they no longer serve to protect the person, but imprison them in an invisible cage. When someone is compelled to reject as an act of felt survival that which moves them, what will make them laugh or let go, even their own too shockingly-felt volition, leaving them helpless, then we have to redefine the boundaries of what is a natural response.

Taking avoidance, diversion or retaliation as language in people without Exposure Anxiety would tell us a lot about someone's feelings, thoughts, likes, dislikes. Taking these responses as 'language' in someone affected by severe Exposure Anxiety is probably inaccurate if the avoidance is coming out where the person is most able to be emotionally moved, or where the person most feels closeness or desires to join in. The dilemma is that avoidance governed by Exposure Anxiety, non-Exposure Anxiety governed avoidance, and diversion and retaliation responses can be happening in the same person. For example, I hated the taste, texture or associations of tripe and was free to express absolute avoidance from and retaliation against the expectation to eat it. At the same time, being offered strawberries, which I very much liked, as a social gesture to get close to me on the part of someone I liked too much would almost always bring the same apparent avoidance, diversion, retaliation responses as the tripe. The same strawberries could be offered by someone I felt indifferent to and I might, rather flippantly, take one. Left on the bench with nobody in the house, I'd likely eat the whole bowl (though I'm also intolerant to the salicylate levels in them). This demonstrates the dilemma. It gets even more confusing when the desperation of a desire itself triggers Exposure Anxiety avoidance, diversion, and retaliation responses. Living in Australia, I desperately wanted to see the snow. Each year I would see the snow fall on the TV up on a mountain but I couldn't ask to go. Finally asked in my adulthood if I wanted to go, all I could say was a flippant 'no'. On an even more practical level I often got into a bath which was burning hot. The quickly felt desperation and desire to get out simply froze me, leaving me to get burned by the hot water to the point I'd become phobic about the whole process. So taking avoidance, diversion and retaliation responses as language is a very problematic thing.

If you gave me something directly, addressed me directly, asked me about choices directly, you got avoidance, diversion, retaliation responses and communications. The more *indirectly*-confrontational others were the more personal communication and expression I had. People learned to give me things by leaving them in my personal space when I was not there and leaving them unwrapped and in positions as though they'd always been there. They learned to leave me out of things in order to provoke my insistence at inclusion. Those who tried to give things to me directly had to prompt me through the opening of them, after which I simply left them, sensing them as invasive 'other' representations of 'their world'.

The language of avoidance, diversion, retaliation responses is that of saying, 'this way is too in my face and is triggering a loss of control over my own behaviour to the degree that like and choice are irrelevant – find a less invasive way'. Similarly, it can say, 'my own passion and desire is so extreme it is triggering a loss of control over my own behaviour to the degree I have to behave indifferently to get it to back off so I can experience self-expression and freedom'. Conversely, the language of avoidance, diversion and retaliation responses may be saying, when I'm out of control, doing something to tune out awareness, trying to join me socially through that very action is likely to extinguish it. This can be very important in helping people to stop doing things which hurt them but which they are compelled by Exposure Anxiety to do.

In late childhood I developed a retaliation-response habit of pre-empting social contact and warning the environment to back off. This involved slamming myself in the stomach suddenly with both clenched fists. My mother found that telling me not to do it didn't stop it at all. In fact, from the inside, in the grip of social provocation of Exposure Anxiety, it worked in the opposite direction. The more she said 'don't do that', the more it was felt as a robbery of control. Instead she stated, 'punch yourself gently'.

The attempt to control the person or say 'no' might work with someone able to reason or control their behaviour but what if they hadn't meant it in the first place? What if the behaviour was simply an involuntary one? For me, though the person was still inside, the 'me' had become the undercurrent, the 'it' had become the tide. The more you appealed to the 'me', the more the 'it' would justify its existence as protector against invasive sense of 'other' and retain its grip on the body. I had developed a response of throwing chairs and spitting when complimented by visitors. Almost always visitors would attempt to engage me by endearing them-selves to me through compliments. 'Oh what a pretty girl', they would start and my hands would clench on the back of the chair, which got thrown in an instant. My mother went from 'Duck!' to heading them off in their tracks. They'd start, 'Oh, what a pretty…' and they'd be interrupted by her quickly pointing at me and enthusiastically pre-empting, 'Wait, here she goes, she's going to throw a chair now, watch'. In retaliative self-protection Exposure Anxiety couldn't abandon the activity quickly enough. It couldn't possibly prove them right, lose the control of the situation.

When I am called in to help with cases where children are self-abusive or violent, I explore what is happening with Exposure Anxiety. If these violent outbursts are to do with information overload and processing backlog I advise in how to reduce the demand for information-processing. I might suggest learning through body rather than mind, keeping things visual and concrete so less interpretation is required, mime, signing, spoken language and written stories. I might suggest reducing overhead lighting, annoying background noises (except rhythmic music), providing space breaks, slowing pace, keeping things in small doses, providing mono and linear activities and making mono approaches. I might train people in using self-regulated rhythm as a self-calming strategy and how to model as though it is for their own beneift. Where I observe violent or self-abusive behaviours to be a mistranslation of sensory exploration, I advise people in how to help people modulate these experiences and use them as bridges to broaden learning. Where I see violent of self-abusive behaviours as related to hypersensitive self-protection mechanisms (Exposure Anxiety) in response to feeling robbed of control by a directly-confrontational social response, I will teach people to use an indirectly-confrontational approach.

Sometimes, especially where someone is addicted to their own Exposure Anxiety-produced adrenaline rushes, I may also mention the possibility of testing for food contributors. Finally, I may advise the environment to treat these violent Exposure Anxiety responses as a language.

A parent asked me about a child who cuts himself with cans and sharp objects. I suggested changing to a generally indirectly-confrontational approach and looking at reducing any chemistry-related provocations. But finally, when 'no' means 'yes', the answer had to be quite surreal, and I advised intervention which scoffed at the use of the sharp object as 'boring and uninteresting', with the enthusiastic offer instead of a piece of rubber or a bendy unbreakable plastic cup, inviting him to learn to use these which were much more exciting. Here, I'd draw public, unafraid attention to the very Exposure Anxiety behaviour in order to inhibit. Using it as a social avenue which progressively would see the person reject it as the only way to stop you trying to be socially involved, whilst at the same time channeling it into something safer, had the potential to address this serious issue where other interventions may offer little help. I had a client whose compulsive vomiting had him put into care and hospitalised when all usual techniques failed. He had had severe Exposure Anxiety all his life and rejected anything others joined him in or praised. I suggested praising the 'artwork' of each vomit and proudly inviting social compliment and conversation on these 'works' before displaying them as art. I also provided hypnotherapy stories for him based on a list of his likes and dislikes. This instilled a sense that food would protect him from the invasion of others by, cleaning his body of all of the effects of 'them' as it passed through.

I don't like these choices. Exposure Anxiety is some opponent. It destorys lives. It can injure. It can even kill. We need to talk honestly and openly about the adrenaline-driven compulsive self-protective drives which can happen, and see them as language providing us with the information to adapt in order to achieve a score for the self of that person. Where someone is attacking the body not because of the sense of social invasion by the environment but purely from crippling, suffocating sensation of self-awareness, it is important not to address the person, but the object. In these cases, addressing the person directly only heightens the self-murderous retaliation. Addressing the hand is neutral. Tell the hand it has no right to hit the person is a statement of fact, not a request or demand. Telling the hand it has the right only to hit itself confuses Exposure Anxiety but is very useful (ever tried to slap your hand with your own same hand? It's quite ridiculous but the rule did work for me). Telling the hand it had no right to pull the hair, only to tug at itself. The leg has no right to kick anything but itself. The teeth only have the right to bite the teeth themselves. Telling the person the hand is in trouble from the teeth and needs the person to take it away and hide it, can help because it addresses things seemingly external to the self, not internal. One thing is for sure, in an adrenaline-driven Exposure Anxiety state, one is a purist. There is little reason, only drive and a purist internal justification of the behaviour that can almost never be countered. You can, however, use this purism against itself. This is speaking the language of Exposure Anxiety.

The use of rhythm seems to work wonderfully in taking the focus back off self and lowering Exposure Anxiety, as well as re-establishing a sense of one's own boundaries so there is nothing to feel invaded about. This *must not*, however, be done as an act of social joining, which will trigger retaliation against it. Similarly, where you give someone a physical rhythm using rocking or tapping, you may progressively be able to turn this into one he can give himself, but this must be a non-verbal experience, involving no social fuss and an extreme solid sense of each other's own boundaries. If you are wanting him to take rhythm over for himself, you stop being a person in relation to him, you become a tool and then you move on to taking care of yourself as your own entity. It is important to bring the rhythm in at a pace similar to the distress, then soften, quieten and slow the rhythm as an alternative flow of expression. It becomes hard for the person to go against this flow.

But retaliation responses, violence and self-abuse are not the only situations in which you can take Exposure Anxiety responses as a kind of language about social interaction and its uses. Diversion responses and diversion communications step up when someone either becomes very enthusiastic about their own topic (signalling 'protect yourself, you are inviting social invasion, you are creating a grating sense of individuality') or when the environment becomes too enthusiastic, waiting, wanting the interaction. Ironically, to help people get their intended communication and behaviour back on track may mean having to turn to the side and begin to hum to yourself in order to lower their Exposure Anxiety. This is extremely hard for parents and carers who associate these 'helpful' behaviours as 'rudeness' or 'negative'. If we realize that some people will sing or hum or rock in order to stand tuning in to what's happening around them, perhaps carers will not take away the only thing that allows involvement and presents the domination of Exposure Anxiety in forms far more difficult to manage. Tuning out in order to calm Exposure Anxiety and stay involved was one of the hardest things in childhood as my very aloofness drew attention and well meaning attempts to 'reach me', only giving further territory to Exposure Anxiety.

Sometimes 'love' means learning a different social language, however much it may be your own social reality turned on its head. Remember that where some people are governed almost always by Exposure Anxiety responses, others are more affected in one environment than another, or regarding one skill more than another (this can include direct eye contact, speech, writing, demonstrating reading ability, using one's body, showing emotion, showing an interest, demonstrating learning). Some are affected by Exposure Anxiety regarding new things but not familiar things in familiar situations. So there is scope for modulating your response – speak your own social reality where Exposure Anxiety is not an issue, speak theirs where you have yet to build bridges.

Other Development Programmes

Exposure Anxiety is a teacher. As an acute anxiety state, it can block the ability to relax and be open in any directly-confrontational way, limiting the person's capacity for the kind of social–emotional feedback that would help them develop in so many ways. This makes Exposure Anxiety the parent, the teacher. It locks the environment out of contact with the internal classroom. The lessons inside affect one's relationship with mind, one's relationship with physical and emotional sensation and one's relationship with the process of letting go control, with developing a tolerance of a sense of audience including to oneself. It affects the development of tolerance of connection with others and the learning of self-calming strategies. In its monopoly on the self it affects something of primary importance: knowing self from the teacher – understanding that one is not purely one's chemistry and mechanisms, and that the self and Exposure Anxiety are not one. In this sense, it attacks and controls the very fibre of identity, removing its only possible internal opponent.

Promoting connection to physical/emotional sensation: getting back body

Acute anxiety teaches the recipient that having a body and having emotional responses to the environment will cause extreme frustration and loss of control. Although self-initiated, self-controlled actions may continue, there is a loss of drive to invite physical and emotional contact initiated by the environment. On the one hand, the person may appear to be playing hard to get, on the other, when the environment responds, the person goes into avoidance, diversion, and retaliation responses. So, how does the environment promote physical contact and emotional sensation without having its relationship with the person monitored and controlled by their Exposure Anxiety? Address the object, issue, not the person. Act as though for your own benefit, not as though for the benefit of the person with Exposure Anxiety. This is not an act – an act can be sensed – it is an emotional space the environment has to find.

It is important to repeat that therapies involving bodywork may be open to sexual abuse. Therapies involving intimate settings and close physical contact have often been subject to abuses. Where this involves non-verbal people deprived of typed communication techniques together with unpredictable responses and communications caused by acute Exposure Anxiety, people are particularly at risk and this needs to be openly acknowledged and addressed in policy. Especially where there is a tendency with Exposure Anxiety for people to feel 'safe' in performed compliance, this makes them particularly vulnerable to being blamed for their own abuse. Similarly, the teasing, aloof, approach-avoidance nature of Exposure Anxiety makes such people a particular target for abusers, who will often then blame the victim's teasing for the abuse having 'got out of control'. Bearing this in mind, body-work can be an essential foundation to sensory cohesion, feelings of social–emotional safety, a cognitive foundation for sequencing and organizing information and a basis for expression of the 'I' and the independence which can spring from it. It would be unfortunate if fear of abuse meant this important area of therapy was avoided as a potential risk.

Reflexology can be done in a directly-confrontational way, but it can also be done using an indirectly-confrontational approach. It doesn't have to address the person, it can address the foot, and can be done as though for the relaxation of the reflexologist. It can be non-verbal and involve only background music as the 'voice' of the situation, or involve the therapist singing whisperingly, quietly to him or herself. For many people with autism, their feet provide their orientation, giving feedback of movement through space, across textures and surfaces, registering changes in body impact from the types of ground surface and the acoustics of these surfaces felt in reverberation through the body. Personally, I trust the feedback through my feet more than that through my hands. So reflexology has an important part to play as a therapy that can begin to convey, in an indirectly-confrontational way, that physical contact is non-invasive. Combined with aromatherapy, music and coloured light in the hands of someone skilled in an indirectly-confrontational approach, it has the capacity to train the relationship between the endocrine system and the brain that physical and emotional sensation are safe realms in which Exposure Anxiety is redundant. This sows a seed in identity and takes away one tiny piece of territory where Exposure Anxiety may have laid claim to the self.

Cranio-sacral therapy involves gentle physical manipulation at the base of the skull to release pressure on the flow of cerebral-spinal fluid – a major source of feedback between the brain and body systems, including those parts involved in digestion, detoxification and immune system responses. So, given that in the majority of cases, people with autism-spectrum conditions have underlying physiological problems, this is a very important tool. But cranio-sacral therapy can also stimulate the release of emotional blocks in the body that can interfere with information-processing on a variety of levels, compounding Exposure Anxiety. It is a very good way of modelling that physical contact can be non-invasive and relaxing, so that Exposure Anxiety responses are experienced as redundant and more annoying than protective – a good point to score in breaking the grip Exposure Anxiety has on identity and self.

Cranio-sacral therapy can be carried out in a social engaging, directly-confrontational way involving verbal contact and eye contact and this may be fine, even reassuring for clients without Exposure Anxiety. Some excellent, flexible, intuitive therapists, however, work in an indirectly-confrontational way. Using little eye contact, little or no verbal language they allow the client to'relax' into their own activity in the room, which for people with Exposure Anxiety may be part of an avoidance, diversion, retaliation response repertoire. They may appear oblivious to what's around them, 'interested' in exploring something (sometimes a set up to provoke a confrontation and prove Exposure Anxiety as justified) or a direct retaliation response which is designed to reassure the person with Exposure Anxiety that the therapist has 'been warned'. A creative therapist can work standing next to the client whilst looking out of the window, as though the therapy just happens to be going on. Many therapists work from behind the client. The therapist can also work lying on the floor where the client has wrapped him or herself up in a sheet. Background music, coloured light or aromatherapy can also be used in conjunction with cranio-sacral therapy if this takes the sense of 'audience' away and helps the person with Exposure Anxiety to be more receptive.

As someone who had little experience of being held or picked up, I had very little sense of the cohesiveness of my body. Combined with the fact I was forced to use my body sense in place of visual processing, I experienced my body as a tool and couldn't stand the kind of physical social contact that was going to confuse this.

Obstacle courses involving climbing, rolling inside tubes, swinging, jumping and falling through space are an important means of encouraging feedback between body and brain, to orient Exposure Anxiety responses to the fact that feedback from body is not a foreign invader. I spent much of my childhood putting myself through programmes of this kind, as though I was craving such experiences. But I would not allow anyone else to be involved. I think, however, the environment could be involved in providing the kinds of materials through which these activities can be done. Exposure Anxiety senses a set up, so I'm not convinced these things are always best in a set up room. I climbed ladders, walk-rolled huge industrial cable spools and walked a tightrope strung between two trees, as well as lines drawn on the ground. I climbed and hung from trees, jumped on cushions and beds, fell through space onto cushioned surfaces, rolled in rolled-up rugs, swung from towels on hooks, jumped from block to block and propelled myself upside-down down the stairs. These things cost no money but developed whatever body sense I had.

The environment can also be involved in modelling the activities in such an obstacle course whilst keeping in mind what that modelling means and involves. If you model in a directly-confrontational way to someone with Exposure Anxiety, you may actually be perceived as 'saying', 'Don't show an interest in this stuff because I can't control my enthusiasm for getting you involved'. This may amount to an equation as follows: 'invasive' sense of other = Exposure Anxiety response = not interested except as passive forced compliance of the performing shell you can have in place of me. The environment can, however, disappear from the person with Exposure Anxiety, as though utterly for their own sake, into such an obstacle course, and when discovered, the environment 'distractedly' exits this 'private' situation. Replayed again, the environment can begin to 'tolerate' its spectator, remaining in the obstacle course in small doses and leaving the area shortly after the person with Exposure Anxiety begins to 'tease' with a demonstration of potential interest. Progressively, the environment remains, behaving with relative indifference to the involvement of the person with Exposure Anxiety, as though both just happen incidentally to be in the same area. This also builds strong foundations for distinguishing between Exposure Anxiety and the self, undermining Exposure Anxiety's potential stranglehold on identity in which the environment is winning by appearing not to 'try' (reducing invasive sense of 'other').

Body brushing, hair brushing, massage and deep pressure can also be useful tools used in an indirectly-confrontational way. Hair brushing can be done as though for your own benefit, in a way that addresses the hair, not the person. It can also be used as a diversion for the introduction of Social Stories told through song the therapist sings gently to him or herself or whispers to him or herself in small doses. The person with Exposure Anxiety can be 'allowed' to listen in indirectly, but the therapist might stop strategically even cutting off midstream to make a cup of tea in order to help build interest and motivation to hear more. Body brushing can be an extension of hair brushing and is an important tool for getting a cohesive sense of body connectedness. Again, this can be done as though incidental and done almost half-heartedly, to counter Exposure Anxiety resistance to sensed 'invasion' provoked by too much enthusiasm on the part of the carer.

Massage is good for toxicity issues, particularly acupressure. It can help boost the immune system and reduce some of the effects of constant high adrenaline levels. Deep pressure is something many people with autism seek and some will try to get in behind the cushions on the sofa, get under heavy rugs, etc. Deep pressure helps give a sense of body cohesion, is good for sensory orientation and helps reduce stress. Rolling and pressing activities involving the use of big vinyl cushions would suffice here, but safety issues are important. Avoiding the person's face is important not only because of the potential of these activities to suffocate, but also because it involves an acute loss of control. When pressure is being used, it must be possible for the person to escape, so as to avoid the acute sense of being robbed of control – and again, safety issues must be considered to avoid injury. Deep pressure doesn't mean crushing. Focusing on the cushion rather than the person may make such an activity less of a social confrontation. Being involved as though for your own fun rather than that of the person with Exposure Anxiety instills a sense of him or herself as an independent empowered human being rather than being the focused upon, special-case 'client'.

Even when I became emotionally unable to dare the use of colour in art (because it would provoke too much feeling), I still could be moved by the use of coloured light. Even when I would not let my feelings out through playing music, had clammed-up singing, stopped playing records, I was still subject to music around me, music which could take me on emotional adventures I had not committed myself to and which I was free to leave. Where the social world is blocked from entry, the abstract world of art and music may be routes of indirectly-confrontational involvement with people with severe Exposure Anxiety.

Mind and consciousness are like a gradual sunrise that takes time to come up. In the meantime, we are not stagnant, waiting for life to happen. We map everything, letting information-processing take care of itself. We map rhythm and pattern, pitch and volume, the form and flow of movements around us, of objects, places, of people. This is the music of life and we feel it with our bodies, long before we identify mind with self. This is the realm of sensing, and we all began there. Some of us stay here longer than others. Exposure Anxiety sets up attack against conscious awareness. As part of the system of sensing, music, art and movement can all be part of the system of sensing and not about mind at all. Through these things we may find expression without noticing we have noticed.

Rhythm, pitch, flow, colour, pattern and form have a particularly special place in the foundations we all came from. Whether we experience this in the footsteps with which an individual crosses the floor, the visual rhythm with which someone holds and puts down a glass or the flow and shifts of how someone sits in their own body, this connection on a preconscious level is everywhere. It is our first language. Even if all that follows so jolts consciousness in the rusty-cog effort of attempting to hold mind, this first language is our base line, our home base.

Music, art and movement have the most important of all places in the lives of those who find the realm of mind a place of rusty cogs and heavy effort – the stuff of overload, shutdown, information-processing delay and the sensory chaos that ensues. Music, colour, pattern and form, in their most primal forms, have the power to restore order in chaos, to reassure that, in spite of an absence of sensory cohesion, something whole and wonderful, flowing, consistent, moving, yet non-invasive, still exists outside of us in the world. Music, art and movement can be a place where those who struggle to keep up with the rate of information, and who are left meaning deaf, meaning blind, still can meet with others in the form of communication and involvement I call 'simply being'. More than this, these realms have the power to convey that, when haywire chemistry tells you that emotion and connection with others signals death, there is at least one social realm that remains safe. Used in an indirectly-confrontational way, these realms of relating can convey an acceptance of the right to 'lose oneself' as an act of self-calming in order to stay.

Coloured lights tickled my emotions, where I would not let human beings so move me. Symmetry and line gave me a sense of cohesion in the face of chaos, and I would place myself in the balance point of great buildings, sites and areas of natural beauty where natural points of symmetry are to be found. Nothing so captures placement and a sense of fitting, of belonging, of being in place, a reassurance that is so necessary yet I was blocked from receiving it from the social world. To know such an experience, by any route, is a great source of comfort in the chaos and isolation of severe Exposure Anxiety. Form gave me physical contact with human beings by proxy. It gave answers to my mind where meaning-blind eyes could not interpret and Exposure Anxiety crippled the ability to ask. I felt everything. Like a blind person starved of experience, I delved into form as if it was social connection. I experienced not only objects, but people through their objects. For someone unable to consistently process visual information and for whom sensory fluctuation left nothing constant, this had to be through sensing form. I felt it at such a deep experiential level, it was like a dialogue through touch. The greatest of these experiences would have to be that of sitting with statues in the cemetery. I lay on these angels, put my body to them, stroked them, put my face to them and sat on their laps as a child might with someone familiar. I did all this, knew these movements in my body, felt my own social desire for contact and inclusion, and because I was alone and they could neither look at me, nor speak to me, nor hold me back. Most children diagnosed with autism will never have such opportunities and Exposure Anxiety will be the one to score the points from such a loss.

Music, art and dance/movement therapy build a safe space, a meeting place, somewhere to feel equal, a foundation of experience in which to remember in our bodies a spectrum of emotion and connection with a process of connection among others equally being in their own space. Through song, we can address topics where directly-confrontational language dare not go (or would not be tolerated with meaning on-line). Through moving with coloured light and pattern, we can incidentally use our bodies, let emotions fly without noticing we have done so. These therapies can show that those in the directly-confrontational self-in-relation-to-other world, can also be indirectly-confrontational in a self-owning way, demonstrating life is not so black and white but has a whole spectrum in between.

Two of the simplest ways of getting people to make friends with body are so straightforward most people forget about them. Fabric, especially clinging, tight fitting, scratchy, dry surfaces, elasticized clothing, feet suffocated in socks and shoes and unable to gain safety and orientation from surface feedback in the absence of visual processing – all create a constant awareness of the invasion of body itself. Many people with autism are already telling the environment through the language of behaviour, 'Get this cladding off me'. In their despair and inability to control this sense of daily invasion, I'm certain the insistence of the environment in keeping this sense of imprisonment and invasion continuing becomes a great source of conflict. Yet clothes which flow, with silken or velvet surfaces, are often tolerated, even adored. Quite simply, if you are driven mad by Exposure Anxiety you become overly focused on all that is invasive and beyond your control. Even if a velvet outfit was worn or made inside out, this might be better than struggling to keep the clothes on to the point someone can no longer even manage their own toilet training. A fluffy toilet seat cover may be better than a lifetime battle over the avoidance of a cold, hard seat. Particularly in the case of people with poor visual processing, attempts to stop people using touch or tapping to compensate will only result in a war over using feet for the same kind of navigation, orientation and reassurance. If you want the shoes kept on, you may have to be understanding about the use of touch for spatial orientation, tracking of movement and object recognition.

Promoting letting go control

Exposure Anxiety constantly instils a feeling of being utterly out of control. Security becomes invested in the reassurance one has control and, conversely, that it is wrong to let go control or allow the environment to cause you to do so.

The opportunities for development in people phobic about loss of control at the hands of the environment can become rigid, inflexible and limited. As the possessive inner protector, director and teacher, wins, the person loses. The person loses choice and, in its place, there is compulsion repetition, reassurance in order and familiarity.

Yet, this in itself meant they inadvertently played hard to get, reducing to some degree the need to protect myself from loss of control. I was allowed to feed myself directly from packets of food in the pantry, from the fridge, from the fruit bowl, from the cupboard (either this or stopping me was futile). I was allowed to take my plate and exit to eat away from the table with no expectation to use cutlery. I wasn't expected to keep shoes on. Though I was exposed to people talking to themselves, I wasn't generally expected to converse. I was expected to use the toilet, which created quite a war with move, counter move. I was not expected to do homework or generally show an interest in particular toys or programmes. I did not perceive the expectation to stay in or return home at any time. I did, however, experience the expectation to say 'Going now' when I was leaving the house, which, as it was not associated with being stopped, I was able to do. My father was brilliant at modelling that it was safe to be expressive in one's own world. He would stand on the snooker table and break into song and Elvis impressions, co-opting lyrics to songs. He would talk to his own snot on his finger as if it was a puppet before chasing me through the house, with it chasing me of its own volition. He broke into almost constant characterizations. He would grab hold of me, swing me up on his shoulders and tear through the house, with me being left to hold on or come flying off. He danced me on his feet. He could make you lose control without seeing it coming, without noticing you had lost it and without being able to directly blame him for causing you to be involved. He was, in these ways, an asset in countering my own compulsive rigidity and insistence on control.

I very much believe in the modelling of communication through song, sung out loud to oneself as a way of promoting the letting go of control. Tickling, trampolining, running, stomping, having a shouting room and a tall throwing box ('gently throwing'), are all excellent ways of developing a good relationship to letting go control. Trampolining and jumping into water are important for the same reason, as well as important in trusting space for those with visual-perceptual problems, and part of learning to trust and rely on kinesthetics when visual perception is unreliable. Horse riding can be important in learning that loss of control can be exciting and freeing, but also subtly convey that this can involve giving up control to something or someone else, with your having the ultimate choice to quit. I spent considerable time in the local cemetery sitting with the statues in a way I could not with moving, reacting human beings. Again, this helped develop a sense that it was safe to let go and relax in the company of others, as this didn't necessarily always result in the chaos provoked by a sense of loss of control.

For developing tolerance to the audience of oneself

There were times I was happiest singing at the top of my voice. It made Exposure Anxiety responses relax, getting off my back, releasing the grip on my stomach. Later, when I realized I enjoyed the sound of my own singing, it became more difficult to sing. Nor could I sing when asked to. There have been phases where either the enjoyment of the environment or my own enjoyment in hearing myself sing has meant, sadly, I am unable to connect to my own voice to do so. It's as though I'm climbing steps from underground, afraid of what awaits me at the top as I break the surface, aware I don't want the chaos of stepping out of line. Yet when the radio is singing, it is sometimes possible; my own singing comes out as non-me and I am a brilliant mimic of the singing of others. Yet the voice I have come to be most moved by, to most love, is my own, singing as me, and I hardly ever hear it. I sometimes wish I could just let it out, without applying myself to the war declaration of insisting on getting it out. To have to do this whilst, exhaustedly, tuning out awareness enough to lessen the internal resistance, playing feigned, self-convinced indifference with my own conscious awareness involves manipulating myself into a position of confusion about drive and commitment to the point I get what I want. It's a subtle dance with the invisible ever-present enemy and it has driven me equally into being a deeply passionate artistic person as it has into something akin to Zen Buddhism.

One of the best tools I've found for developing tolerance to the audience of oneself is a mirror. It's not so much about the mirror as how the mirror is introduced. Introduce it as a 'trap' for social contact and Exposure Anxiety will block attraction to it and social contact through it. But if it just 'appears' there one day, as though it had a volition of its own, this is far less likely to trigger Exposure Anxiety. I would touch hands with my reflection, whisper and chatter to it, put my face to 'her face' and look deeply into her eyes. I wished for her to save me from being in the world, to let me into her world under glass. She always kept my secrets, she always reflected understanding of my feelings, shared cheekiness in my playfulness. We even fought with each other when she reflected what I didn't want her showing anyone. It was a full social and interactive relationship.

Later, intentionally or not, I don't know, my mother used mirrors in other rooms of the house. This facilitated the extension of this relationship between me and myself in a way which had me feel just as secure and in company in the mirrored rooms throughout the house, and progressively this trust extended down the street to shop windows. I began to relate to people in the reflected world, addressing their 'safe' under-glass reflections and eventually jumping between the world and the mirror world under glass. At no time, did anyone try to deliberately and directly join me in the mirror. In time, had they eventually joined themselves in the mirror, this may have instilled a sense of normality without triggering invasion. Talking to oneself in the mirror can be a indirectly-confrontational form of counselling in addressing the object/issue rather than the person, especially if what's being expressed is kept visual and concrete by either being played out to oneself via objects or augmented by gestural signing.

There are fairly affordable talk-back toys which mimic sound back at you. Starting with non-verbal sounds in small doses and done for one's own benefit, this might inspire curiosity in the person with Exposure Anxiety to also explore such a controllable self-initiated 'dialogue' with something external. The fact that what comes back requires no information-processing means there is nothing for Exposure Anxiety to jump in and protect against. Of course, being in someone's face, full of hope and the need to make a connection, is a very quick way of saying, to a non-verbal person with Exposure Anxiety 'Whatever you do, don't use this'. It may be giving the message, 'Use this and I'll likely jump on the first indication you might open up'. It might be saying, 'Feel my eagerness and know I'll seek to extend that into such a loss of control you will dread you ever started'. And it may be saying this without even the added issue of directly-confrontational 'praise' as a potential damaging factor to taking on new skills. It's not just the goods that matter, it's the form of delivery. Playing, as though for your own sake, with resonant and whispering sounds through long cardboard tubes such as those for tin foil or carpet rolls can inspire quite a wish to get free and try such a buzz through voice. But get in someone's face with this and you may be ensuring failure. Make your noises in small doses at people on the TV, addressing those who come to the front door, saying goodbye to the contents of the toilet bowl before flushing, this is good fun, and children, especially distressed, controlled, anxious or depressed children, need surrealism, daring and humour. Be self owning in your surrealism and silliness. Walk off afterwards and don't stand there waiting for a response.

Facilitated expression can be used to dress, to help oneself to the cupboard, to use a key in a door, to put on a video, to begin pointing out 'picture sentences' through a communication book, right through to facilitated typing. Facilitated expression involves shadowing the person with Exposure Anxiety so that there is a hand-over-hand control with the focus on the activity and not the person. The activity is a generally silent one unless the dialogue is carried on between Mr Hand, Mrs Foot and with the clothes, the cupboard door, the key, the letters on the keyboard, etc. Gradually, as the person with Exposure Anxiety feels comfortable to be more able 'as' the other person, the facilitator begins to fade out support, become slower, more intermittent, more half-hearted, sloppier in her support. The person with Exposure Anxiety becomes bossier in trying to get the facilitator to facilitate 'properly' and, in doing so, asserts himself more strongly in their expression and activity. This is an ebb and flow relationship, but, played masterfully, it has been known to lead to expressive independence.

For developing tolerance of connection with others

Tolerating a sense of audience to self is only half the battle. It is another thing to be able to stand a sense of others directly and being part of this interactively, tolerating a sense of connection with others.

I felt my world was 'contaminated' when something 'mine' was commented on, complimented, discussed or used by others. I was then compelled to disown it, however much it spited me or created a loss to do so. Then I could carry on, having severed it from my life. Otherwise, I had to go through disassembly, disintegration rituals to somehow 'purify' my things from contact, make them again 'my world'. This was not so when I was very young, because before the age of nine I had such severe difficulty understanding language with meaning that such things had little impact. But once I began to move from a world of sensing into one of interpretation, self-consciousness and possessiveness of my own world interplayed with Exposure Anxiety and meaning in a behavioural cocktail that had me labelled disturbed.

Building up tolerance of connection to others was a gradual process which I undertook of my own accord merely because in an extremely challenging environment, my difficulties compounded a sense of trapped helplessness. I began daring to let things be unsymmetrical, even if it was only for a few seconds, just to feel my own terror of loss of control before correcting the disorder and chaos. Progressively, I could stand more and more minutes and as an adult even intentionally allow visual chaos, asymmetry and mess. I began to dare falling through space, daring to let go control, and then taking this to people and falling straight over onto them like a toppled block, daring to let go control in relation to others. I began telephoning random numbers from the phone book and allowing people to trigger expression out of me before hanging up. I started to watch others through the mirror in the lounge room and, at ten, was given responsibility for my three-year-old brother who could not converse, was extremely compulsive, very ADHD and this gave me a feeling of normality and equality. I studied situation comedies and replayed them throughout the house as an extension of my verbal repertoire.

My father and mother helped me build up the tolerance to connection with others through the indirectly-confrontational ways they communicated through with me. What I learned was not, 'I can't stand contact with others', but 'I can't stand directly-confrontational, other-initiated, contact with others'. So I was able to maintain a relatively healthier approach to social contact than Exposure Anxiety might otherwise have allowed me.

People as 'statues', self-owned modelling of improvised wild creative movement, indirectly-confrontational 'music therapy', 'art therapy', and meeting through buzzing on the experience of patterns are all wonderful bridges to building up tolerance of connection to others. More important, all involve inspiring through self-owning activity, rather than compliance activities that too often get dumped later.

Learning calmness

How do you learn to calm yourself down when you are in a highly provoked state of self-protectiveness and everything in you says, shutdown, run, hide, fight? This is especially so when others try to calm you down in such a state; their caring and fuss adds fuel to the fire as these actions pierce the individual with impressions of 'invasion', 'being externally controlled'. So learning calmness is extremely important, but it's far more important how you provide such modelling. You can't easily calm a drug addict.

When it comes to calming, the first place to look is prevention. If a child is pale, with dark circles under his or her eyes and lives on a diet high in Salicylates, colourings, flavourings and preservatives, have you done all you can to reduce anxiety through diet? If, like so many children with asthma, excema, have you looked at altering dairy intake (keeping in mind soy can be equally a problem for many children, especially with low IgA)? If you are looking at a child with recurrent ear, nose or throat infection, have you looked at the effect of sugar and refined carbohydrates on anxiety? In children with signs of irritable bowel, have you looked into gluten intolerance as a key to reducing anxiety in general? Has anyone done a test for B vitamin, zinc, magnesium and fatty acid levels so necessary to managing anxiety? Has anyone tested for subclinical phenylketonuria? Has a simple urine analysis for dopamine, seratonin, tryptophan and noradrenaline levels been done to find out whether hormone balance is adding fuel to the fire? It is my strong view these areas should be properly explored by nutritional therapists experienced in these conditions in people with autism before embarking on long-term use of psychiatric or behaviour-suppressant drugs. Many psychiatric drugs have side effects, often increasing stress on an already overburdened liver. Many of these are prescribed not because the person is psychotic but simply because the therapist cannot manage the client's behaviour. Chronic stress in a myalgia sufferer, however, is likely to have an even more detrimental effect on the liver than a well managed low dose of a drug which is used to address neurotransmitter imbalance and correct the effects of chronic stress. It's a matter of open-mindedly balancing the two sides without letting knee-jerk reactions close the door on possibilites in the fight against adrenaline addiction on the Exposure Anxiety it provokes. When it comes to the use of drugs to promote calmness, herbal preparations such as Valerian, Passiflora or the Bach flower remedy, Rescue Remedy, could in milder cases be conventional psychiatric drugs.

Adrenaline is about energy, and very wild energy at that. Attempts to still someone who needs to purge this build of adrenaline might see you on the receiving end of the purge. It might be more sensible, when you are stressed, to model trampolining, jumping on a cushion or running on the spot. The jumping cushion is a message that there is a time and a place for this kind of jumping. The self-calming has a focus. It's important, in a state of high Exposure Anxiety, not to assume that the right way is to offer help directly. This can provoke some people to reject the very thing that might help them, as well as to attack the giver. This is why modelling self-calming for your own benefit, when you, yourself, are stressed, and without making this an obvious 'lesson', can be very helpful to the person with Exposure Anxiety. Where physical intervention is required, walking off often has a better, less inflaming effect on getting someone to move than trying to control them in a high adrenaline state which only makes them dig in further, jeopardizing your relationship with them as a mutually respecting 'equal'.

Singing very quietly to yourself can model self-calming, humming a pattern over and over again, getting progressively quieter, slower, more intermittent till you phase your humming out can help people tune out to their own heightened and uncomfortable self-consciousness and restore a sense of cohesion. The person with Exposure Anxiety now doesn't feel they were force-fed or 'given to' when they hadn't asked, but instead that they had 'discovered' or 'picked up' a pattern that just happened to have occurred in the environment. Classical music works for some people, rhythmic, Celtic or drumming patterns work for others. It's a matter of using these things intermittently to reduce the disruptive consequences of heightened self-consciousness. Using music in small intermittent doses of about fifteen minutes at a time, can be like diffusing the self-consciousness in order to relax about what you are doing. You may then need the focus of no music for the next fifteen minutes before self-consciousness again begins to peak once overload accumulates, due to delayed processing.

Knowing self from Exposure Anxiety: It starts with just one crack in the wall

Knowing self from Exposure Anxiety is the key to inspiring the self to challenge and manage this self-saboteur. The dilemma is that you can't do this in a way that provokes self-consciousness or your attempts become the 'invasion' and your actions inadvertently compound and 'justify' the person siding with their own self-protection responses instead of against them. An indirectly-confrontational approach is designed to do this but it is an art . Go easy on yourself if you don't get it right. You won't be an expert overnight. It is like any skill and if you are someone who doesn't have chronic Exposure Anxiety, remember that you are working 'blind'. That's a very brave and adventurous thing to dare. If you find your own directly-confrontational self-in-relation-to-other social–emotional orientation is sabotaging you in spite of your psychological conviction to using an indirectly-confrontational approach, you may need help. Your mind may be clear about your goals but your own social–emotional orientation may be heading in the other direction. Creative visualization techniques used by a qualified hypnotherapist may help you to let go and find the self-ownership and detachment you need to sit comfortably in the inspiring and empowering role of parent, professional or partner. It may be that some turning around is needed on both sides in order to be able to meet on that bridge you envision.

Making the cage visible: The strategy of exposing Exposure Anxiety

After dietary intervention in my twenties I began to use disclosure to counter my predicted impending self-sabotage. In effect, I exposed the Exposure Anxiety to provoke it into abandoning me, as if to say 'Exposure Anxiety? What Exposure Anxiety?'

I used to find it excruciating to speak about my personal life, clamming up or diverting people in every possible direction to deflect self-consciousness. In my mid to late twenties I learned, however, to announce to people that I may not be able to speak directly to them because I'd end up saying everything I didn't mean or clamming up. The result was that although I then began to communicate through writing, my communication was concise, warm, personal, cohesive and focused. I was even publicly criticized and demeaned for this apparent 'regression' by someone, who for his own interests, stalked me via his manipulation of the media. I stuck to my own needs. Because of my disclosure of my Exposure Anxiety, I became progressively able to defy my own disclosed difficulties. I became gradually secure and fluent in speaking off my notes, more and more directly with the public, yet retaining the same wholeness, the same cohesion, the same focus, conciseness and personal quality to my interactive speaking as

I had had to my typed communication. Though this ability is limited to the topics I've spoken on often, I now use this same developmental path for all kinds of personal communication.

Being public, vocal, open and up-front about how someone's Exposure Anxiety probably won't let them do X or answer Y can work the same way. Saying something 'won't let them' isn't the same as saying the person 'can't'. It is basically telling them, 'You are being controlled by your own mechanisms'. The Exposure Anxiety dynamics themselves exposed creates a feeling of nakedness before others, provoking the compulsion to hide the truth of the disclosure. Ironically, this can leave the person more, not less able. Taking this approach may seem like ridicule, but ridicule is expressed in a tone and this approach doesn't have to be done in a demeaning way. Such disclosure can be very 'neutral' and matter-of-fact. If it provokes a 'I'll show you who controls who' response, then that may just be great. It's important, however, not to follow this achievement with praise, however glad you might be. This would be like rubbing salt into an open wound. To someone with Exposure Anxiety it may be akin to saying, 'Tricked you, I won. I'm so impressed by your gullibility.' So, if you want to promote what has been achieved, it may be best to shut up and act as if nothing amazing happened.

Relaxing with unknown knowing

To allow the individual to fly in spite of Exposure Anxiety, you as the environment need to promote the modelled impression that you trust a lack of self-consciousness. You need to model that you know there is more to learning than interpretation and awareness and that you accept that mapping pattern is a form of unknown knowing that is vast and can be a functional database if it isn't used in a consciousness-jolting way. You need to model that life isn't primarily based on proof and that you know some people don't need to 'know', only trust in the 'doing'. For me, God is that internal self where we cannot go with consciousness and mind, and trusting unknown knowing is like trusting God; you let that database surprise you with who is in there because you are not expected to call it 'you'. There is nobody waiting to put your name to it, to praise you for it; your achievements are allowed to be utterly impermanent, to just 'be' and to have been worth it purely in the 'doing', not always in the 'having'.

I was asked about a boy with severe Exposure Anxiety who only 'scribbles' but is thought well capable of art. I pointed out, what was the point of trying if the compliment only offends by its intrusiveness? I pointed out that sometimes it is easier to do art using sand which will blow away than paint which will last because then, something in you knows it is just for you, just 'in the doing' and not something self-in-relation-to-other. I ran play workshops and I loved the fact that when people left, all the work was within them. There was no 'proof'. It was just theirs. For those with severe Exposure Anxiety compelled to put such energy into defending personal space and a sense of boundary, is this better than losing ninety-five per cent of conventional learning time because it was spent in self-defence against the delivery and packaging of the learning? I think so.

Bach flower remedies and emotional support in the cage

In my view, Bach Flower remedies can help people through the developmental entanglements in themselves as a result of living with Exposure Anxiety and also in addressing the entanglements between them and the environment. They can help the person living or working with someone with Exposure Anxiety to work towards the warm detachment and self-ownership necessary to easing into the use of an indirectly-confrontational approach.

The flower remedies, like many plants, have known physical and emotional effects. The Bach range was developed by Dr Edward Bach (1886-1936) who 'discovered flower remedies that would help feelings such as grief, worry and irritation'. The remedies are believed to have impact on specific emotional states in helping people not to suppress emotion but to restore balance by increasing the emotional solution or opposite to the problematic excess going on. The transcript below is adapted from the write up by Healing Herbs (email: healing-herbs@healing-herbs.co.uk), a company which produce flower remedies based on Dr Bach's work. Their range and the descriptions of each is as follows:

For fright:

- *Rock Rose:* for feeling alarmed, intensely scared, horror, dread: the courage to face an emergency.
- *Mimulus:* for fright of specific known things – animals, heights, pain etc, for nervous, shy people: bravery.
- *Cherry Plum:* for the thought of losing control and doing dreaded things: calmness and sanity.
- *Aspen:* Vague, unknown, haunting apprehension and premonitions: trusting the unknown.
- *Red Chestnut:* worry for others, anticipating misfortune, projecting worry: trusting to life.

For uncertainty:

- *Cerato:* distrust of self and intuition, easily led and misguided: confidently seek individuality.
- *Scleranthus:* cannot resolve two choices, indecision, alternating: balance and determination.
- *Gentian:* discouragement, doubt, despondency: take heart and have faith.
- *Gorse:* no hope, accepting the difficulty, pointless to try: the sunshine of renewed hope.
- *Hornbeam:* feels weary and thinks can't cope: strengthens and supports.
- *Wild Oat:* lack of direction, unfulfilled, drifting: becoming definite and purposeful.

For insufficient interest in present circumstances:

- *Clematis:* dreamers, drowsy, absent-minded: brings down to earth.
- *Honeysuckle:* living in memories: involved in present.
- *Wild Rose:* lack of interest, resignation, no love or point in life: the spirit of joy and adventure.
- *Olive:* exhausted, no more strength, need physical and mental renewal: rested and supported.
- *White Chestnut:* unresolved circling thoughts: a calm, clear mind.
- *Mustard:* gloom suddenly clouds us over for no apparent reason: clarity.
- *Chestnut Bud:* failing to learn from life, repeating mistakes, lack of observation: learning from experience.

For loneliness:

- *Water Violet*: Withdrawn, aloof, proud, self-reliant, quiet grief: peaceful and calm, wise in service.

- *Impatiens*: irritated by constraints, quick, tense, impatient: gentle and forgiving.

- *Heather*: longing for company, overconcern with self: tranquility and kinship with all life.

Oversensitive to ideas and influences:

- *Agrimony*: worry hidden by a carefree mask, apparently jovial but suffering: steadfast peace.

- *Centaury*: kind, quiet, gentle, anxious to serve, weak, dominated: an active and positive worker.

- *Walnut*: protection from outside influences, for change and the stages of development: the link breaker.

- *Holly*: jealousy, envy, revenge, anger, suspicion: the conquest of all will be through love.

Despondency and despair:

- *Larch*: expect failure, lack confidence and will to succeed: self-confident, try anything.

- *Pine*: self-critical, self-reproach, assuming blame, apologetic: relieves a sense of guilt.

- *Elm*: capable people, with responsibility who falter, temporarily overwhelmed: the strength to perform duty.

- *Sweet Chestnut*: unendurable desolation: a light shining in the darkness.

- *Star of Bethlehem*: for consolation and comfort in grief, after a fright or sudden alarm

- *Willow*: dissatisfied, bitter, resentful, life is unfair, unjust: uncomplaining acceptance.

- *Oak*: persevering despite difficulties, strong, patient, never giving in: admitting to limitation.

- *Crab Apple*: feeling unclean, self-disgust, small things out of proportion: the cleansing remedy.

Overcare for the welfare of others:

- *Chicory*: demanding, self-pity, self-love, possessive, hurt and tearful: love and care that gives freely to others.
- *Vervain*: insistent, willful, fervent, enthusiastic, stressed: quiet and tranquility.
- *Vine*: dominating, tyrant, bully, demands obedience: loving leader and teacher, setting all at liberty.
- *Beech*: intolerant, critical, fussy: seeing more good in the world
- *Rockwater*: self-denial, stricture, rigidity, purist: broad outlook, understanding.

Getting them to do half the work

Exposure Anxiety is nothing to be ashamed of. It may dictate a self-in-relation-to-self, indirectly-confrontational orientation which runs counter to the self-in-relation-to-other, directly-confrontational social–emotional orientation of most people, but being a minority doesn't mean you don't deserve understanding, equality and real help. If that help isn't there, it's the unfortunate fact that the person with Exposure Anxiety is one of the pioneers who will help to build the understanding and help that they themselves and those like them need. Those who live with the condition themselves have often tried to teach the world around them how to help, not realizing that the world has never fully heard what the differences are. Without knowing this, behavioural, even typed or verbal cries for help are met with 'deaf' ears or a response that is worse than none at all. This is not a reason to give up asking the environment to do half the work. However difficult for them, the environment can usually learn an indirectly-confrontational approach, if only in interaction with the person who needs it. It's not easy to learn a new skill, a new way of relating or experiencing dialogue, company or interaction. The environment needs the person with Exposure Anxiety to be patient with them and understand they are trying, just maybe need time to learn to try in a way which works. With patience, each side can build bridges in order to move forward as whole people with whole lives.

Forgiving yourself and others

One of the consequences of understanding Exposure Anxiety in yourself may be that you are angry about lost time. It may also be you feel angry that the world didn't understand, couldn't understand, or is not 'like you'. Remember that reading this book alone won't make an indirectly- confrontational approach instantly understandable to those without chronic Exposure Anxiety, but it may be a big step in their finding out such an approach exists. For them, such an approach may be like new shoes that take time to get used to and relax in. It's hard to be patient if you've spent your whole life blaming yourself for not being like 'everyone else' and realize your state of being is shared, comprehensible and manageable to some degree. It's understandable when you've lived with great discomfort in managing the simplest of things that you feel that if the environment can help in a way which works, it 'should'. But an indirectly-confrontational approach isn't merely a behaviour, an act, it's a way of being. It stems from a way we relate to ourselves. It is part of our social–emotional development as people with chronic Exposure Anxiety. Others have been self-in-relation-to-other from the time they were only weeks old. They can't turn that around overnight and they may feel really sad and frustrated about that. They may need time and patience and understanding from the person with Exposure Anxiety that they didn't mean to 'invade' or 'control' or provoke excessively intolerable self-consciousness just by trying to share. As someone with Exposure Anxiety you may have experienced their way as purely 'tolerable', or even 'toxic'. But from their world, the 'sharing', 'giving', 'noticing', 'complimenting' of the non-autistic self-in-relation-to-other, directly-confrontational person, may be about warmth and comes from good feelings within them. It just maybe doesn't feel good on the receiving end. So, it is up to you to translate.

One of the consequences of understanding the mechanics of Exposure Anxiety in others is that you may be angry at yourself. This may be for not having been able to see past your own social–emotional orientation to understand the dynamics of Exposure Anxiety before, or because you unquestioningly followed those 'experts' who promoted an approach which made no sense of the condition. You may wish you were the same as the person with Exposure Anxiety so you didn't feel like 'an infliction' or even wish yourself absent. Remember that many people with Exposure Anxiety, though they may experience connection as uncomfortable, nevertheless may sense that, however confusing your directly-confrontational approach may seem, it is done from good motives. They may still know you are 'a good person' even if this means they then 'blame themselves' for not being 'like you', someone without the invisible jacket of pins they cannot remove. It is not a matter of right or wrong, it is a matter of connecting in a way that works for both parties. Being riddled with guilt or shame or regret will only drive you further to needing to 'break through', to 'give', to 'prove you are a good person' and that won't help you or the person with Exposure Anxiety. So, take some space, look at and name the negative feelings and let them go. Don't carry them around in your back pocket like some whipping stick you have to attack yourself. The learning of an indirectly-confrontational approach is not for the person with Exposure Anxiety. It is for you. It is your own adventure in believing you deserve a sense of personal space, to do 'for you' and your belief in yourself as someone who can be an inspiration through modelling daring and doing 'for one's own sake'. Remember that just because you learn an indirectly-confrontational approach, you are not stuck there. By the environment learning it, eventually some people with Exposure Anxiety have crossed into a more self-in-relation-to-other, directly- confrontational social–emotional reality and some have simply developed more functional indirectly-confrontational lives among others. Remember that you can still be around those who work by your own natural system. You won't lose 'you', you just take on 'a second language of being', 'a second language of behaviour'. Remember it's OK to ask for help. Explain your approach to others if that helps. Be open about how foreign or challenging you are finding it. If you can't share with others, keep a dialogue with yourself. Don't feel alone. Learning to use an indirectly-confrontational approach shouldn't leave you isolated.

In a nutshell

Exposure Anxiety in your own child is probably one of the hardest things a parent can live with. It can give some parents a feeling of being excluded, of being a failure and this same feeling can be felt by teachers, carers and the partner of the person with Exposure Anxiety. But Exposure Anxiety is not intended as an insult to others or a reflection on them personally. Exposure Anxiety is about adrenaline and adrenaline is about chemistry, chemistry that is running too high. When that chemistry runs too high, it can impact on impulse control, involuntary behaviours and health and that can alter those first stages in development and the social–emotional, cognitive, communication and behaviour patterns that follow. The approach of the environment can make such development easier to navigate and can model patterns that are useful in self-management in living, oneself, with chronic acute Exposure Anxiety and minimize the intensity and frequency of involuntary defensive reactiveness. It can do this by using a method of interacting and communicating which acknowledges the chemistry problems of the person with Exposure Anxiety in provoking them too quickly into self-protective responses in the face of simple everyday attempts to connect.

Society can help by listening to parents of children with Exposure Anxiety and not being overly prescriptive in its one-size-fits all expectation that a directly-confrontational, self-in-relation-to-other way is the only, or only loving and empathic way to relate to one's child. All children are different and children with acute chronic Exposure Anxiety may not need more or bigger of the same, they may need something quite different. Teachers can help in being creative and empowering in their delivery of 'learning', broadening in their ideas of 'experience' and 'learning', open to their importance as inspiring models of responses rather than prompting machines inadvertently promoting and reinforcing co-dependency as 'helping'. Partners can help in being open-minded that there may be more than one way to 'get through' to someone with Exposure Anxiety and that pressure, expectation, pity and co-dependency may hinder more than help whilst they themselves may enjoy the relationship more by trying in a very different way.

People with Exposure Anxiety can help themselves by addressing the underlying causes of their own adrenaline highs. They can also make an effort to apply themselves to counter what may be a long-established addiction to their own adrenaline. They can recognize this addiction as driving a phobic take on connection with others in order to feel the rush that comes from the 'threat' and the power of the survival response to it. There is a world beyond this compulsive self-protectiveness.

Ultimately, however high the mountain, we can still, by contrast, adjust the ground. When it comes to the involuntary compulsive self-imprisonment of Exposure Anxiety, we cannot save anyone else, we can only inspire them through the model of our own lives, that it is possible, even challenging and adventurous to save ourselves. I throw down the gauntlet to those in the grip of acute chronic Exposure Anxiety.

If the world is so 'invasive', 'so robbing of control', 'so threatening' in the psyched up state of Exposure Anxiety, then surely someone who has survived so well by closing the world out, has incredible guts and endurance. If such a survivor has such guts, such endurance, then surely a way out, offered on their own terms is hardly a challenge. If such a survivor cannot even dare to look at what's on offer, running instead like a coward into the shadow land within, then there can be no strength, no solace in being such a coward. Exposure Anxiety, the prison warder, the would-be saviour, has lied to you, and you have been gullible and listened.

I wrote a poem which I later made into a song I recorded. The original lyrics appeared in the opening page of the autobiography, *Nobody Nowhere* and it can be heard on a CD of the same name. The poem was about the internal relationship of the self in the grip of Exposure Anxiety. It is a taunting song to the self, a reminder of the great empty promise of Exposure Anxiety. Here I translate it, for clarity, in the context of this book.

In a room without windows, in the company of shadows,
The prison warder never forgets you, he'll take you in.
Emotionally shattered, here you needn't ask if it mattered,
It was of their world, you don't let that touch you,
As if it never happened, just start again.

Take advice, said the prison warder, don't look for the answers,
Watch you don't connect out there, you just might listen,
Come, run into here, inside,
Here in the shadow lands, beyond the realm of mind.
Be warmed in the great promise of your guaranteed aloneness,

There…just like a Nobody Nowhere.

Index

can't do it
    as myself 22, 32–8
    by myself 22, 38–42
    for myself 22, 23–32
Carol (internal character) 34, 38, 143
Cerato (Bach Flower Remedy) 85, 320
change, oversensitivity to 271
Cherry Plum (Bach Flower Remedy) 85, 271, 295, 320
Chestnut Bud (Bach Flower Remedy) 320
Chicory (Bach Flower Remedy) 85, 295, 322
choking rituals 185
Chris (D.W.'s husband) 69, 78, 172
chronic stress 18, 73, 76, 92, 255, 285
clapping, sharp warning-like 91
claustrophobia 26
Clematis (Bach Flower Remedy) 320
clenched jaws and fists 91
clinginess 92–3
coloured light bulbs 72
communication
    experiencing as self 35
    through objects 47
    through someone else's voice 17
    typed 49
        and overload 79–80
compartmentalising incoming information 51
complementary medicine 75
completing circuits 185
compliments
    that hurt 117
    violent response to 56
compulsive behaviour 13–14, 22
confidence 321
consciousness and EA 50–61
    adaptation of mono 51
    adaptation of using preconsciousness and
        peripheral use of senses, 52–4
    information overload and EA 54–6
    problem of 'knowing' 57–8
    proof and EA 58–9
    system of sensing and EA 56–7
    why some indirectly-confrontational
        approaches have worked 60–1
constraints, irritated by 85
context removal tactics 92
control
    freaks 22
    friendships and letting go 206–7
    promoting letting go 309–10

controlling EA by addressing overload 71–2
copying others (echopraxia) 24, 36–7
counselling
    isolation and inner world disputes 213–15
    on issue of self 119–23
    on issue of social–emotional expression in
        'world' 108
    and other people's needs 166
    support people and social safety 170–1
Crab Apple (Bach Flower Remedy) 85, 321
crime and punishment of want and need
    102–3
curriculum, teaching with people with EA
    244–6

dairy intolerance 45, 74, 76, 256
DAN list of Autism Research International
    190, 284
dance, drama, music, writing 251–3
Danczac, Dr 287
definitive statements 29
depersonalisation 125–7
desensitisation, developmental programs for
    123–5
desensitising EA 50, 55
despair 23, 84, 321
despondency 84, 320, 321
detachment
    and EA 125–7
    'mathematical structuralism' and concept of
        'insight' 140
detachment, depersonalisation, performing and
    other useful tools and their saboteurs
    125–7
determination 85, 320
developing mind as technique for managing
    overload 76–8
developing tolerance
    of connection with others 313–14
    to audience of oneself 311–13
development of social face 177–215
developmental programs
    for desensitisation 123–5
    other 301–2
    for working with identity as key to
        motivation 155
diet
    digestion, immunity and EA 73–6
    school dinners, sugar and impact of 256–7
digestive system problems 74, 143